LONDON'S UNDERGROUND

AN ILLUSTRATED HISTORY OF
THE WORLD'S PREMIER UNDERGROUND SYSTEM

LONDON'S UNDERGROUND

AN ILLUSTRATED HISTORY OF
THE WORLD'S PREMIER UNDERGROUND SYSTEM

EIGHTH EDITION

JOHN GLOVER

IAN ALLAN
Publishing

Front cover:
A train of 'A' stock emerges from the tunnel at Surrey Quays on the East London Line in June 1990. *John Glover*

London Underground map courtesy of London Regional Transport.
Registered User No 95/2265

Back cover:
Views of the new 1992 stock for the Central Line taken at North Acton in July 1994. *John Glover*

Half-title page:
Home-going commuters at Barbican on a refurbished 'A' stock train. *John Glover*

Title page:
The District Line 'D' stock was for a time covering the East London Line service. Here a three-car set arrives at Whitechapel. The station here is perhaps close to its original condition, as once shared by many Metropolitan and District Railway stations. *John Glover*

First published 1951
Second edition 1959
Third edition 1961
Fourth edition 1967
Fifth edition 1981
Sixth edition 1986
Seventh edition 1991
Eighth edition 1996

ISBN 0 7110 2416 2

Published by Ian Allan Publishing

an imprint of Ian Allan Ltd, Terminal House, Station Approach, Shepperton, Surrey TW17 8AS. Printed by Ian Allan Printing Ltd, Coombelands House, Coombelands Lane, Addlestone, Surrey KT15 1HY.

Contents

Foreword

*by Denis Tunnicliffe CBE
Managing Director, London
Underground Ltd*

I am delighted to welcome this new edition of John Glover's comprehensive history of London's Underground. It is a detailed account ranging from the earliest days of the world's first underground railway to the issues we face today.

He has achieved a chronicle which is scholarly, meticulously researched and, for that legendary but not yet extinct creature, the intelligent general reader, a fascinating and entertaining read.

Anyone who takes a serious interest in the quality of life in our capital city understands the importance of an efficient modern transport system. It is essential to London's economic health and prosperity. In a competitive world, it is vital if we are not to be relegated from the premier league of world cities.

The vision of the pioneers who built the world's first Underground railway in the last century brought a new standard to urban transport. The modern-isers and designers who followed established standards of excellence in architecture and design, creating a transport system for our capital which was the envy of the world.

As traffic congestion and air pollution threaten the quality of life in the metropolis, the virtues and value of good public transport are back on the agenda.

London Underground has detailed plans to conserve the best of the past while developing new transport links for the future. I am optimistic that the years to come will add more important chapters to the story of London's Underground.

Denis Tunnicliffe
Managing Director
London Underground Ltd

Introduction

'He who is tired of London Transport is tired of life.' Thus stated a 1995 leader in *The Times*, with distinct overtones of the 18th century critic, Samuel Johnson. The newspaper's comment was entitled 'Mind the Gap', in which *The Times* discussed ministerial perceptions of the Underground, and their justification or otherwise.

Forty-five years ago, the first edition of Henry Howson's *London's Underground* became one of the original hardback books to be published by the fledgling Ian Allan organisation. The present author can just remember seeing it for sale, and wondering why anybody should want to buy a book about holes in the ground through which trains chased one another at more or less regular intervals! Yet the confidence of author and publisher was well founded, and the book has seldom been out of print as edition has followed edition over the years. The Underground railways of London have a long and distinguished history in the service of the capital, their fortunes waxing and waning as they struggled to match the changing demands made on them.

In 1863, the first element of the Underground system was born into an era of horse bus and hansom cab, of steam railways… and traffic congestion. Despite all the technical problems in those early days, it became clear that the most effective means of allowing people to move in and about the capital city was by railways beneath the streets. The system expanded slowly until the turn of the century, when the advent of electric traction suddenly offered, literally, new horizons. There was a frenzied period of construction. This was private capital being employed for private gain, even if the profits turned out to be somewhat illusory. Criss-crossing of the central area was completed in 1906, after which the promoters concentrated on extensions into what became the suburbs. Later, tunnels were enlarged and station platforms lengthened to cope with the growing traffic. The deep level 'tubes' vastly enhanced the travel opportunities in the built-up area, but by pushing out beyond it were also instrumental in the creation and nurturing of suburban London.

These excursions to the boundaries were not welcomed universally. The planning profession was distraught: 'The influence of electric trains on suburban growth was deplorable. "Live in Metroland" was the slogan of mutually supporting rail and building interests in exploitation of the house-in-the-country hunger of London workers and those in the new factory estates…'. That *cri de coeur* was written in 1962, but the plain fact that the provision of public transport, and particularly rail services, had made a decisive impact on the form and growth of London, was there for all to see.

Thus the Underground had a powerful effect on land use patterns and development, but its own evolution from the 1920s onwards was dependent on at least some support from public funds. Perhaps the long drawn out postwar hiatus in the 1950s was due to lack of agreement as to what the Underground was there to achieve. The Victoria Line was 20 years in gestation before it was opened in stages from 1968 to 1971, the operators by that time having exhausted their ingenuity for devising improved means of handling the traffic on offer. Its opening coincided with the solution of passing the problem to local politicians in 1970, which then proceeded to demonstrate how wide a gulf there could be between opposing, albeit sincerely held, political views. Unfortunately, a system as complex, permanent, and with such long lead times as an Underground railway, is among the least able to adapt quickly to political whim.

Technical refinements accompanied the physical development. The trains became more sophisticated, with greater space being devoted to passengers rather than equipment, while the coming of the sliding door dispensed with the need for gatemen to be stationed at the ends of cars. Rubber springs needed less maintenance than steel. At stations, the escalator replaced the lift. Technology assisted the development of traffic control systems while, out on the track, signalling systems were perfected, and the welding of rails did much to reduce rail wear. Ticket machines enabled passengers to serve themselves long before the checkout became commonplace in the retail trade. Good industrial design became the hallmark of the system, epitomised by the roundel.

Since 1984, London Underground has been a subsidiary business of London Regional Transport, a state-owned corporation. Today, the Underground is far from a monopoly provider, with two million private cars registered in the Greater London area alone.

Neither does the Underground have a monopoly in the geographical sense. Thus, only 28 of the 270 stations on the lines presently served by the Underground are south of the river. This is due to a combination of geological conditions and, in the formative years, the Underground's competitive position compared with the main line railways. Might future changes produce a more flexible railway network? The Underground is in no sense a minor railway; in the last decade, with the exception of one year only, more passenger journeys have been made on London Underground than on the whole of British Rail.

As the reader will find in the following pages, this is principally a physical record of the Underground's development, concentrating on the growth of a whole system of lines out of a short stretch of smoky steam railway. Its creation has been an outstanding achievement, notwithstanding the criticisms which may fairly be made. Perhaps the most remarkable aspect is that the Underground works today as well as it does; the credit for this lies almost entirely with the management and the 17,500 staff of all grades, whose collective business it is to run the railway.

Acknowledgements

A book of this nature draws its material from many sources, but my greatest debt is to the original author, the late Henry Howson. In presenting this eighth edition, I have taken the opportunity of advancing the story by a few years. Some suggestions for further reading from the vast amount of available literature are listed in the back of the book. I am grateful to Denis Tunnicliffe, Managing Director of the last large public sector company, for his willingness to contribute the foreword. My thanks are due also to the editor of *Underground News* for permission to reproduce extracts from 'The Phantom of Aldenham' by T. Handorff, and my thanks go to all who have contributed in any way. Naming individuals is always potentially unjust to others, but I would mention especially Derek Mercer, whose photographic printing does more than justice to my negatives. Finally, it has only been the support of my own family which has allowed this new edition to be produced, and their help and encouragement are much appreciated.

John Glover
Worcester Park
Surrey
November 1995

Chapter 1

The Coming of the Underground

Above:
The original stations of the Metropolitan Railway were constructed with much use of horses, as seen in this picture of Aldersgate Street station (today's Barbican) under construction. The brick retaining walls remain, but the curved iron and glass roof has long since been removed.
London Transport Museum H3952

The site of London was originally selected way back in Roman times, offering as it did good drinking water and suitable locations at which to construct quays. A good 30 miles up the Thames estuary, London offered a degree of inland penetration by waterborne transport, which was far preferable to the muddy tracks on land which were, initially, the only alternatives for the occupying armies. The Thames thus became a major highway, and also a divider; hence London's axis has always been east-west. This influenced the detailed layout, but London was able to develop in all directions unlike, say, Liverpool,

bounded by the Irish Sea and the Mersey. All principal streets like The Strand and Piccadilly run broadly parallel to the river. Industry was situated to the east, so that the prevailing westerly winds carried the resulting smoke away from the city; as a result the west end became 'superior'. On the south bank, the alluvial deposits delayed the building of roads. Thus, the north bank with its better natural drainage was developed first, and it has always retained its pre-eminence in commercial, business, court and governmental terms.

In 1500 the population was 75,000, considerably smaller than Paris and the Mediterranean centres. In the 17th century it grew from 200,000 to 575,000 and in 1800 was over one million; by 1900 it was over six million, and is about seven million today.

The growth was made possible by the agricultural and industrial revolutions, and the development of foreign trade. It was reflected in the river and street traffic; street improvements, slum clearance and more bridges across the Thames went hand in hand. After the Napoleonic wars the need for enhancement of

street facilities became ever more pressing as London continued to spread outwards beyond the previously built-up area. There was money to be made out of transporting people, and in 1829 George Shillibeer used horse buses for the first successful route between Marylebone, King's Cross, Old Street and Bank. A fixed timetable was operated with no pre-booking, both novelties in comparison with the hackney cabs. However, horse buses were expensive, and most suburban dwellers from Camden or Camberwell walked to work.

The first railways built for local traffic were the London & Greenwich, opened in 1836–38, and the London & Blackwall, opened from 1840. Oriented to passenger traffic, as were subsequent lines constructed to the south and east of the city, they contrasted with the main line railways to the north and west where short distance traffic was discouraged by few local stations and fewer trains. In time, this led to uneven development of the urban railways, in the form of the Underground, which were devised and built to fill the vacuum left by the main lines.

Above:
The East London Line utilises the Brunels' Thames Tunnel, seen here at the Wapping end with an 'A' stock train from Whitechapel disappearing into it. The station platforms are noticeably narrow. All connections with the main line railways have been severed, although extension plans may see reconnection taking place. *John Glover*

The northern main line railways had been excluded from central London, siting their terminals along the New Road, today's Euston Road and its continuation along City Road to the east and Marylebone Road to the west. In the south the barrier was the river. Attempts by the companies to extend their lines into the centre to get better access were turned down by a Royal Commission in 1846; with few exceptions (notably Charing Cross), that decision stood. The railways were thus not going to be allowed to contribute to solving central London's by now chronic traffic problems. Rather, they would henceforth be adding to it, by disgorging passengers onto the road system at what were then the outskirts. However, had they been given the go-ahead to approach the heart of London more closely, it is an open question as to the extent they would have done so, given the relatively enormous costs of property acquisition and demolition, or tunnelling — to say nothing of the investments represented by their existing termini which would then have become redundant.

In 1855, a Parliamentary Select Committee had been set up to consider how to combat the congestion. It was estimated that over 750,000 people were entering London every day, whether by

main line railway or by road, and the streets were being blocked by a variety of iron-tyred vehicles — omnibuses, coaches, hackney carriages, drays and so forth — all making a vast din on the cobbled roads. With frayed nerves and tempers Londoners looked around for alleviation, and the Press were vocal in their denunciation of the 'scandalous state of London's transport facilities'. Grandiose and, one fears, ultimately impractical ideas were abundant. One of the most ambitious was the construction of a tile-lined glass arcade encircling central London. There would have been a street above and a railway below; trains on no less than four tracks would be powered by atmospheric pressure. This came from Sir Joseph Paxton of Crystal Palace fame, and was to have been titled the 'Great Victorian Way'. The Committee, though, seem to have had their feet firmly on the ground, and their recommendations included the removal of river bridge tolls, and the linking of street improvements with underground railway building.

Some improvement in road passenger transport was afforded by the formation of the Paris-based London General Omnibus Co in 1856, which led to a shake-out of the multiplicity of horse-bus operators competing one with another, and to an altogether more orderly situation. Somewhat later, from 1870 onwards, the development in earnest of the rival horse tram offered the prospect of a cheaper operation, as the use of rails allowed the haulage of greater loads. In addition, all horse transport was given a boost through the importation of cheaper grain from abroad. But by then there was a new phenomenon in London, in the form of the Metropolitan Railway.

In his evidence to the Royal Commission, Charles Pearson, solicitor to the City of London, had presented his proposals for his Arcade Railway &

Central City Terminus Co. 'Ingenious' said the Commission, and left it at that. But Pearson was undoubtedly right in his championing the cause of railways as a means of offering relief to London's streets, and it is thus of no surprise to find him as a leading light in the promotion of the Metropolitan. The first authoritative notice of the enterprise which founded the Metropolitan Railway was to '... encircle the Metropolis with a tunnel to be in communication with all the railway termini, without forcing the public to traverse the streets in order to arrive at their destination'.

With the help of John Stevens, Architect and Surveyor to the City (Western Section), Pearson evolved a plan for a steam-operated underground railway to run the 3¾ miles between Farringdon Street and Bishop's Road, Paddington. This was to follow Farringdon Road and King's Cross Road to King's Cross, and then run more or less beneath the course of Euston Road, Marylebone Road and Praed Street to Paddington. Thus it would serve as a link between three main line railway termini: the Great Western at Paddington, the London & North Western at Euston, and the Great Northern at King's Cross. It did in fact eventually serve St Pancras as well when that station was built in 1868; prior to this Midland trains had used the Great Northern's premises at King's Cross via a now long-defunct connection between Bedford and Hitchin.

Farringdon Street was chosen as the site for the eastern terminus principally because the City Cattle Market, then occupying the site, was about to be moved to the Copenhagen Fields, Islington. The Act of Parliament obtained by the North Metropolitan Railway Company in 1853, however, only authorised the construction of the section between Edgware Road and Battle Bridge. Here, it is said, Queen Boadicea routed the Roman legions before putting

locomotive itself to maintain a working pressure. Regrettably, although having the desired effect in getting the Bill enacted, the technical problems proved to be altogether too much. A prototype was constructed by Robert Stephenson, but it languished in the sheds after being christened 'Fowler's Ghost'. Thus the Metropolitan opened for traffic on 10 January 1863 using conventional steam locomotives.

It had been a considerable feat to obtain finance for such a novel undertaking, the costs of construction of which were inevitably huge in comparison with its length. But an even greater potential hurdle must have been the attitude of the public to being hauled through glorified sewers by smoke-belching monsters. Pearson had been indefatigable in his promotion of the project, and it is sad to record that he died too soon to see the realisation of his ambitions. Nevertheless, much interest had been created by the very visible construction methods, and private viewing days were laid on for Mr and Mrs Gladstone and other notables, who rode through the newly-built tunnels in open wagons! On 9 January 1863, less than three remarkable years after construction started, the formal opening was celebrated by a banquet held at Farringdon Street. Special trains as they approached the station were heralded by music from a band.

Despite a sceptical Press, the Metropolitan was well patronised from the start. With fares of up to 9d (3.75p) for a First Class return, as much as £850 was taken on the first day. Patronage was 9,500,000 in the first year and 12,000,000 in the second, and did not look back.

From the start of services proper on 10 January, closed carriages were used. This original section of Metropolitan track was laid to the mixed gauge of standard and the Great Western's broad gauge of 7ft 0¼in. At first, the GWR supplied the motive power, rolling stock and personnel. Twenty-two coke-burning 2-4-0Ts of Gooch design were fitted with condensing apparatus, whereby nuisance from atmospheric pollution was to be attenuated. They were named after insects, foreign rulers and flowers, in true Great Western fashion. These were complemented by 45 eight-wheeled coaches of various origins, but all were lit by coal gas as were the stations.

The Great Western proved to be an uncertain partner for the Metropolitan. The Metropolitan management were anxious to increase service frequency from the basic four trains an hour to cope with a traffic running at 27,000 journeys daily, but the cautious Great Western objected to the effect of the additional working costs. Only two months after opening, payments were being withheld; then, outraged at not receiving an allotment of shares in the Moorgate Street extension, the GWR used this as a lever to bring the Metropolitan to heel. Or so they hoped. Late in July 1863, an ultimatum was issued by Paddington that the GWR would cease all operations from 30 September, a date then advanced to 11 August. Furthermore, they would not sell the locomotives and rolling stock to the Metropolitan for that company to run the service itself.

Both the Great Western and the City of London

London to fire and the sword. Battle Bridge became the more prosaic King's Cross when in 1830 a tall octagonal building surmounted by a statue of King George IV was erected. Though demolished only 15 years later, the name stuck. Further Acts were thus necessary for the construction of the original line.

Work began in 1860, and it was always envisaged as being a complex task. Although the construction of bored tunnels had been well practised with the canals and main line railways, this was something new. The method of digging a trench for the trains and then roofing it over became known as 'cut and cover' construction. Finding and diverting sewers, gas and water mains and drains was followed by the excavation of vast chasms in the streets 30ft wide and 15ft deep or more, to be lined with brickwork and roofed over, followed finally by the re-laying of the streets for surface traffic. Although the method minimised interference with private property and avoided the need for its purchase as the law then required, the effects on the road traffic in the vicinity must have been disastrous. Generally, damage to buildings was minimal, although owners were not slow in claiming for any structural defects which could possibly have been caused by 'the digging of an enormous ditch' in front of their properties.

A severe setback occurred in June 1862 when the

Fleet River, which had been diverted into a ditch alongside the railway, burst. This flooded the workings to a depth of 10ft between Farringdon and King's Cross, and the opening was put back to the following year partly as a result of this mishap, but also because of the need for signalling alterations to satisfy the Board of Trade.

Operationally, 'it is intended to run light trains at short intervals, and calling at perhaps alternate stations, and all risk of collision will be avoided by telegraphing the arrival and departure of each train from station to station, so that there will always be an interval of at least one station between the trains'. Thus, the *Illustrated London News* in 1860, sought to reassure its readers.

The means of traction was debated while the Bill was in Parliament. John Fowler, the Engineer, was said to have at first envisaged that trains should be blown through an airtight tunnel using giant compressors at each terminus. Such a system was being used on a mail-carrying narrow gauge railway in the City, but as with Brunel's atmospheric railway in South Devon before it, the difficulties of maintaining a satisfactory seal proved insurmountable. Thus Fowler opted for a fireless locomotive, to be recharged with high pressure steam at each terminus, and assisted with a firebrick heater on the

Above:

The pair of dummy houses in Leinster Gardens, Bayswater, was built at the railway's expense to preserve the dignity of the neighbourhood, for the railway passes directly underneath. Environmental pressures are not of recent origin. This 1995 view shows the blank windows distinctly. *John Glover*

Corporation had put up substantial sums for the Metropolitan, the GWR seeing advantage in the access to the City which it otherwise had no hope of reaching. The Corporation wanted the removal of carts from the streets. Both it and the GWR were thus keen to see rail access constructed to the new market at Smithfield. Fortunately for the Metropolitan, arrangements had also been entered into with the Great Northern, as a result of which connections had been provided to that company's lines. Hence it was to the Great Northern that the Metropolitan turned in their hour of need. It transpired that the Great Northern was not averse to scoring a few points off Paddington. By a superhuman effort in concert with the London & North Western Co, the GNR managed to assemble sufficient rolling stock to work the services from 11 August on the standard gauge,

which had so fortuitously been provided.

With scratch crews unfamiliar with the line, service quality went downhill rapidly. On the first day alone, six trains were derailed due to misalignment of the hitherto unused standard gauge rails, but order was soon restored. The arrangement could only be a stop gap, and the Metropolitan hurriedly ordered locomotives and coaches of their own.

The locomotives were outside-cylindered 4-4-0Ts built by Beyer Peacock & Co of Manchester, and were an adapted version of a design supplied for export to Spain. There was no cab roof, only a cab plate, which on later versions carried a top lip which was bent back to afford a little more protection for the crew. The engines were painted green, with the typical Beyer Peacock fittings of polished brass domes and numbers on the copper capped chimneys; each weighed just over 42 tons. The first order for 18 of the 'A' class was later expanded to 44 over several batches delivered from 1864 to 1870. The improved 'B' class followed, and ran to 22 locomotives between 1879 and 1885. The Metropolitan replaced the green livery with maroon from 1885. This outstandingly successful class was further multiplied for the Metropolitan District Railway which secured 54, making 120 in all. The principal (and important) difference was the Metropolitan's use of the

automatic vacuum brake, having first experimented with the Clark & Webb chain brake, whereas the District used the incompatible Westinghouse air system. The Metropolitan District used their locomotives exclusively up until the end of steam traction in 1905, but the Metropolitan went on to purchase and build a number of other types of tank engines for general work.

One of the biggest problems confronting the engineers of the underground steam railways was to provide and maintain a supply of breathable air in tunnels and stations. The Metropolitan engines burned coke, which is clean but gives off poisonous fumes, and after abortive trials with additional ventilation at the stations, the railway went over to coal. This had the immediate result of an extremely smoky atmosphere. It reached its worst at Gower Street (today's Euston Square). As a remedy, certain openings originally provided in the covered way at King's Cross and elsewhere for lighting purposes were adapted as smoke vents, and finally 'blow holes' were bored all along the route between King's Cross and Edgware Road. They were covered by gratings in the roadways above, and were prone to sudden belchings of steamy vapour which startled the passing horses.

The locomotives were fitted with condensing gear, which gave the driver a means of diverting exhaust steam from the chimney outlet into the water tanks, where the steam condensed, leaving the tunnels more or less clear of smoke and vapour. The trouble was that the blast on the fire was much reduced, and the power of the engine correspondingly impaired, whereas to maintain schedules between closely spaced stations needed a pretty lively engine. By rule the driver would operate his condensing lever on approaching a tunnel section, and restore the chimney exhaust wherever the line was not enclosed. From the sulphurous state of the tunnels, which some passengers found actively nauseating, it seems that the rule was not always obeyed. Matters were bearable initially, but conditions worsened as the frequency of service increased, and niceties such as the replacement of the warmed condensing water with cold at the end of each journey were abandoned.

The first of the new coaches was delivered by the Ashbury Railway Carriage Co on 1 October 1863. They were finished externally in varnished teak. First Class accommodation was distinguished by being painted white above the waist, and was fitted with carpets, mirrors and well-upholstered seats. No doubt this offset to some extent the discomfort caused by penetrating smoke in such confined spaces. Furnishings decreased in elegance according to the class, as did the space allotted per person, and one imagines that the third class passenger was usually glad to resurface, somewhat stiff after a ride during which all the windows had to be kept closed. It seems a little incongruous that after all this there should have been a 'No Smoking' rule applied impartially across all three classes, though this was later rescinded.

For the locomotive crews, the experience of driving steam locomotives underground, even with rather more openings to the sky than remain today, was not pleasant. 'In the summer you could hardly breathe going through the tunnels, it was so hot. It was enough to boil you on the footplate. You took your jacket off and stripped down to your shirt. There was a terrific wind and smoke going through the tunnels ... I'd shovel about two hundredweight in a day's work: it was a dirty, hot, sweaty job, but we

Above:
The Metropolitan Railway façade in the station at Praed Street, Paddington today disguises a station at which only Circle and District Line services call. This rebuilding dates from 1915, and was carried out to provide commercial letting space on two floors. J. Lyons is now a bookmakers, while the tobacconists has become a *Bureau de Change*. Remarkably, though, the 'Fresh Cut Flowers' sign and the business remains. The photograph is dated 25 July 1946.

Great Western Railway

had to put up with it.' This was George Spiller, in the early years of the present century. Nevertheless, the locomotives performed a grand job, and it is pleasing to relate that one of the 66 constructed, No 23, has survived, to find a permanent resting place in the London Transport Museum.

The broad gauge trains had disappeared for good from central London, and their rails were totally removed by 1873. The GWR left behind only a few rather more widely spaced running lines than might otherwise have been there.

The Metropolitan was run first and foremost as a passenger railway, and carried 9½ million passengers in its first year, a figure which rose to 28 million by 1868. Workmen's trains were introduced at a fare of 1d (0.4p) per single journey, but the line remained peripheral to central London. It was, however, outstandingly successful in revenue yield per route mile, when compared with its contemporaries, as Table 1 shows.

Murky and grimy the Metropolitan may have been, but that did not deter the good people of west London from pressing for an equivalent. At least the journey could be accomplished in the warm and dry, and more quickly than along the streets. The latter bore copious evidence of the use of horses, which made them especially unpleasant in wet weather. A few years after the opening of the Metropolitan, the District started operations with an east to west route

running through the heart of the capital. Thereafter, each line carried out a programme of extension with the same object in view: to bring the suburbs and the underdeveloped country beyond into direct rail communication with central London.

The first section of the Metropolitan District Railway opened in 1868 between South Kensington and Westminster, a distance of just over two miles. Construction was not without difficulty; the Westbourne River had to be contained and carried over Sloane Square station in a conduit, and the Company had to take special precautions to ensure that Westminster Abbey did not vanish into the 'cut and cover' construction. History often has a knack of

repeating itself, with the construction of the Jubilee Line Extension being blamed in recent times for slight movements in Big Ben.

Concurrent developments saw what became known as the Inner Circle begin to take shape. The Metropolitan extended from a junction west of Edgware Road, with a new line turning south through Notting Hill Gate to meet the Metropolitan District in an end-on junction at South Kensington. Environmental objections overcame the original intention to run across Kensington Gardens and Hyde Park on the surface, and the present route was selected instead. Here too, the susceptibilities of the residents of the area were involved, and in Leinster Gardens, Bayswater, the railway was forced to build a dummy pair of houses, Nos 23 and 24. Although identical to the adjacent houses, they are merely façades 5ft-thick, complete with false windows and front doors (minus letter boxes). Their purpose was to fill what would otherwise have been an ugly gap in the uniform, dignified, frontage of the row of buildings, for at this point the Metropolitan Railway

TABLE 1:		
Passenger Receipts per route mile per week		
Railway	**Miles**	**Revenue/route mile (£)**
London & North Western	1,274	41.15
Great Western	1,269	27.98
Great Eastern	673	22.16
London & South Western	490	34.40
South Eastern	306	53.42
London, Chatham & Dover	84	79.67
London, Tilbury & Southend	42	28.47
Metropolitan	3.75	720.80

passes beneath.

For the first two and a half years, the whole line through to Westminster was worked by Metropolitan stock, under an agreement between the two companies, but in the meantime the District (as it quickly became known) extended its lines eastward under Victoria Embankment to Blackfriars. Bearing in mind the smoke problem, the later District Railway engineers built their line in open cutting wherever possible and avoided much of the nuisance. This was not practicable along the Embankment and City sections, and here ventilators proved essential and unduly costly because of the need for camouflage. In the neighbourhood of Temple Gardens all surface evidence of an underground railway was frowned on, excepting Temple station itself, and the pump house chimney stack there had to be carried horizontally right along the station wall and up the side of a neighbouring building. Here it was decently screened by the wall and could smoke without giving offence. The Embankment and this portion of the District were built together, the railway opening in May 1870 and the road six weeks later.

In the meantime, extension westward was contemplated. Projection to West Brompton over the District's own tracks took place in 1869 though the purpose, which was to connect physically with the West London Extension Railway, was never fulfilled. Kensington still lay on the western outskirts, and beyond was practically open country, with places like Hammersmith and Chiswick still villages but rapidly growing. Extension became a fruitful proposition; District trains reaching Hammersmith in 1874.

The suburbs were seen as the key to prosperity, and the District pressed on westwards. A short link at Hammersmith gained access to the tracks of the London & South Western Railway and thus to Richmond in 1877, with a branch leaving this line at Turnham Green and continuing to Ealing Broadway (1879). The West Brompton stub was pushed south

to Putney Bridge in 1880, while arrangements were made to work the independently sponsored Hounslow branch from Acton Town in 1883. The District's last westward extension in the 19th century was over the Thames at Putney in 1889, to join with an L&SWR anxious to preserve 'its' territory, and on to Wimbledon.

Meanwhile the Metropolitan had been driving steadily east and west, with its ends both pointing towards the Thames, and an eastern extension to Moorgate was opened in 1865. In the west a railway between Hammersmith Broadway and Bishops Road (Paddington) was opened in 1864 by the independent Hammersmith & City Railway, which made working arrangements with both the Metropolitan and the Great Western. Somewhat unwisely, the GWR had allowed this railway to cross their main line on the level; a dive-under was subsequently constructed between Royal Oak and Westbourne Park, and opened in 1878. A service was also provided from Latimer Road to Kensington (Olympia), then known as Addison Road, on the West London Railway. It was worked by portions detached from Hammersmith trains and ultimately gave access to the District at Earl's Court. As from 1872, after the District had struggled eastwards as far as Mansion House, it became part of the meandering 'Outer Circle' worked by the L&NWR between Mansion House and Broad Street via Addison Road and Willesden. By a connection at Grove Road Junction, Hammersmith, the Metropolitan gained access to Richmond from 1877.

The District's arrangements with the Metropolitan for that company to operate its trains meant that in return the Metropolitan received 55% of the receipts. However, this proportion was tied to a given service level, and if the District wanted more trains (as it did), it had to pay out more to the Metropolitan. Hoping to escape from what it considered to be an excessive outpayment to the other company, the

Above:
The ubiquitous 4-4-0T locomotives of Beyer Peacock were found all over both the Metropolitan and District Railways; this is No 26, a Metropolitan Railway version with the later addition of a full cab. As pictured, it has the final cast-iron chimney and no condensing gear. Built by Beyer Peacock in 1868, No 26 lasted in Metropolitan service until 1926. It passed then to Pelaw Main Colliery, where it survived until 1948.
H. C. Casserley

Top Right:
The greatest extent of the Metropolitan Railway.

District determined to work its own trains, and gave notice to that effect. It thus built for itself a depot at West Brompton, now known as the Engineers' Depot at Lillie Bridge. Additionally, use of the Metropolitan's facilities would be avoided wherever possible, and to this end the District created its own separate running lines westwards from South Kensington. The upshot was a prolonged 'who does what' battle on the 1872 Circle service between Mansion House and Moorgate; eventually the Metropolitan agreed that it would accept District trains providing half the Circle service on Metropolitan metals. The District also worked its own lines. Although a solution had been found, further altercations followed on matters such as the division of receipts for bookings to the South Kensington exhibitions held annually on what is now the Imperial Institute site, and of which the

'Exhibition Subway' is a tangible reminder. The quarrels enriched nobody.

The District also provided decent rolling stock. This company too used coal gas lighting, but rather than copying the Metropolitan system of carrying gas in long rubber bags in a clerestory on the carriage roofs, the District pioneered a distinct improvement in 1878 by substituting oil-gas compressed into wrought-iron cylinders hung below the carriages. The gas was produced at Lillie Bridge depot and transported at night in mobile containers to various points on the system, where the carriage cylinders could be recharged. The use of compressed oil-gas later became general in Britain.

While all this was going on, the Metropolitan began its long excursions into northwest London and the land beyond, a journey that was to take it eventually to Verney Junction in darkest Buckinghamshire and over 50 miles from Baker Street. The promoters of the Aylesbury & Buckingham Railway could hardly have imagined that their railway, remote and unconnected with the London Underground system as it was, would one day become part of that distant and greater whole. Yet both the A&BR and the independent St John's Wood Railway which built a single line from Baker Street to Swiss Cottage were opened in 1868.

The Swiss Cottage appendage was forced to operate as a shuttle, the Metropolitan declining the use of the Baker Street Junction to enable trains to be projected towards the City. A passing loop had been provided at St John's Wood, and pilotmen were employed for the two sections each side of the loop to act as the authority to proceed. One wore a red cap and the other blue, and St John's Wood became a noted place for acrobatics. Here, each man changed over to the other's train, which he had to pilot to his original starting point, and seconds counted. On drawing level with the train waiting at the opposite platform face, the incoming pilotman would leap nimbly off the moving locomotive and join the outgoing footplate. The more prosaic wooden token, held by the guard rather than the driver, soon

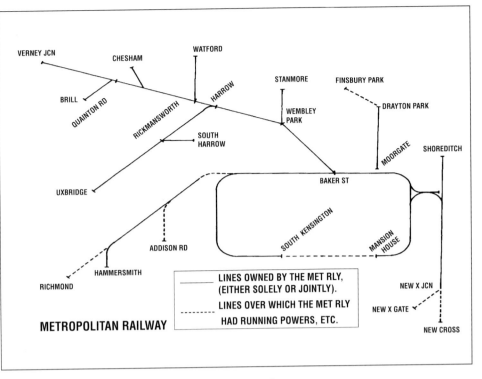

METROPOLITAN RAILWAY

LINES OWNED BY THE MET RLY,
(EITHER SOLELY OR JOINTLY).
LINES OVER WHICH THE MET RLY
HAD RUNNING POWERS, ETC.

Below:
At platform level, retaining largely its original appearance, the District Railway station at Fulham Broadway was opened as Walham Green. Many London Underground stations have a decidedly dated appearance, which does not match today's market-led approach too well. This picture was taken in 1983.
John Glover

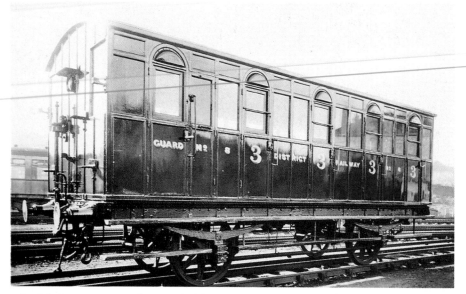

replaced the human one. Five 0-6-0Ts were built for this service by the Worcester Engine Co to cope with the steep gradients, but these turned out to be overpowered and were substituted by the standard 4-4-0Ts.

Meanwhile, the prospect of trains from the Great Northern and elsewhere converging on its tracks and disrupting its traffic had been exercising the Metropolitan, and it was decided to construct a second pair of tracks between King's Cross and Moorgate. The 'Widened Lines' dipped down through a second Clerkenwell Tunnel, passing beneath the Metropolitan which was carried above them on the 'Ray Street Gridiron'. This was a remarkable skew bridge of wrought-iron which also acted as a strut between the walls of the deep cutting. When all work was complete in 1869, a cross-London route was in place serving the Great Western, the Midland (via a connection to its new main line north of St Pancras) and the London Chatham & Dover (by a spur to Farringdon from Blackfriars), as well as the Great Northern. All were thus enabled to reach Smithfield meat market. The Midland got to Moorgate with trains from Bedford in July 1868, nearly three months before St Pancras was ready, and Moorgate thus became the Company's first terminus.

The Metropolitan reached east to the Great Eastern at Liverpool Street in 1875, making connections with the main line as well as building its own station. Ironically, in view of the constructional and subsequent operational complexities which ensued for the GER's Liverpool Street terminus, the connecting tunnel saw next to no use; the extension of Metropolitan services to Walthamstow over Great Eastern metals was not to be. A century later, the tunnel housed the BR Staff Dining Club, but it is now buried in the Broadgate development. The terminus at Aldgate was reached in 1876.

For the time being, that was it as far as the Inner Circle was concerned. The principal cause was that the Metropolitan was now under the control of the redoubtable Sir Edward Watkin, while the neighbouring District which had generally been considered a natural business partner and likely to fall under the same ownership, was headed by James Staat Forbes. With conflicting railway interests in Kent, these two men were personal enemies; what price therefore the construction of an inordinately expensive piece of linking railway 1.15 miles long under the City, which could only be worked satisfactorily in close co-operation?

Even without Watkin, relationships between the companies had been strained. Yet the public clamour for completion of the Inner Circle could not be resisted indefinitely. The necessary parliamentary powers were in existence, and eventually the City Lines and Extensions Act received Royal Assent in 1879.

Mindful of the disruption that 'cut and cover' construction could cause, it was stipulated in the Act that during construction the streets must be kept open for road traffic from 0600 to 1800. Consequently, the excavations had to be covered with a timber roof as they advanced; eventually work proceeded at 20ft a night. Completion was achieved on 6 October 1884.

Operation of the Circle was not straightforward. To make sure that the intentions of the legislators were carried out, the Act had laid statutory obligations on the companies to maintain the Circle Line service once it had been established. This was perhaps wise, as the ability of the two companies to agree showed no signs of improving, especially as the financial results of the completion of the Circle project were

1884

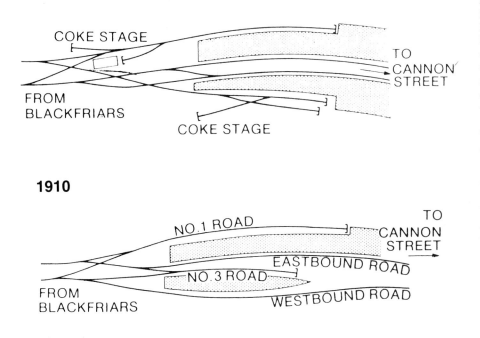

COKE STAGE

FROM BLACKFRIARS

COKE STAGE

TO CANNON STREET

1910

NO.1 ROAD

NO.3 ROAD

EASTBOUND ROAD

WESTBOUND ROAD

FROM BLACKFRIARS

TO CANNON STREET

disappointing. But there were fundamental difficulties in running a railway without a terminus: how would locomotives be coaled and watered, and the carriages 'gassed'? The practical solution was a two-minute stop at Aldgate for all trains to have the condensing water changed, with locomotives removed for servicing at South Kensington (Metropolitan) or High Street Kensington (District). The locomotives were then reattached to the following trains. The problem of how to recover from delays without the benefit of a terminal layover was tackled in part by an examination of the cause. Most trains using the Circle tracks originated and terminated on the many branches which radiated from that core, using it as a kind of overgrown carousel, and the system in the early days was overstretched. Eventually, a compromise of six Circle trains an hour instead of the eight intended enabled a workable result to be achieved. During busy parts of the day, the Metropolitan still managed to run an extra 13 trains an hour of its own along the northern side, a quite remarkable feat in the age of steam.

The City Lines and Extensions Act had also authorised both companies to extend eastwards and link with the East London Railway and its outlets to the south; the District also built its own eastern terminal at Whitechapel. The East London company had bought up the Thames Tunnel which was in use as a pedestrian subway in 1865, converted it to railway use and arranged with the London, Brighton & South Coast Railway to operate a service from New Cross to Wapping from 1869. Connections to the South Eastern and Great Eastern companies followed, the latter via Whitechapel and Bishopsgate Junction to Liverpool Street main line. A curve at St Mary's, Whitechapel, linked to the Underground railways from 1884, and from that time the Metropolitan and the District provided the local services under a working agreement. The main line companies all worked freight trains through the tunnel, and a passenger service terminated at Liverpool Street. It was said that Forbes, Chairman of the District, envisaged trains starting at New Cross and, having reached Aldgate East, running round the Circle in each direction alternately, and back to New Cross! It was no wonder that the operating managers

of the day had difficulties.

If the completion of the Inner Circle was something which had to be virtually forced out of the companies, the same could not be said of the Metropolitan's bid for main line status. Sir Edward Watkin, chairman from 1872 to 1894, also controlled the Manchester, Sheffield and Lincolnshire, the East London, and South Eastern Railways, as well as having Channel Tunnel interests. It was not therefore altogether surprising to find him championing the Metropolitan as part of a great trunk railway from the Midlands and the North, across London to Dover, and thence to the Continent. The shareholders found that the short urban railway in which they had placed their savings was now intent on greater things. No matter; by 1879, the Swiss Cottage appendage was extended to Willesden Green, and less than a year later to Harrow-on-the-Hill. At Neasden, a site was earmarked for workshops to replace what must have been desperately cramped facilities at Edgware Road. The tunnel section from Baker Street to Finchley Road was doubled in 1882.

Pausing shortly for breath at Harrow, it was not until 1885 that Watkin got his railway to Pinner, followed by Rickmansworth in 1887. By now, the Metropolitan had a main line 17½ miles in length, which amounted to a very long country tail to wag the urban dog. From Rickmansworth began the unremitting climb for steam traction into the Chilterns at a ruling gradient of 1 in 105. Though Aylesbury was the traffic objective and the company had the necessary powers to build the line, finance could not be raised and the railway was instead diverted to Chesham. Here, the grateful inhabitants presented the Metropolitan with the land required for the last half-mile into the terminus to enable a town centre site to be found for the station. Chesham was reached in 1889.

Finally, the section from Chalfont & Latimer, which became the branch junction, to Amersham and Aylesbury was completed in 1892. From Aylesbury, further possibilities arose. For this was the starting point of the Aylesbury and Buckingham line, which to Quainton Road provided a natural extension of the Metropolitan, before turning north to Verney Junction on the Oxford–Bletchley railway. The

A&BR's single line was promptly taken over by the Metropolitan, and doubled. The stage was now set for what was shortly to be renamed the Great Central Railway, formerly the Manchester, Sheffield and Lincolnshire, to press south and gain running powers over what were now Metropolitan tracks from Quainton Road. This was duly agreed, although separate running lines for Marylebone trains were constructed south from Harrow-on-the-Hill. This work was completed in 1899.

There remained the oddity of the Wotton Tramway, or the Brill branch, and a more unlikely concern to have become part of London Transport in 1933 can hardly be imagined. It started life as a private single-track railway owned by the Duke of Buckingham, and was constructed to carry staff and goods between Quainton Road station and the Duke's estate at Wotton. The line was 6½ miles long, with intermediate stations at Waddesdon, Westcott, Wotton, Church Siding and Wood Siding; trains took all of 1½ hours for the journey, including stops. Construction started in 1870; the first section from Quainton Road to Wotton was brought into use on 1 April 1871, and the whole line completed to Brill by the summer of 1872.

The first locomotives were a pair of thoroughly unconventional Aveling & Porter 0-4-0 geared locomotives, supplied at a cost of £400 each. Each 10-ton locomotive had a single overslung cylinder, 7¾in x 10in, connected through a countershaft and pinion to further pinions on the axles. Their maximum speed was about 8mph.

Operation was at first contracted out, while maintenance work was undertaken by the Duke's staff. Signalling was primitive, but only one engine was in use at a time. The operating regulations were notably strict, and a rule book was published in 1873. This contained a list of fines which might be levied on staff for misdemeanours. Thus, 'If the train be late at Quainton Junction (sic) in consequence of a late Start, the fault of the driver in not having his engine ready, a fine of Half a day's Pay to be imposed'.

On the death of the Duke in 1894, the tramway passed as part of the estate to Earl Temple, and in that year the working of the line was taken over by the Oxford & Aylesbury Tramroad Co. This company set about improving the line, replacing the original light rails laid on longitudinal sleepers with flat-bottomed rails spiked direct to transverse sleepers. The rolling stock was also replaced, and the two original locomotives sold to the Nether Heyford brickworks, near Weedon, Northants.

Not wishing to miss any expansion potential in the area, the Metropolitan was pleased to lease the railway and purchase the rolling stock when approached; the company assumed control on 1 December 1899. The Metropolitan had already provided a new coach, much higher off the ground than the original offerings. Station platforms were raised, but to avoid the expense of complete rebuilding they were altered at one end only, retaining the 1894 tramroad buildings at the old level.

By the turn of the century, steam operation had nearly reached its zenith; only the Whitechapel & Bow extension of the District in a joint venture with the London, Tilbury & Southend Railway remained to be completed (in 1902), and the Uxbridge branch of the Metropolitan from Harrow-on-the-Hill. Steam trains began to work that line in 1904, but as a temporary expedient only; they were replaced by electric traction within six months.

Chapter 2

The First Tube Railways

Above:
The City & South London Railway's sole surviving locomotive rests at the Science Museum, London. They were built in several batches by a variety of manufacturers; this is No 13 of 1890, built by Beyer Peacock and equipped by Mather & Platt. The four wheels are only 27in in diameter and the wheelbase 6ft. The 14ft long locomotive weighed about 12 tons; with its 50hp motor, it was capable of moving its 40-ton train at an average 12mph. Maximum speed was 20–25mph. *John Glover*

Top right:
This delightful drawing shows a train of 'padded cell' cars with their minimal window openings. The sideways-facing driving position of the City & South London Railway locomotives can be seen; this must have been somewhat disconcerting for passengers waiting on the platforms.
Author's collection.

The basic process of driving a large tunnel without disturbing the surface directly above is old. The first significant example for the London Underground was completed in 1843, although there was then no intention of putting it to railway use.

In March of that year, the first tunnel beneath the Thames was opened, connecting Rotherhithe on the south bank with Wapping on the north, without impeding river traffic. Its length was 1,200ft. In fact, it was the first tunnel for public traffic ever to be driven beneath a river anywhere in the world. The engineer responsible was Sir Marc Isambard Brunel, with the assistance of his even more illustrious son.

Brunel's method of tunnel construction was inspired by a study of the shipworm, *teredo navalis*. A shell, scored with parallel rows of small teeth that resemble the cutting edges of a file, forms the head of the shipworm. As the shipworm burrows its way inward, the wood dust is passed through its body and a secretion containing carbonate of lime is deposited. This lines the tunnel created with a whitish, shell-like substance. Brunel patented a process for tunnelling based on the mollusc's own

principle.

The result was a shield forced into the earth and excavated from within. Although primitive by modern standards, it worked, and the idea has yet to be bettered. For the Thames Tunnel, Brunel employed a rectangular shield made of iron, shaped like a huge box with open ends, and furnished with projecting teeth. It was placed at the working face of the tunnel, and as the face was gradually excavated the shield was moved forward, protecting the men within against the great pressure of the ground above them. The shield was honeycombed with compartments wherein worked miners and bricklayers, and as it moved forward beneath the river bed, the miner excavated the soil and strengthened the cavity he made. The bricklayer followed and lined it with bricks.

This tunnel was intended to expedite the work of the London Docks and to save horse-drawn traffic from making the long detour via London Bridge. Long sloping approaches would have been necessary for this purpose, but when the tunnel was completed after a series of misfortunes, the

THE FIRST ELECTRIC TUBE RAILWAY, 1890.

promoting company had no funds left. The only access was by stairways down the circular shafts which had been used for construction purposes, and usage was thus confined to pedestrians. It was an extremely costly project which took 18 years to complete, including a seven year period during which it was abandoned through lack of funds. This followed an accident in which the Thames had burst through the roof, flooding the workings and

drowning seven men; the project also claimed the health of Marc Brunel.

As early as 1832, it was stated that 'it is confidently hoped that the public approbation and admiration which have hitherto encouraged the labours of those who have designed and undertaken this magnificent work, will not be withheld'. The 1843 opening saw a band of the Coldstream Guards at the head of a procession in which Brunel took

part, but the tunnel was quickly dubbed a white elephant by a sceptical public. It languished until it was acquired, as already related, by the East London

Below:
All the City & South London stations were provided with a pair of hydraulic lifts, but of the domes containing the winding gear only that at Kennington survives. This picture was taken in 1990. *John Glover*

was only 7ft in diameter when completed, which severely limited its usefulness. Barlow's shield was driven forward through the earth by levers and jacks, cutting into clay and averaging 5ft progress a day.

Both the method of tunnelling and the tunnel itself are notable in railway history, for Barlow's iron-lined tube was the first of its kind in the world. Since it also contained a small railway, it was also the very first tube railway. Passengers descended a shaft in a lift, and at the bottom took their seats in a car which was drawn through the tube by cable, worked by a small stationary engine. The rail track gauge was 2ft 6in and the car held 12 passengers. After a life of only three months, the company went bankrupt and the lifts and the cable car were removed. It lingered on as a pedestrian walkway until the opening of Tower Bridge in 1894, since which time it has been used to carry hydraulic power and water mains under the river.

From these two beginnings evolved the famous Greathead shield, which cut most of London's subsequent tube tunnels. James Henry Greathead drove the tunnels for the King William Street–Stockwell tube railway in 1886, using a shield of his own design. It differed from Barlow's in so far as it was driven forward into the earth by

hydraulic rams working at a pressure generally of 1 ton/sq in, although the larger Greathead shield used for the Blackwall (road) tunnel worked at a pressure of 2¾ ton/sq in. The rams pressed against the tunnel segments already fixed in place and forced the 12ft diameter shield into the earth, enclosing a great core which was then removed by the miners. The excavated section of tunnel was sprayed with liquid cement, and after a ring of iron plates was placed in position, more cement was forced through the holes in the plates to fill the small intervening spaces; the process was known as grouting.

The driving of tunnels required a great deal of precision if they were to meet accurately, since an error of only ¹⁄₁₆in in sighting would throw the actual

Left:
The C&SLR later abandoned the small windows for its passenger vehicles; this internal view is of the first enlarged window car type.
J. A. Rosser collection

Top right:
An 1898 view of the Waterloo terminus of the London & South Western Railway's Waterloo & City line, to which finishing touches are being made. The separate arrival and departure platforms were needed to avoid the arches supporting the main line station above, though a combined arch spanned the connections to the reversing siding and the depot roads.
Crown Copyright/National Railway Museum LSW245

Bottom right:
The Central London Railway used these handsome camel-back locomotives initially, though with unhappy results. No 19 is seen at the Wood Lane depot with a train of gate stock in the early days.
Bucknall collection/ Ian Allan Library

Below:
The Northern Line passing under Hampstead, 1907.

Railway. Nevertheless, Brunel had shown a way which many others would follow, and in 1869 Peter Barlow was engaged to drive a second Thames tunnel, this time between the Tower and Bermondsey. He improved on Brunel's method, using a circular shield and dispensing with brickwork, lining the tunnel instead with cast iron segments bolted flange to flange. The Tower Subway, as it was named, had a minimum depth of 22ft as against the shallower Rotherhithe tunnel, but

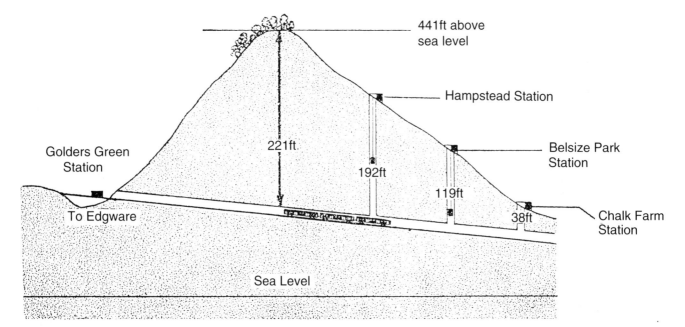

441ft above sea level

Hampstead Station

Belsize Park Station

Golders Green Station

221ft.

192ft

119ft

38ft

Chalk Farm Station

To Edgware

Sea Level

driving seriously out of alignment. Sufficient was now known to enable the whole of the tube network to be cut accurately.

Along the line of route, a series of vertical shafts was sunk, from which headings were driven at right angles. To find the exact centre line along which to bore the running tunnel, a theodolite (an instrument for measuring angles by optical means) was set on the surface over the end of a heading and precisely over the subterranean line of route, but way above it. Two plumb lines were next hung down the working shaft and exactly aligned with a sight on the instrument. The theodolite, thus set, was taken to the bottom of the shaft, and its position adjusted until this time it agreed with the plumb lines already adjusted from above. In other words, a sight line taken above ground was about to be transferred below, and it was then only necessary to determine a true right angle off the vertical plummets and to fix a true depth. When the correct distance along the heading had been measured, and the true right angle determined, the point and direction of the running tunnel's centre line was known, and work could begin. The shield was erected in position in a chamber formed by several rings of iron lining, and a short excavation made in the working face of the running tunnel. Provided the earth was soft enough for the purpose, piles were inserted between it and the edge of the shield, and a forward thrust of the shield drove the piles into the face and broke up the earth for easy removal. With the Greathead type of shield it was necessary thereafter to cut a small chamber in the face in advance of the shield, so that the earth enclosed by the ring of the shield after each forward thrust might collapse into the space made.

On certain sections of the London tubes, the

tunnels may be seen to dip on leaving the stations and to rise on approach to them; by looking through the end windows of a car where a sight along the interior of several successive cars can be had, the bend of the train on meeting each change in direction is perceptible. It has become the practice that running tunnels should be so graded for the double purpose of accelerating the departure of a train and retarding its speed on approach. The falling gradient of about 1 in 30 results in a saving in current consumption, and conversely the rising gradient, which is made rather less acute, results in an economy on brake wear. With modern trains possessing reserves of tractive power and powerful brakes these switchbacks are less important, although they still augment appreciably the overall speed when stations are closely spaced. The double reverse curve encountered on the Piccadilly Line at South Kensington though, and the fearsome bend on the Central Line at Bank, stem from a different reason, in that the builders preferred to follow the street patterns above rather than tussle with property owners over possible compensation problems.

On various occasions when driving tunnels, engineers have had to contend with more than clay or workable earth. They have encountered waterlogged sand or have had to tunnel below rivers and streams where normal methods would have quickly resulted in flooded workings. The general procedure is to construct airtight working chambers and compress the air within them, so that there is sufficient pressure to keep out the water or, in certain cases, to help support the periphery of the tunnel face. If a waterlogged stratum is met when sinking a shaft, a vertical chamber is constructed; and if a tunnel has to be driven through a bed of soaked sand, for instance, then a horizontal chamber is made. In both cases a smaller compartment is constructed at the entrance to the pressure chamber to form an airlock, so that men and material do not enter or leave the pressure chamber direct from the outer air. The move from atmospheric pressure is thus via a chamber in which pressure can be increased until it equals that at the work face. On tube construction work, air pressures vary up to 35lb/sq in, but the average is around 10lb/sq in.

The greater proportion of tunnelling for London's tubes has been driven through what is known as London clay, varying in colour from grey-green to yellow, and which lies on top of the chalk and sand that once formed a sea bed. The tunnels burrow beneath shallow beds of gravel and river drift which the Thames and its tributaries have deposited over the clay during the ages. Roughly north of a line represented by Euston Road, the London clay comes to the surface, and stretches out as far as the chalk of the Chiltern hills. In central and southern districts of London, pockets of sand and gravel, often waterlogged, are found lying beneath layers of 'made ground' formed by the foundations of older London. The depth of the made ground is as much as 24ft at Farringdon. Under a few parts of London the predominant clay is shallow in depth, and chalk is encountered, but generally London rests on a very thick layer of clay which is anything up to 450ft deep.

Little of this was known to the tube pioneers, but

even in Victorian London it was clear that the 'cut and cover' method of railway construction was unacceptably disruptive to normal day-to-day living. At the same time, the need to improve transport facilities within the central area, that is within the area of London encompassed by the Circle Line, became ever more pressing. An effective tunnelling method was therefore a prerequisite for the expansion which was to follow.

Another necessary technical development was the means of traction. Cable haulage had been used since the earliest days of railways, until it was supplanted by the steam locomotive. Could cables be used satisfactorily for underground railways?

The City & South London Railway was built on the premise that they could. With an original route length of 1½ miles, quickly extended to three miles after work started when it was realised that the full potential of the line was unlikely to be developed otherwise, the C&SLR was to be powered by a stationary engine at Elephant & Castle. Two cables were to be provided, one at 10mph on the sharply curving section north to King William Street, the other at 12mph on the straighter and easier Stockwell section. Contracts were signed, but the work was never carried out as in the meantime the decision was made to adopt electricity as the motive power. This promised to offer a higher average speed and, ultimately, to be a cheaper medium than cable. Thus in 1890 the C&SLR opened for public traffic, its trains of three bogie trailer cars hauled by 12-ton electric locomotives at an average speed of 11½ mph.

Only by their freedom from steam and smoke could these early trains have commended themselves to travellers. Unlike the creature comforts of the traditional steam-hauled rolling stock found on the Metropolitan and District railways, the City & South London offered little amenity. It was a railway designed for a purpose, without the constraints of the compatibility needed for an installation which was part of a system. Its function as the 'Sardine-box Railway', a name bestowed on it by Punch, was to take passengers from one station to another, avoiding the delays from road traffic.

This it did with remarkable success, and within three years of its opening was carrying 15,000 passengers each day. The coaches, appropriately nicknamed 'padded cells', were a mere 6ft 10in wide, designed for a tunnel purposely made as small as possible to reduce construction costs. Passengers sat on longitudinal benches, above which were tiny windows that were little more than ventilators, so that in the absence of advertisements passengers could do little more than sit and stare at one another. Electric lighting was provided, which was a luxury compared with the gas lights in the Metropolitan and District stock, so perhaps the fortunates who sat below one of the low powered bulbs were able to read their newspapers. A curious notice on the inside of all cars read: 'No passenger shall be permitted to ride on the roof on penalty of 40s (£2) fine'.

If the general description seems less than enticing, the tram alternative had oil lamps, and seats with negligible upholstery. The two guards on

each train were responsible for control of the gates at the ends of the cars and also for informing passengers of the names of the stations. It seems that ridicule as much as anything else persuaded the company to build their future stock with larger windows; the fleet reached 170 cars by 1908. Describing a journey on the C&SLR between Monument and Bank, Punch said: 'The train rocked alarmingly. It was so packed with people that getting in and out was a regular scrimmage. We entirely endorse the railway company's advertisement in that it is the "warmest line in London".'

There were basically two types of locomotives, represented by Nos 1–14 with flat sides, distinguished from later builds with rounded sides which gave more space for housing the air brake reservoirs. This was a matter of some moment, since the locomotives at first carried no compressors, and for their braking had to rely on a fresh supply of compressed air taken in at the terminus. The train pipe of the braking system was routed over the roof of the locomotive and its cars. The first 14 locomotives were built by Mather & Platt of Manchester, Nos 15–16 by Siemens, and most of the others by Crompton. The maximum fleet of 52 was in service in 1901. All were driven by a pair of 50hp motors; No 22 was subsequently remotored in 1912 with two 120hp interpole units and was thus the most powerful on the line. The four-wheeled locomotives were minute, being only 14ft long, 6ft 6in wide and 8ft 6in high. Even so, the driving cabs extended from front to rear of the locomotive, with the driver facing sideways. Passengers waiting on

Top left:
The incorporation of station names in the platform wall tiling was a splendid idea — unless management wished subsequently to change the station name! Arsenal today displays the name the station carried from 1906 until 1932. Another notable survival is Great Central, today's Marylebone.
John Glover

Bottom left:
Edgware Road station on the Bakerloo Line remains today at street level much as it was when it opened in 1907. The facing is of ruby-glazed blocks in the style of Leslie Green.
John Glover

Above:
Barons Court station opened for District Line services in 1905, being served also by the Great Northern, Piccadilly & Brompton Railway when that opened from Finsbury Park to Hammersmith the following year.
John Glover

platforms were thus presented with the odd sight of the driver facing them as the train rumbled in. Perhaps it was as well that he was provided with an assistant.

These midgets of locomotives were designed for an uncomplicated run under known conditions, and were therefore both simple in design and sturdy in build, with a minimum of fittings which could give trouble. There was no reduction gear in the drive, and the motor armature was mounted directly on the axle. Wiring was equally simple; the traction current merely passed from the collector shoes to a fuse cut-out and main switch, thence to a rheostat (or variable control), and through the motors back to earth via the axlebox, wheel and rail. In short, the locomotives were the absolute embodiment of electric motors on wheels. This highly practical engineering approach was rewarded by many years of hard work, hauling 40-ton trains at speeds of up to 25mph.

The whole of the running line was below ground, as much as 105ft down at the Thames crossing and never less than 45ft. The workshops and depot were on the surface, reached by a 1 in 3½ inclined ramp at Stockwell. Later, and after an unfortunate mishap when the tow rope broke and a car took a headlong flight back to the main line, a hoist similar to the one which graced the Waterloo & City Line was installed. The up and down running lines were in their own separate tunnels of 10ft 2in diameter north of the Elephant and 10ft 6in to the south. This reflected the 2mph greater speed planned with cable haulage on the southern section and which would thus increase the sway of the trains! Today's engineers refer grandly to the 'kinematic envelope'; this was an early practical response to the problem.

At the termini, the running tunnels merged into one larger elliptical tunnel. Locomotives had to be placed on the other end of the trains, and this was carried out by 'stepping back' each incoming train locomotive so that it returned with the subsequent train. Coupling and uncoupling were jobs for the driver's assistant. The stations and passages were entirely lined with white tiles, except where space was monopolised by advertisements, and the effect was recorded as being 'to provide a bright and cheerful gleam under the artificial light'.

Adequate passenger access to the deep level tube platforms was the remaining technical necessity. All the original stations were furnished with hydraulic lifts, later stations having electric ones.

Power for the system was taken from the company's own power house at Stockwell, where three dynamos were belt-driven by steam engines with massive 14ft-diameter flywheels. The current was taken along the tunnels by feeder cable to signal cabins at each station, where other cables led to the conductor rails.

The City & South London Railway proved so popular during peak hours that capacity became a real problem. It was decided to raise the 2d (0.8p) flat fare during the morning peak, but modification of the signalling system allowed more trains to be run and this early example of a peak hour surcharge was not proceeded with. However, passenger traffic continued to grow, so that the small single road terminus at King William Street, which had been designed for use with cable haulage, became overcrowded. The company's solution here was to abandon the terminus with its steeply inclined approaches, and to build a replacement at Bank. The extension diverged from the old line at London Bridge and was opened in 1900. In the next two years the tube was extended south to Clapham Common and north to Moorgate, after which it continued beneath the line of City Road to the Angel at Islington, and subsequently reached King's

Cross and then Euston by following the slope of Pentonville Road. This final section opened in 1907.

Traffic continued to increase in the years preceding World War 1, until it became obvious that the C&SLR would have to be completely modernised. This was the penalty for the pioneer, upon whose work others had subsequently improved. It meant the installation of a new signalling system, the enlargement of the stations to take longer trains, and the reconstruction of the tunnels to what became the increased standard diameter of 11ft 8¼in. Such work was well beyond the financial capabilities of the company to carry out unaided, and an agreement was sought with the Underground Electric Railways Company of London which by then controlled most of the other underground lines in London. Consequently, control of the C&SLR passed to the UERL in 1913, although the war delayed a start on the expansion work for a further nine years.

Since tube railway schemes were now coming before Parliament in some numbers, an attempt was made to set out some ground rules. With the example of the C&SLR no doubt in mind, a Parliamentary Committee of 1892 suggested that future tubes should be of a minimum 11ft 6in in diameter. They also proposed that the principle which required companies to purchase properties they passed beneath should be abandoned, and replaced by a wayleave system. The ability to obtain such permission might avoid some of the tortuous curves which resulted in following the streets above, although it would still leave the companies open to claims of extortionate compensation

payments. Wayleaves would be granted free of charge when running under public streets. These sensible reforms were to be of benefit to London, although they did not solve the problems of funding high capital intensive railway construction.

The completion of the Circle Line in 1882 had

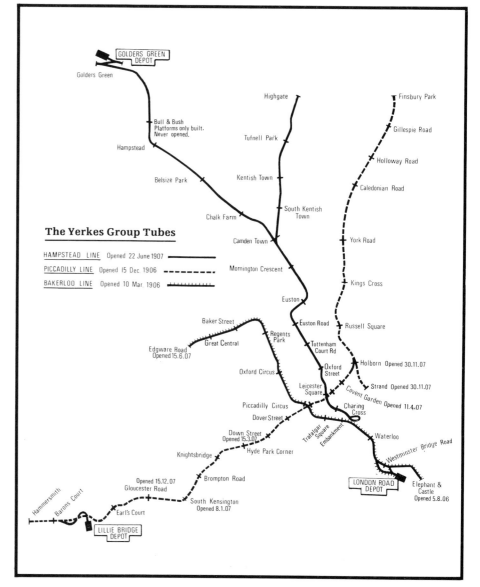

The Yerkes Group Tubes

HAMPSTEAD LINE Opened 22 June 1907 ——————
PICCADILLY LINE Opened 15 Dec. 1906 - - - - - -
BAKERLOO LINE Opened 10 Mar. 1906 ++++++++

resulted in the linking of all the main line railway termini to the City that were not within walking distance; all, that is, except Waterloo. In the days when the West End was of less importance, this was a serious shortcoming as far as the London & South Western Railway was concerned, and to remedy it they promoted a direct tube link using the newly developed technology and backed with that Company's substantial resources.

The second tube railway in the capital was opened in 1898 after a construction period of less than four years. Completely self-contained and with the two stations at Waterloo and Bank only, this 1.6-mile line crosses beneath the Thames near Blackfriars Bridge. An inclined tunnel which meant a long wearisome walk formed the exit from the system at Bank, and remained thus for the next 62 years. The line's power station and sidings were at Waterloo, where a hoist brought cars to the surface.

This was the first tube line to use rolling stock with motor cars instead of locomotives. The bodywork of the 22 cars was built in America by Jackson and Sharpe, with electrical equipment by Siemens and bogies from the L&SWR workshops at Eastleigh where the vehicles were assembled. The open saloons were of distinctively transatlantic appearance, and the seats were formed of perforated plywood without any upholstery. To reduce the cost of operation during the day when traffic was light, five additional single unit motor cars were supplied by Dick, Kerr of Preston the following year.

Current collection was from a centre conductor rail, and the trains were formed of a pair of motor cars with two intermediate trailers. Eight power cables ran along the roofs of the trailers to connect the power cars, a feature which was not allowed on any other tube railway. Commendably, all electrical gear was arranged so that it did not reduce the length of the vehicles which was available for passenger use, although the truly massive motor bogies with their 33in diameter wheels had a raised floor level above them.

A Siemens shunting locomotive was provided to work in the sidings at Waterloo.

Historically, the line never had any formal connection with the Underground railways or London Transport. The Waterloo & City remained with the L&SWR and their successors until it passed to London Underground in 1994. The original system proved to be sound both in design and construction, and few changes were made until the next generation of rolling stock was acquired in 1940.

The C&SLR and the W&C came; the public saw; the Central London Railway conquered. At nearly six miles in length, what became the heart of today's Central Line ran through the heart of London in an area which until then had not seen a railway of any kind. It deserved to be, and was, an instant success, and managed to avoid falling into the trap of

catering for business traffic only. By tapping the theatre, shopping and hotel areas of the West End as well, it attracted over 40 million passengers in its first full year of operation in 1901. This was eight times the numbers generated by the City & South London after a similar period. It was a tremendous improvement on the Metropolitan, still wedded to steam. Hamilton Ellis recalled that Punch published 'a happy cartoon of sweet little Fairy Electra riding on a sort of sparkling Catherine wheel, waving a minatory wand at a hideous demon with a smoking chimney hat, and remarking that now people had seen her, she fancied his days were numbered'. However, the Central London too had its share of technical problems.

Its route was from Bank, westward in a straight line to Shepherd's Bush. There were 11 intermediate stations. It was decided not to use the island platform arrangement favoured by the C&SLR (and still to be seen today at Clapham North and Clapham Common), and instead to separate the twin tubes widely enough to allow a platform for each direction, joined to its neighbour by cross

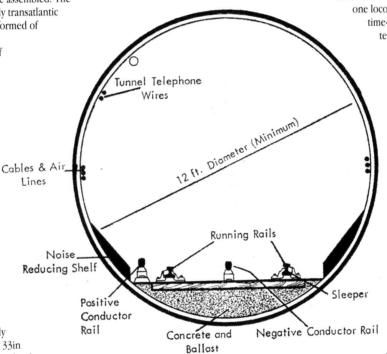

passages. Where the streets were narrow as at Notting Hill Gate, Chancery Lane and St Paul's (formerly Post Office), one tube was placed directly above the other to take advantage of the free wayleaves thus obtained. In the anxiety not to incur compensation costs as a result of undermining buildings, some ferocious curves were introduced between St Paul's and Bank, so much so that the tunnel diameter had to be increased by up to 9in to accommodate the 'throwover' of the cars as they negotiated the line. This has proved to be a lasting nuisance, particularly at Bank station where the train-to-platform gap can be excessive.

The stations were finished with white tiling, and

had large nameboards in white enamel picked out in blue, but in addition the train guards were instructed to call out the name of the next station on leaving the previous one, and repeat it on arrival. (A voice synthesised version is incorporated in the current 1992 rolling stock; such is scientific progress!) Electric arc lamps illuminated the platforms, which were reached by electric lifts, offering an altogether more attractive environment than the C&SLR. This superiority was continued in the 170 cars, which were built by Ashbury and Brush to take full advantage of the increased tunnel size. These were long, low vehicles with a platform at each end enclosed by a lattice gate structure, with slightly bowed sides and clerestory roof. Although the intention had been to use the recommended 11ft 6in diameter tunnels, a later decision not to line the cast-iron segments of the tubes resulted in an effective diameter of 11ft 8¼in, which became the standard.

The platforms were 325ft long, and it was envisaged that a locomotive would be provided at each end of the seven car trains. This was vetoed by the Board of Trade's Railway Department, who this time refused to allow power cables to run between the two. So the Company had to confine itself to one locomotive per train, which then required time-wasting shunting movements at each terminus and restricted the minimum service interval to 3½ minutes or 17 trains/hr (tph).

There were other disadvantages. Locomotives required the use of valuable platform space but, more seriously, they gave rise to complaints of vibration. Fortunately, a technical solution was at hand thanks to the work of Frank J. Sprague in Chicago. Sprague is credited with the invention of multiple unit working, whereby a single master controller uses a low voltage circuit to achieve simultaneous control of all the traction motors in a train. This overcomes concerns about the wisdom of allowing high current traction power to be transferred by cable along the length of the train. Experimentally, four trailers were converted to driving motors cars with two motors in each, and sandwiching four trailers in between. Success led to an order for 64 new motor cars, and these were delivered in 1903 from the Metropolitan Railway Carriage & Wagon Co and the Birmingham Railway Carriage & Wagon Co. However, much valuable space was still taken up by the control equipment and switchgear, which were housed above the car frame. Another worthwhile outcome was the ability to run trains at two-minute intervals (30tph) if required, thanks to the quick turnrounds which could be achieved.

The electric locomotives were scrapped, apart from two which were fitted with trolley poles and sent to join the Company's pair of steam locomotives, which had been built by Hunslet to tube gauge. These condensing 0-6-0Ts were used for shunting duties at the Wood Lane depot beyond the Shepherd's Bush terminus, and for maintenance

work in the tunnels when the power was off. The power station was also located here.

The first extension to the Central London Railway was opened in 1908 to serve the Franco-British Exhibition at White City. In view of the existing depot connections, the terminal loop provided was negotiated in an anticlockwise direction, with a single platform at Wood Lane situated on the loop. This introduced some operating and technical problems, since cars were 'handed' depending on the direction they faced and they could now be turned in the course of their journeys. The importance of 'handing' lies in the electrical and air pipe connections made between cars, since unless these are arranged symmetrically about the centre (and are thus expensively duplicated), a car to be coupled to another cannot reverse. The penalty for not providing full reversibility is the constraint in limiting what may be coupled to what.

At the eastern end, the line to Liverpool Street was completed in 1912.

Motor bus competition ate into receipts from 1905 onwards, and the Central London Railway was drawn inexorably into closer co-operation with the Underground Group, under whose control it fell in 1913. Commercially, it was known by the nickname 'Twopenny Tube' long after graduated fares were adopted. From 1911 the Company decided to carry parcels in compartments set aside on the trains. A porter sorted these during the journey, and they were then delivered by messenger boys on tricycles. Parcels could be up to 56lb in weight and not

exceeding 4ft x 2½ft x 1ft in size, with a collection and delivery radius of ½-mile from any station. Passengers were also wooed with season tickets, with reduced rates for those under 18. The company also indicated how a model passenger should behave 'in order to aid in rendering the service expeditious, clean and comfortable for all':

- ■ To enter and pass along the lifts quickly and not congregate around the entrances.
- ■ To be ready to leave the train immediately on arrival at destination.
- ■ To be careful to extinguish matches, cigar and cigarette ends before throwing them away.
- ■ To refrain from spitting.
- ■ To refrain from smoking in the lifts.

By far the most massive of all tube construction in London resulted in the building of the big 16ft-diameter bores of the Great Northern & City Railway, between Finsbury Park and Moorgate. The original intention was to allow Great Northern trains to reach the City direct via a connection at Drayton Park which would have rendered the continuation to the underground station below the GNR premises unnecessary, but this ambition was frustrated for over 70 years.

The 3½-mile long line was built by using an extra powerful Greathead shield, but as the shield progressed the lower cast-iron segments were removed and replaced by a blue brick invert as an economy. It was the only economy which was practised, since the stations were built to a full 420ft long (and 450ft at the termini), in the fond hope that one day they would be needed by Great Northern trains. They appeared immense and deserted, as indeed they mostly were, with trains occupying only a small portion of the platform length during the slack hours.

The line was electrified from the outset using multiple-units on the Sprague principle; it opened in 1904. The conductor rails followed closely the arrangement used in the earlier Metropolitan and District trials to be described in the next chapter, with both positive and negative rails placed 10in outside the running rails and 2in above their level. This ensured that no traction currents were present in the running rails. For the first time, these were being used to carry track circuits in the modern sense and provide automatic signalling using treadles. The conductor rail arrangement remained in use until the original cars were replaced in 1939.

Thirty-two motor and 44 trailer cars were built for the service by Brush and Dick, Kerr. Trains of six cars operated in the peak, and two cars at other times. The cars had open end platforms where the guard stood and worked the lattice gates by levers. There were also sliding doors in the centre of each car, but these were opened only from the outside, and then only at the termini, by porters specially detailed for the job. The line had its own power station near Essex Road, which allowed for direct cables to be run to four connections along the line, thus making substations unnecessary.

The line was acquired by the Metropolitan Railway in 1913, and the new owners promptly abandoned the power station and provided their own supplies from Neasden.

Success for entrepreneurs in the promotion of underground railways was thus far from a foregone conclusion, and many lesser schemes fell by the wayside. Nevertheless, all the interest now being shown resulted in some which were deserving of being built (having obtained their necessary powers), but found themselves struggling. The common denominator was a lack of sufficient backing, but this they were to find in the person of the American financier, Charles Tyson Yerkes.

Yerkes was already involved in the District, confirmed by his taking a controlling stake in 1901. His interests quickly expanded. The Metropolitan District Electric Traction Co was created for the purpose of electrifying that railway and the building of a power station at Lots Road, Chelsea, to supply it. Within a year the Company had bought out the Charing Cross, Euston & Hampstead Railway interests, the Brompton & Piccadilly Circus and the Great Northern & Strand (which were combined and enhanced to become the Great Northern, Piccadilly & Brompton) and the partially constructed Baker Street & Waterloo. In 1902 the MDET was revamped as the Underground Electric Railway Company of London Ltd. Yerkes was its Chairman, and although some variations to schemes already authorised were approved, no underground railway proposals outside the UERL empire survived to be built.

Yerkes' backer was Edgar Speyer, the American-born son of a German-Jewish banker. Through his international banking concern and the Old Colony Trust of Boston, Massachusetts, it proved possible for Yerkes and the UERL to raise the capital to build the lines. To what extent financial chicanery was resorted to remains unclear, but the result was that central London gained a network of underground lines about 80ft below ground level, which was to remain in its 1907 form for a further 60 years. Yerkes died in 1905 before any of his tubes were opened; he was succeeded by Speyer, while George Gibb of the North Eastern Railway was brought into manage the undertaking.

The 'Bakerloo', to which the name of the Baker Street and Waterloo was quickly corrupted, opened to traffic in March 1906 between Baker Street and what is now Lambeth North; by June 1907 the Piccadilly and Hampstead tubes had also come in to being, leaving only the Aldwych (previously named Strand) spur from Holborn, which opened on 30 November that year. Using current station names, the Yerkes tube lines therefore were:

- Edgware Road and Elephant & Castle
- Finsbury Park and Hammersmith, with a branch from Holborn to Aldwych;
- Golders Green and Charing Cross, with a branch from Camden Town to Archway.

Common ownership had brought a number of common features, one of the most distinctive being the stations. Designed by Leslie Green, many of the 'ox-blood' coloured tiles cladding steel-framed buildings, sometimes with further offices above, were designed to draw attention. At platform level (there were no islands), tiles on the walls spelt out the station name in large letters and the tiled surrounds were colour coded to aid station recognition.

On the track itself, the rails were carried on sleepers of Jarrah and Karri wood, which is practically non-combustible, and the spaces between sleepers filled with concrete so that passengers might have no difficulty in walking to stations in the event of trains being held up in the tunnels. All platforms were constructed of concrete slabs.

The Yerkes tube lines were all fitted with automatic signalling which relied on track circuits, with the additional refinement of the automatic train stop. In this the practice of the District was followed.

With a requirement for nearly 500 tube stock cars in the space of a couple of years, many manufacturers were involved, though there was little enough British input. The major orders were fulfilled by the American Car & Foundry Co of Pennsylvania, Les Ateliers de Construction du Nord de la France, and the Hungarian Carriage & Wagon Works. Considerable attention was paid to fire-proofing the system in general and the cars in particular, which had steel body shells.

The spring-loaded 'dead man's handle' was fitted, thus enabling the trains to be worked by a motorman only and without an assistant. The 'gate stock' as it was called required staffing by a man between each pair of cars to open the twin saloon doors and the gates on to the platforms. A single stroke bell was provided on each car platform, operated from the platform at the other end of the car. When the train was ready to start, the guard at the rear passed a signal to the motorman via each of the gatemen *en route*.

The cars were all compatible with each other, although this was of limited importance as there was no physical connection between any of the lines. Cars were 50ft long, but an 8ft or 12ft section of the body of the motor cars was taken up with a control compartment. Doors were provided at the ends of the cars only, leading to the platforms, but the interiors were already adopting the 'transverse seats in the centre with longitudinal seats over the bogies in the ends' approach, which would be familiar to succeeding generations. Depots were provided at London Road for the Bakerloo, the only part of that line which was above ground in the beginning; Lillie Bridge for the Piccadilly, which needed to run over District tracks to gain access; and at Golders Green for the Hampstead tube. This rural crossroads, later described in group advertising as 'a place of delightful prospects' made an ideal site, and thus the story that Yerkes made a spot decision to extend his line beyond Hampstead on the basis of a chance trip with his coachman is perhaps an exaggeration. Whatever the reason, the judgement was not flawed, and 10 million passengers a year (from 5,000 new homes) were using the associated station by the outbreak of World War 1.

The onset of competition from the electric tramways and motor buses in the latter part of the decade depressed the fortunes of all the underground railways. Further American involvement came with the appointment of Albert Stanley, a young tramway expert from New Jersey, to support Gibb and who ultimately succeeded him.

Later Lord Ashfield, he was to be the future driving force.

Financially, the situation was slowly restored, helped on its way by the establishment of the London Traffic Conference (or operator cartel). Fares were gradually forced up to avoid the ruinous competition which was taking place, and the companies agreed to a joint marketing policy with the use of the word 'Underground'. Thus Frank Pick entered the scene; from that time on, the contribution of good design was to be exploited wherever possible.

In 1910 the Yerkes tubes were formally merged. Now under the guidance of Stanley, the UERL began to swallow up buses and tramway companies. The UERL became known as the 'Combine', and co-ordination with the development of through fares became the order of the day. Of the underground railways, only the Metropolitan with its newly acquired Great Northern & City stood apart.

An early result was the promotion of a terminal loop for the Hampstead tube. Projection beyond (present names) Charing Cross in a terminal loop running under the Thames and calling at what is now the northbound Northern Line platform at Embankment offered interchange with both the District and Bakerloo. It was opened in 1914 as part of a rebuilding scheme for the station. It followed a projection of the Bakerloo to Paddington in 1913, after the Great Western with some agonising had brought itself to make a contribution towards the cost. The London & North Western Railway followed suit and provided the capital needed for a further extension to Queen's Park. This was to enable an integrated service to be offered with its own electric trains using the 'New Line' built to tap the suburban potential of local services out as far as Watford. Bakerloo trains were extended as electrification permitted, reaching Watford Junction in 1917. This was the first time that a tube line had come into direct contact with a main line railway, and this raised some floor height compatibility problems. Due to the war, cars from the unfinished Central London extension were used initially, together with gate stock. The guards' and conductors' positions on these cars were provided with a sort of footstep, which enabled them to help passengers mount the large difference in platform heights. The Joint Stock compromised and the floor level of the new trains, which were finished in L&NWR livery, was 4½in higher. Incidentally, when the same problem arose later because of joint running between the District and Piccadilly lines, the track was raised so that the difference was spread between the two floor heights.

A number of other schemes were started before the onset of hostilities, but completion had to wait for a while. War brought with it traffic growth and staff loss to the forces; female labour was employed for the first time, but strictly for the duration only. Damage to the system was negligible. The use of the tube stations as shelters during Zeppelin raids caused minor chaos, but this was nothing to what was to be experienced in the next conflict.

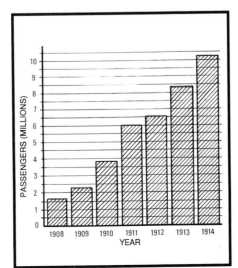

Left:
Number of passengers using Golders Green Station, 1908 to 1914.

Chapter 3

The System Reaches Maturity

MOTOR CARRIAGE CONSTRUCTED FOR THE EXPERIMENTAL ELECTRIC TRAIN OF THE
METROPOLITAN DISTRICT RAILWAY.

Above:
Motor coach of the Earl's Court–High Street Kensington experimental train, with Siemens electrical equipment. This six-car train consisted of two motor coaches and four trailers; half was owned by the District and half by the Metropolitan Railway.
J. A. Rosser collection

So far, this book has examined the origins of the steam railways and the electric tube lines which supplemented them in the central area. The latter put the offerings of the surface railways to shame, and it was at the turn of the century that serious talk began of converting the Metropolitan and its District counterpart to the joys of electric traction. It was almost a case of electrification or die, for with steam power their position was deteriorating rapidly in the face of competition from the tubes and rapidly evolving road transport. But what system of electrification should they choose? Logic dictated compatibility, and it was agreed to conduct an experiment.

The two lines decided to electrify both tracks between Earl's Court and High Street Kensington. This joint decision was taken in 1898, and conductor rails were laid each side of the running rails and electrified at 600V dc. It was decided to purchase a new six-coach train rather than convert existing stock, and this consisted of two motor coaches and four intermediate trailers. Through control lines were not installed, and thus only the leading motor coach provided power. The experimental service commenced at the close of 1899, and a premium fare of one shilling (5p) was charged as against 2d to 4d (0.8p to 1.7p) by steam train. It was thought that people would pay extra for

the privilege of riding in an electric train, but in fact the novelty had already worn off since the City & South London had by now been running for a decade.

The train was retired a year later, with (inevitably!) three cars reverting to each company. It had fulfilled its purpose by proving the case for low voltage dc traction — or so it seemed. Yet when the tenders came in, the one which most impressed the adjudicators of the committee of the two companies was that submitted by Ganz of Budapest. This system used three phase alternating current at 3,000V, supplied by a pair of overhead copper wires insulated from each other and with separate collection devices for each, with the third phase provided by the running rails. It was however untried in any conditions remotely like those of London, and when the Board of Trade demanded a demonstration, the companies were unwilling to finance it.

The Metropolitan remained firmly behind the Ganz option on the grounds of economy, since it would require only simple substations and no heavy conductor rail. It did, however, require a pair of overhead wires instead. Another claimed advantage was that the static transformers would not need attendants and could be left to look after themselves. The District, on the other hand, favoured the British Thomson-Houston Company's dc system. There was, however, an element of unreality in the argument for, truth to tell, the District was all but bankrupt. The Metropolitan offered terms for acquisition, but was rebuffed.

In the end, a growing American influence was consolidated by the arrival of Yerkes and his acquisition of the ailing District. With electrification

as a top priority, Yerkes rejected the 'expert' advice he was offered, and sent his engineers to find out for themselves. By then Ganz's experimental section of line had been dismantled, but they were able to inspect the 67-mile Valtellina line in Italy from Lecco to Sondrio, then all but complete. However, Yerkes remained unconvinced of the merits of untried ac systems, having seen what dc traction could achieve in his native USA. The Metropolitan fought a rearguard action on the merits of the Ganz system, pursuing it even to arbitration. The Board of Trade gave judgement for the dc system, albeit with some hard words to say on how the District had conducted itself in the process. The tremendous jobs of building the power stations at Lots Road and Neasden, many substations, and laying miles of cable, were at last put in hand.

Some 26 route miles of the Metropolitan were electrified in three years, a very creditable performance considering the line was clear for work to take place in only about six hours out of every 24. The length of the District to be electrified was even greater. At first an experimental electrified line between Acton Town and South Harrow was laid down and used both for testing the installation and training crews to operate the new electric trains. Two seven-car trains of the open saloon type, seating an average of 46 passengers a car, were run on the 5½-mile length of District track to South Harrow. Larger and heavier than any tube stock, and with three 175hp motor cars in each train, a top speed of 60mph was claimed for them. They were fitted with hand-operated sliding doors in the middle and gates at each end platform. Both electrical and braking equipment came from different sources to compare the results. These

District cars, with their angular appearance and open platforms, bore unmistakable signs of their American origins. This influence remained in future building, and henceforth carriages became cars, and bogies became trucks.

Once these cars had proved themselves, mass production was undertaken, although two thirds of the 420 cars ordered were constructed in France. Sliding doors were provided throughout, and pneumatic cylinders were installed to allow their operation by the gateman. However, this turned out to be over-ambitious for the technology of the era, and the apparatus was removed.

Whilst this was going on, the work of electrification was proceeding steadily, and eventually, on 22 September 1905, the last steam train puffed around the Inner Circle. Not many months after its exit, the major programme of electrification of both railways was completed. Henceforth there were long, well-lit saloon coaches for the delectation of passengers, and the stuffy compartment coaches were withdrawn. It was as if the authorities wished to wipe the memories of steam trains from the minds of their passengers, for stations and tunnels were thoroughly cleaned of accumulated layers of soot and grime, and there was much repainting and a general brightening up. Such, some would observe, is the value of competition.

The District committed itself to total electrification, and purchased 10 electric locomotives which normally worked in pairs. In appearance, these were among the nearest to boxes on wheels ever to run in Britain. Built to haul L&NWR trains on the Outer Circle service between Mansion House and Earl's Court where engines were changed, the locomotives found new employment in 1910 in conjunction with the Tilbury line. The basic services out to Barking were provided by jointly owned trains of a similar type to those already owned by the District. For the new services, the London, Tilbury & Southend company constructed two rather splendid trains of

District was felt to be inappropriate. Steam traction would continue, albeit on a much curtailed basis. Although the 'A' class 4-4-0Ts had provided the brunt of the steam services, there were other small classes of locomotives which saw most use on the main line. Of these, the five 0-4-4Ts of the 'E' class built from 1896 were notably successful, as were the four similar 'F' class 0-6-2T locomotives for freight working which followed them. The third of the 'E' class, No 1, was built at Neasden and has survived into preservation in working order.

Further steam locomotive building saw four massive 'G' class 0-6-4Ts in 1915 for freight, and which the Metropolitan took the unusual step of

the Metropolitan quickly found BTH equipment to be much more reliable than that offered by the Westinghouse company. Unfortunately, by the time this became apparent, the Metropolitan were lumbered with a substantial number of orders for Westinghouse traction controls which they were unable to cancel. These cars were later converted to trailers to operate with new motor cars.

The Metropolitan provided all the outer rail trains on the Circle and some of the inner rail ones as well, since it owned the greater part of the mileage. From 1907, it took over the whole service provision, and this hastened the conversion of some of the steam stock, built only a few years previously,

Above:
A District Railway 'B' stock train at South Kensington, 3 May 1925.
J. A. Rosser collection

naming. Eight graceful 'H' class 4-4-4Ts for express passenger work were built in 1920/21, and finally six locomotives were constructed from the parts manufactured at Woolwich Arsenal to a South

to electric operation. These later vehicles had been constructed with bogies, as opposed to the rigid eight-wheeler designs previously used.

A further 20 trains, later increased to 24, were built for the joint Metropolitan and GWR Hammersmith & City electrification, completed in 1906; this included the branch to Addison Road. For this, the GWR built its own power station at Park Royal and became the owner of some of the trains, although all were maintained by the Metropolitan.

The first electric locomotives for the Metropolitan were of Bo-Bo centre cab type and built between 1904 and 1906. They were intended for hauling through Great Western main line trains from origins such as Windsor on the Bishop's Road and Aldgate section. A second type, for domestic Metropolitan use, resembled those supplied to the District. Neither design lasted long, all 20 being replaced by new machines built by Metropolitan Vickers at Barrow in 1922 to handle the increasingly heavy trains on the main line out to Harrow and, from 1925 when electrification was extended, to Rickmansworth.

These celebrated locomotives were equipped with 300hp motors, one geared to each of the four axles, with electro-magnetic control to provide special slow speed control for shunting purposes. Besides the 12 current collector shoes on the locomotives, other shoes were fitted to the guards' vehicles at the extreme ends of the rakes and connected by power cable, to ensure that the whole was not brought to an unseemly halt by the locomotive becoming 'gapped' at a break in the

Table 2:
Services, Ealing Broadway to Mansion House

Traction	Year	Trains per day, each way	Fare	Journey time
Steam	1891	n/a	10d	49min
Steam	1901	40	7d	48min
Electric	1913	187	5d	35min

gangwayed stock with sliding doors and, be it noted, retention toilets; these were put into service between Ealing Broadway and Southend. The District locomotives hauled these trains as far as Barking, then the limit of electrification. The new coaches entered service in 1912, and the operation continued until 1939.

There is little doubt that electrification did much for the railways and their passengers. A comparison of what was offered as the years advanced and technology developed is revealing (see above table).

Today there is less than half the 1913 number of trains, while journey times have been eased slightly.

The Metropolitan had other preoccupations. Its various lines differed greatly in type and requirements, and the blanket solution applied by the

Eastern & Chatham design after World War 1. Bearing a strong resemblance to Maunsell's 'K' and 'N' classes (which they in effect were), their main purpose was freight work. These 18 locomotives all went to the London & North Eastern Railway in 1937, when that company assumed responsibility for non-electric passenger haulage on what was by then London Transport.

The Metropolitan's main interest now was in electric traction. Deliveries of multiple-units were in batches from a variety of British manufacturers; however, they differed fundamentally from the District stock in that the latter opted for a single motor bogie and associated equipment, whereas the Metropolitan's motor cars had two motor bogies and thus no trailing bogie. Like the District, though,

31

conductor rail at junctions. In such subtle ways had the excellent steam 'Dreadnought' compartment stock to be modified for electric traction! The other change was the fitting of electric heating.

The overall length of the locomotives was 39½ft, and their weight 61½ tons. Double-ended, they were fitted with dual Westinghouse compressed air and vacuum brakes, also trip cocks for train control (a separate one for each brake type). In 25 seconds 20mph was attainable, with 180 tons in tow, and a maximum speed of 65mph on the level. No 15 was exhibited, with some rolling stock, at the Wembley Empire Exhibition in 1925 (an event of considerable commercial significance for the Metropolitan), and carried a commemorative nameplate. The whole

class received names, the others all being of people (some fictional) associated in some way with the area served. When the locomotives were retired, the nameplates of No 2 *Thomas Lord* (its second name), No 6 *William Penn*, No 8 *Sherlock Holmes* and No 18 *Michael Faraday* were presented to, respectively: the Marylebone Cricket Club, the Pennsylvania Museum in Harrisburg USA, the Sherlock Holmes Society, and the Institution of Electrical Engineers. Locomotive No 12 *Sarah Siddons* remains in the service stock fleet today, while No 5 *John Hampden* is in the LT Museum at Covent Garden.

The addition of the Uxbridge branch to the Metropolitan at Harrow had proved successful in

Above:
Through trains from the District Railway to the London, Tilbury & Southend were double-headed by the District's BTH electric locomotives as far as Barking. This, however, is a train of four-wheelers from Ealing Broadway to Pitsea. It was photographed near Acton Town on 9 May 1925. J. A. Rosser collection

Below:
A Metropolitan Railway Westinghouse locomotive of 1904, with giant roller blind, at Wembley Park. J. A. Rosser collection

Top right:
A third-class motor car of Metropolitan Railway MW stock, with hand-worked sliding doors and complete with luggage compartment.
Bucknall collection/Ian Allan Library

generating traffic, to the extent that quadrupling of the double track north of Finchley Road was undertaken as far as Wembley Park by 1915. Similar capacity constraints had affected the District, and west of Hammersmith the sharing of the L&SWR's tracks was producing unacceptable delays. Consequently, the District quadrupled this section in 1911, only to find the L&SWR withdrawing its service five years later. As matters turned out, this was to much simplify the subsequent westward extension of the Piccadilly, so the work was not wasted. What this activity did achieve was to establish the need for additional trains, and both the surface railways had new stock delivered in this period.

Although the small bore tube railways had never contemplated more than one class of

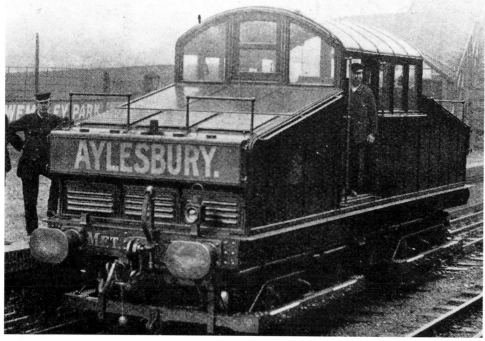

travel, the Metropolitan and District continued to provide selectively for First Class passengers until 1942. The Metropolitan indeed were prepared to go to considerable lengths for their important customers. The Rothschild saloon was a 1905 reconstruction of two luxury six-wheeled vehicles built 10 years earlier for the use of Ferdinand de Rothschild, who lived at Wendover. It became the Company's Directors' Saloon, its last official duty being to form an inspection special over the Brill branch before services were withdrawn in 1935.

Of greater fame were the legendary Pullman Cars constructed by the Birmingham RCW Co for Pullman, but fitted out to Metropolitan

specifications. Built to Circle Line gauge, they entered service in 1910 and were retained until 1939. Mayflower and Galatea were the Metropolitan's response to Great Central competition, and although initially they ran in ordinary trains throughout the day, including a late night theatre train arriving back at Aylesbury at 0055, lack of patronage soon restricted their use to the principal business services. Their value was in the publicity they gave the company, seen as a matter of increasing importance, rather than the revenue they generated.

By the 1920s, the Underground map was beginning to look familiar to modern eyes, though

as yet the extensive incursions into what became vast swathes of suburbs had hardly begun. The experience of Golders Green in the Edwardian era had however shown the potential for suburban development, and this decade witnessed further extensions. The first to get under way were projects which had been deferred by the war.

The Central London had been determined to press on westwards, and agreement was secured with the Great Western that it would construct the Ealing & Shepherd's Bush Railway. Reconstruction

Below:
Train and tunnel profiles, City & South London and Yerkes tubes compared.

City & South London and Yerkes Tubes

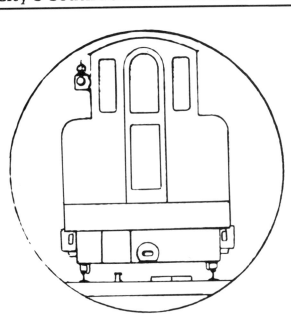

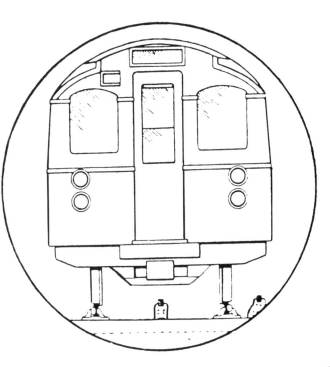

of the terminal loop was called for, especially in view of the opening of White City Stadium. The platform on the outside of the sharp curve was causing delays to trains, as there was a very substantial gap between the doors newly installed in the centre of the cars (replacing those at the ends), and the platform edge. The platform on the inside of the curve could take only six cars, due to the positioning of the depot entrance and exit roads, and was not used in consequence. The solution adopted was to construct a movable 35ft extension to the short platform, which was capable of being swivelled through a 4ft arc away from the tracks when use of the depot roads was required. Movement was electro-pneumatic, controlled from the signalbox and interlocked in the normal way. This ingenious contraption lasted from 1920 when the Ealing extension was brought into use, until 1947.

The two tracks which continued west from Wood Lane were arranged for right-hand running, so a flyover was constructed to restore the normal rule of the road before the next station at East Acton was reached. Electric power came from the GWR's plant at Park Royal.

Legal powers to project the Hampstead tube northwards had been obtained as early as 1902, but it was late in 1923 that the extension to Hendon Central was opened, and August 1924 by the time the tube reached Edgware. The tardiness had cost the Combine dear, as land values had risen (due, one imagines, almost entirely to its own efforts), and some demolition was needed before the railway could proceed on brick arches and viaduct, north from Golders Green. These gave way to cutting as the line reached Brent (now Brent Cross), and the formation widened. Later, passing loops to be used for express working would be provided each side of the tracks serving the island platform. Crossing the North Circular Road on viaduct again, the line reached Hendon Central. As with others on the extension, this station was finished in a Georgian style to complement the suburban housing developments.

The twin tunnels at The Burroughs, Hendon, took the new railway under the Midland main line and today's M1. Above the northern end of the tunnel was sited a semaphore signal, but not for train control purposes. It offered a range of positions, most of which were unknown in the railway rule book. Viewed from Colindale station 1,000yd distant, this was an eyesight test for train drivers. Not being allowed to wear spectacles, failing an eyesight medical was a serious matter for the individual, who was entitled to demand this practical test if he did not pass.

Continuing to Edgware, the line passed through the embankment of the Great Northern Railway, to make its own island platform terminus with an overall roof which covered also a pair of adjoining sidings. Additional sidings and a car shed were also provided. A frequent snappy Underground service was to galvanise Edgware's growth in a way that the modest offerings by the longer GNR route could never have done; in 1919, ordinary bookings from Edgware GNR were as low as 20 per day.

Bolstered by the allocation of cheap money from the government, the much needed rehabilitation of the City & South London and its integration into the Hampstead tube began at last in 1922. Two distinct elements were involved: the enlargement of the old tunnels to standard bore, and the construction of the complex series of underground junctions at

Right:
Camden Town junctions construction, 1926.

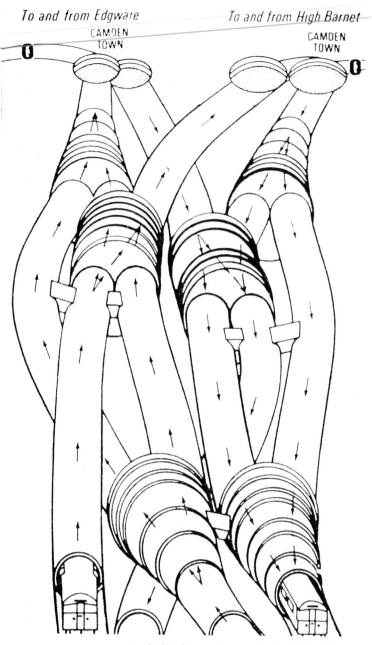

Camden Town. While work was in progress, further powers were obtained to extend south from Clapham to Morden, and to construct a new link from Embankment under the river to Waterloo and to junctions at Kennington. With the Edgware extension under way as well, the 'Edgware, Highgate and Morden Line', one of the names by which the combination was uneasily known, largely assumed its present Northern Line form.

The C&SLR's tunnels were built to a mixture of dimensions, successively 10ft 6in (Euston to Moorgate), 11ft 6in (Moorgate to Borough Junction), 10ft 2in (Borough Junction to Elephant), and 10ft 6in Elephant to Clapham Common. To enable the enlargement work to be carried out, the line north of Moorgate was closed completely, while trains continued to run on the southern section. This latter policy came to grief in November 1923 when a minor roof fall stopped a northbound train near Elephant & Castle. Fortunately the driver was able to remove the obstruction and reach Borough station before large quantities of earth cascaded into the tunnel and blocked it completely. After this episode, it was decided to close the line until work was finished. The substitute bus service was increased to a one minute headway as a result.

Where the tunnel diameter was 11ft 6in, hand enlargement and use of larger key pieces in the tunnel linings was sufficient, but elsewhere the existing lining rings were removed and shields used to bore out the tunnels to the standard 11ft 8¼in diameter. The ring-like shields were designed to allow the diminutive trains to continue to run; perhaps the odd C&SLR rule forbidding passengers to ride on the roof of trains had some relevance after all! Four new segment pieces replacing originals were enough for the 10ft 6in tunnels, even if the result was hardly circular, but the smallest tunnels had new linings throughout. There were some realignments to eliminate speed restrictions.

Modernisation also covered the installation of standard Underground automatic signalling and the conversion of the power supply to fourth rail. Station platform tunnels were lengthened to 350ft (a standard C&SLR three-car train was only 110ft long). The stations themselves were suitably updated, many being provided with escalators. Alone, City Road station between Euston and Angel did not reopen. The reconstruction effected a major improvement, and with new rolling stock as well, the running time between Euston and Clapham Common was reduced by one quarter from 31½ to 23½ minutes.

At Camden Town the requirement was to insert junctions between the Hampstead tube's two diverging northern branches and the C&SLR's Euston terminus. Since the latter was aligned east-west and well below the newer tube, and there was less than a mile in which to effect a junction, steep gradients at a maximum of 1 in 40 uphill and 1 in 30 down were needed. The 'stomach diagram' of this complex of underground lines which enables parallel and non-conflicting movements to be made throughout was proudly publicised. Interestingly, this junction has since been claimed to be the major

limitation to expanding train frequencies. The work was completed in April 1924, and a through service between Golders Green and Moorgate instituted.

The Morden extension was the result of horse trading with the Southern Railway interests, who drew a physical as well as a metaphorical line across the tube's path with the building of the Wimbledon & Sutton Railway. As so often in south London, tube construction was problematic due to waterlogged ground; nowhere was this more apparent than at Tooting Broadway. In the past, the village of Tooting had been noted for its plentiful water supply, and the tube station lay over what amounted to an underground lake. The station and its approaches

had to be built under compressed air conditions, work being first conducted from beneath air locks in vertical working shafts, and then from behind horizontal air locks in the sections of tunnel completed. From a final 'cut and cover' section due to wet ground, the tube emerged to an open-air cutting at Morden, where a three-track/five-platform face layout was built. The tracks continued beyond to extensive stabling facilities on the surface. A conscious effort was made to make all the stations on the extension conspicuous, and the angular surface buildings made much use of Portland stone in their construction.

Calls from time to time to extend the Underground fell on deaf ears; in consequence Morden station forecourt has remained a busy and important bus-rail interchange point. In any event, it is doubtful whether the Northern Line has the capacity to carry much additional traffic over this section.

Work on the last piece in the jigsaw began immediately after the Camden Town junctions were opened. Immediately south of Charing Cross (then Strand), the new southbound line forged straight ahead to Embankment (then Charing Cross), through the return part of the loop at a point below the river, and on to Waterloo and Kennington. Here, the new connection divided and rose each side of the City Line platforms, giving easy interchange. Connections enabled trains to continue south and a

conventional turnback siding was provided between the running tunnels. However, a terminal loop was and is the principal means of reversing direction, and the author admits to having watched a train disappear into the tunnel at the end of Platform 2 and then nipping across to Platform 1 to see if the same train really would reappear! Terminal loops are not all they might be from the operator's point of view, and are discussed later.

Opening of the Kennington extension coincided with the completion to Morden, and on 13 September 1926 work was finished for the time being. (Balham station opening was delayed to December). These extensions created what was then the world's longest rail tunnel, from Golders Green to Morden via Bank, a distance of 16 miles, 1,100yd. This was subsequently exceeded by the High Barnet branch of the Northern Line, whose East Finchley to Morden via Bank distance is 17 miles 528yd.

The following year a single track link was made at King's Cross between the eastbound Piccadilly and the northbound City Line, both in a trailing direction. This was purely for rolling stock and engineering train movements, and gave the Northern access to Acton Works.

Jointly with the Great Central Railway, the Metropolitan built a two-mile branch from Moor Park to Croxley Green and Watford. Or rather, the line was built to the edge of Cassiobury Park, through which the railway was not allowed to pass.

This unsatisfactory terminal arrangement severely limited the practical usefulness of the line, which has always remained something of a backwater. Services commenced in 1925. A triangular junction was built to provide direct access to Rickmansworth, but full passenger operation over the north curve lasted only until 1933. Since then it has seen occasional use only. Future possibilities in this area are discussed in Chapter 13.

The housing boom of the inter-war years transformed great expanses of open country around London into street upon street of detached and semi-detached houses. This growth was not confined to any particular area, but went on at a rapid pace wherever there was easy access to London. Perhaps the most sustained attempt to stimulate suburban living was the building of Metro-Land. This is an extract from a 'Live in Metro-Land' press advertisement of 1931:

'The delightful residential area served by the Metropolitan Railway claims the serious attention of every Home Seeker ... The train service provided is unequalled for frequency and rapidity; the educational and shopping facilities are unlimited; the Season Ticket rates are low and the local

Below:
Rebuilding west of Hammersmith, 1911 and 1932.

housing developments especially attractive. Residents in this district also have the added advantage of being able to travel to and from the City without change of carriage ...'

During the interwar period, 4,000 homes were built in Middlesex and Buckinghamshire on the back of the Metropolitan Railway Co, with the concurrent expansion of the railway facilities. That this was possible was in large measure due to the Metropolitan's ability to exploit its excessive land holdings in the area to the benefit of the railway's finances. This was achieved through the associated Metropolitan Railway Country Estates Ltd. British railway companies were generally discouraged or forbidden from ownership of land which they did not require for carrying on their main business.

Continued congestion on the Metropolitan main line resulted in the four tracking reaching out to Harrow by 1932, the same year in which the 4½ mile-long Stanmore branch was completed. The latter was designed to tap the housing spreading out from Edgware, Canons Park station being only a mile's bus ride from Edgware tube. However, the Metropolitan's relatively high fares policy compared with the Underground group acted as a disincentive to traffic growth, and single-car units transferred from the Rickmansworth–Watford service sufficed for the limited off-peak traffic between Wembley Park and Stanmore. In view of the two track

bottleneck between Finchley Road and Baker Street, growth was the last thing the Metropolitan really needed. Both schemes were financed by cheap government money, provided for the relief of unemployment.

In the east, the District extended its interests another 7¾ miles from Barking to Upminster in 1932; this was to serve the vast Becontree housing estate. Two additional lines were laid in to the north of the Tilbury tracks (now owned by the London Midland and Scottish Railway) for the new service, with additional stations provided at Upney and Dagenham Heathway; also at Upminster Bridge (1934) and Elm Park (1935).

The Great Northern, Piccadilly & Brompton Railway, to give the line its earlier title, had provided a direct connection from its northern terminus at Finsbury Park with the West End from 1906. Finsbury Park was one massive, not to say notorious, interchange, with passengers in those days arriving by Great Northern suburban services from Edgware, High Barnet and Dunstable, as well as today's Hatfield and Hertford lines. To this was added the traffic from the extensive tram and motor bus systems. The tube terminus was built on Great Northern property, and one of the consequences had been an undertaking given in 1902 that the Piccadilly would not be extended northwards without GNR consent.

By 1925, with 30,000 passengers changing

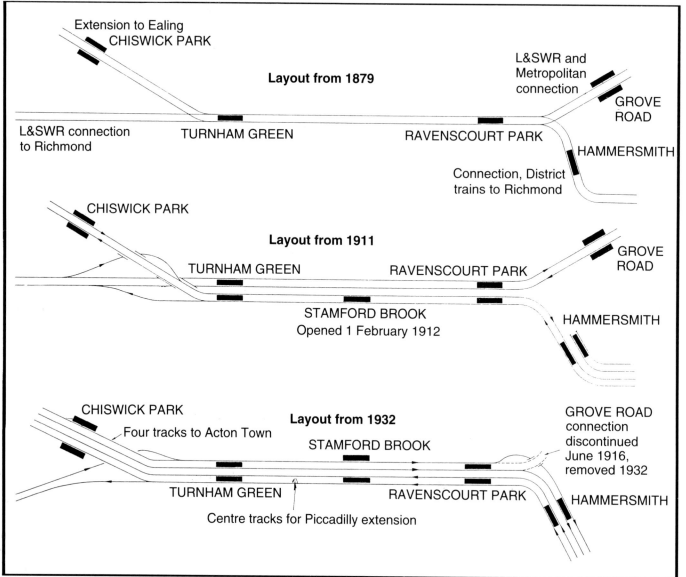

between different forms of transport daily, the public pressure to relieve the congestion was intense. 'There is enormous overcrowding on the trams and on the other vehicles during the peak hours of the day, and there is no possibility of inaugurating accommodation save by providing increased railway accommodation either by tube or electrification of existing lines or by introducing electric

Left:
Tooting Bec station, originally Trinity Road, was designed by the architect Charles Holden; in its Portland stone, it is typical of the stations on the C&SLR extension work. The line from Clapham Common to Morden was opened in 1926. John Glover

Below:
F. H. Stingemore's map of London Underground, 1926.

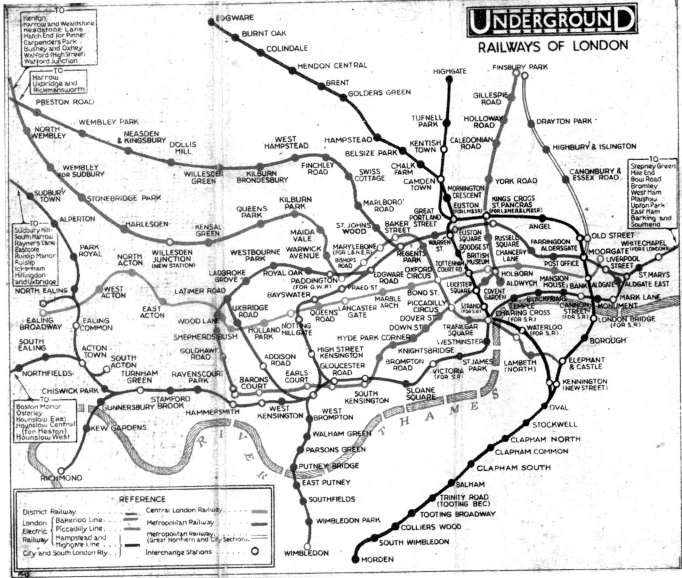

Above:
Four-tracking between Turnham Green and Acton Town in 1932 meant that the embankment between had to be widened to carry the additional tracks. This picture, west of Turnham Green before the work took place, shows the Ealing line crossing over the Southern Railway lines to Grove Road. On the right is the District Line route to Richmond.
Modern Transport/Ian Allan Library

Right:
Approaching Hammersmith from the west, the 1932 work also required the removal of the Grove Road branch. Its remains are seen centre; both westbound and the Piccadilly eastbound tracks are on the far side of the remains of the embankment. This view of a 'D' stock train for Upminster was taken on 13 March 1995.
John Glover

signalling,' Sir Henry Maybury told the Royal Commission. Part of the problem was finance. The Underground Chairman, Lord Ashfield, noting the disparity of traffic between the peak and what was then often termed the 'valley hours' was blunt: 'It may be a great surprise to you to know that the Underground railways in London have never been, in their whole career, a financial success. In other words, they have failed to earn anything approaching a reasonable return on capital invested in them ...'. One result was the Act of 1927 under which the Underground Group was able to borrow capital at 3% to finance the Piccadilly improvements, which were started in 1930, following the waiving (under protest) of the L&NER veto five years earlier.

As might be expected of a line which runs partly in tube, and partly across undulating country, the Cockfosters extension has several interesting features. For four miles to a point between Bounds Green and Arnos Grove, it runs in twin tunnels

driven beneath Seven Sisters Road to Manor House, where they swing north through a 15-chain radius curve (the sharpest on this line of otherwise easy curvature), and continue beneath Green Lanes to Bounds Green. The gradient falls all the way to Turnpike Lane, and then rises at an average of 1 in 60 to the summit at Enfield.

Where the tube emerges at Tewkesbury Road, the tunnel is enlarged to 16ft, and bell-mouthed to reduce the air pressure on trains entering at speed. Just after the line leaves the twin tunnel, it is carried obliquely across the North Circular Road on a 175ft girder bridge, followed by a long viaduct to reach Arnos Grove station. It then enters a half-mile tunnel, towards the far end of which is Southgate station. Cutting followed by viaduct and embankment takes the line to Oakwood and Cockfosters terminus, between which points the highest and coldest car sheds on the Underground system, 275ft above sea level, are passed on the west side of the line.

The tunnelling was through the yielding London clay, using a variety of shields and pneumatically operated shovels. One particularly delicate operation involved strengthening the brick tunnel through which the New River flowed at Bounds Green. Here it was necessary to insert an iron lining for a distance of 90ft, as the railway was to pass 25ft below the river bed.

The naming of the stations produced a flurry of local excitement. Perhaps unwisely, the Underground Group invited the public to respond to ideas put forward by the Group for the names of most of the stations. The new line extended well beyond the built up area, partly to reach a suitable depot site. The route was carefully chosen to split the distance between the two existing Great Northern Railway suburban branches, and as a result the stations initially served nowhere in particular. The most controversial choice proved to be the present Oakwood, for which the suggested

alternatives were Merryhills (a nearby public house) and East Barnet (then the name of the road alongside the station). However, the Group then determined to call the station Enfield West, which upset the sensibilities of the Southgate Urban District Council on the grounds that the station was nearly a quarter of a mile outside the Enfield UDC area and the name would confuse passengers. Alternatives of Southgate North and Oakwood Park were rejected by the Group, who stuck to their intentions and opened the station as Enfield West in 1933. But offence of this nature, once given, does not lie down, and a year later the station became Enfield West (Oakwood). It took the UDC until 1946 to secure the final adoption of plain Oakwood.

As the country filled up in the northern districts of Southgate and beyond, so it did in places like Hounslow, Ealing and Harrow, and it was considered advisable to balance the working of the Piccadilly Line by extending it at the other end also.

Services were projected concurrently to the west and northwest, not so much by breaking fresh ground but by the adaptation of existing lines. In 1932, the Piccadilly was extended from Hammersmith to South Harrow, then to Northfields in 1933, and later the same year to Hounslow West. Finally, in October 1933, the Piccadilly was extended from South Harrow to Uxbridge, where it replaced the District shuttle from Acton Town, itself inaugurated in 1910.

The District tracks already extended through Hammersmith to Hounslow, and from Northfields onwards it was simply a matter of Piccadilly trains using the District Line. But the District tracks as far as Turnham Green, on the way to Northfields, were far too busy to accommodate additional Piccadilly trains, plus a lesser number of Richmond trains, and some major work was called for. The problem was solved by constructing a new tunnel by 'cut and cover' methods under Hammersmith Broadway for two new tracks, completely rebuilding the station as

Top left:
The old Wembley Park station, probably in 1923 or 1924, with trains for the Cup Final.
Modern Transport/Ian Allan Library

Bottom left:
A train of the 1920/21 'F' stock approaches Pinner on a special working around 1959. These trains were built by the Metropolitan Carriage & Wagon Co for the District Railway and were renowned for their ability to move large crowds with a triple set of doors.
G. M. Kichenside

Left:
In the cab of an 'F' stock train, 23 July 1959. The round driver's windows of this stock were also highly distinctive. *J. A. Rosser*

Below:
Interior of a District Railway 'N' class car, albeit still with hand-worked doors as evidenced by their handles. This stock was built as part of the updating programme. *Author's collection*

Next spread-Top left
Hendon Central was another of the Underground's conquests. It was the railhead for the short period from 19 November 1923 until 18 August 1924, when the rest of the line through to Edgware opened. It was during this short period that this photograph was taken; it is no longer a country retreat.
London Transport Museum U2907

Next spread-Bottom left
The drum-shaped listed station building of Arnos Grove, 1932, is the first on the eastern end of the Piccadilly Line to be in the open air; a three-track station lies below in cutting. *John Glover*

Next spread-Top right:
The Metropolitan Line 'T' stock electric compartment stock was introduced in 1927 for Watford and Rickmansworth line services. A standard six-car formation is seen arriving at Harrow-on-the-Hill. This fleet, previously designated 'MV', consisted of motor cars sandwiching slightly older steam-hauled vehicles. The last survived in passenger service until 1962.
Ian Allan Library

Next spread-Bottom right:
A typically mixed train of rolling stock types, with a 'K' class Birmingham-built motor car bringing up the rear, leaves Ealing Common for Ealing Broadway. The date is 18 March 1963. This train probably ran from Mansion House; the upturned destination plate is a lazy driver's way of avoiding finding the correct item.
J. A. Rosser

Above:
Steam locomotives were still being acquired shortly before the formation of the London Passenger Transport Board in 1933. This Hunslet 0-6-0T was one of a pair purchased by the District Railway in 1930, seen here at Lillie Bridge depot on 25 August 1956.
G. Clarke

well for good measure, and then adapting the disused Southern Railway viaduct which had once given L&SWR trains from Richmond access to Kensington and included a connection to the Metropolitan's Hammersmith & City line.

The rebuilding was designed to offer complete physical separation between the Piccadilly trains which were to use the two centre tracks, and those of the District Line which flanked them. The latter had junctions to accommodate both the Ealing Broadway and Richmond services, and the diagram shows how the changes in the layout were made. This also illustrates how it came to be that Stamford Brook station, which was opened in 1912 and never had platforms on the L&SWR line, has no platform today on the eastbound Piccadilly Line.

West of Turnham Green junction, the tracks were quadrupled through Acton Town to Northfields by widening works; between Northfields and Boston Manor, a new car depot was built, with access from the running lines via a flyover junction. Services to Uxbridge from Acton Town used a grade separated

junction, and followed the District and then the Metropolitan tracks to reach their objective. Thus the western extensions used existing lines almost throughout.

The layout between Hammersmith and Acton Town required a different stopping pattern for the two lines, the Piccadilly providing the non-stop service and gaining a modest couple of minutes in the process. The four tracks west of Acton Town have proved less useful, particularly since withdrawal of District Line services on this section in 1964. Nowadays, the former District eastbound track between South Ealing and Acton Town is devoted to testing purposes.

The extensions brought renewed pressure on the central London section of the Piccadilly, and extensive rebuilding of Leicester Square, Green Park (formerly Dover Street), Hyde Park Corner and Knightsbridge followed. The classic rebuilding was that of Piccadilly Circus, completed in 1928. The old station which dealt with 1½ million passengers in 1907 could now look forward to a traffic of anything up to 50 million journeys annually, and total reconstruction was called for. The solution was to create a 15,000sq ft booking hall 15ft below the surface of the Circus itself, surrounded by a circular area which was accessed from five subways leading to the street and directly into the basement of Swan & Edgar's prestigious department store. (It is now a branch of Tower Records, but the facility remains). 'Passimeter' ticket offices with the clerks in the

middle like goldfish in a bowl were installed, as were no less than 26 self-service ticket machines. Five escalators in two shafts led down to a common landing 57ft below ground level, from which two sets of triple escalators led to the Piccadilly and Bakerloo Lines respectively. The booking hall was intended to recall Nash's Circus, obliterated by Edwardian rebuilding. Shops and showcases lined the perimeter, which was lit by lanterns on the red scagliola columns. Fitments were in bronze, and travertine marble was used for surrounds. A 'world clock' built at Lillie Bridge workshops was installed, as were the 'see how they run' indicators from which service regularity could be observed by the public. It was a masterpiece of its time.

Also on the agenda was the closing of three of the lesser-used stations, thus speeding up the services. Brompton Road, Down Street and York Road all ceased to trade between 1932 and 1934.

Rebuilding at Holborn, completed in 1933, was to make it an interchange station between the Central Line, which had previously served British Museum station, and the Piccadilly. The new platform tunnels were built around the running tunnels, so that until the old tunnels were dismantled trains were running in a tube within a tube. At the same time, escalator tunnels had to be built to connect the lines to each other and to the surface booking hall.

The Combine had always been keen on publicising its services; the following gem of logic

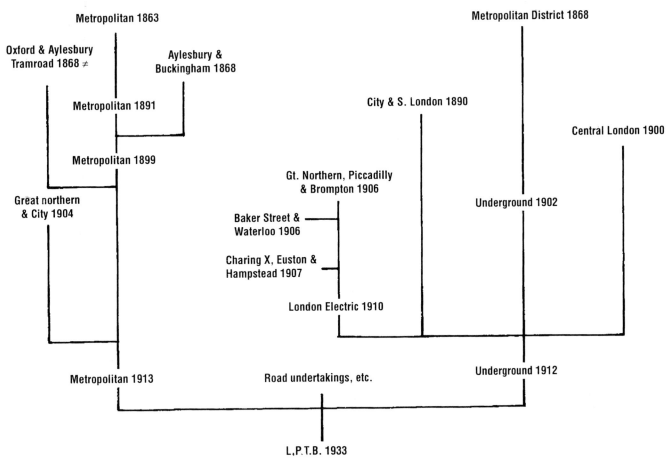

Metropolitan 1863

Oxford & Aylesbury
Tramroad 1868 ≠

Aylesbury &
Buckingham 1868

Metropolitan District 1868

Metropolitan 1891

City & S. London 1890

Central London 1900

Metropolitan 1899

Gt. Northern, Piccadilly
& Brompton 1906

Underground 1902

Great northern
& City 1904

Baker Street &
Waterloo 1906

Charing X, Euston &
Hampstead 1907

London Electric 1910

Metropolitan 1913

Road undertakings, etc.

Underground 1912

L.P.T.B. 1933

≠ HORSE TRACTION WAS ORIGINALLY EMPLOYED

Above:
The railway company amalgamations which led,
eventually, to the formation of the London
Passenger Transport Board.

came from the 1928 Diary:

HOW MUCH DOES IT COST YOU TO WALK?
The average man walks three miles a day or
1,095 miles a year.
The average man buys two pairs of boots a
year, say 30/- (£1.50) a year.
Boots must be soled and heeled — 15/-
(£0.75) a year is a reasonable allowance.
On this basis the cost of footwear works out
at 0.822d (0.343p) per mile.
The cost of Underground travel averages
0.796d (0.332p) per mile.
THEREFORE IT IS CHEAPER TO RIDE THAN
WALK IN THE LONG RUN.

The general thrust of legislation in the 19th
century had been to preserve as many small and
competing industries as possible, with the ever-
present fears of monopoly power and consequent
exploitation of the public being uppermost.
However, views changed in the present century.
1915 saw the London Electric Railways Facilities Act;
this allowed the C&SLR, CLR, LER, MDR and also
the LGOC to create a pooled revenue agreement
into which all moneys collected would be paid, and
each would draw upon in agreed proportions. The
first steps by government to co-ordinate London's
transport were taken by the setting up of the

Ministry of Transport in 1919, and the benefits of
mass production and the planned approach became
part of the general ethos. By 1931, it was possible
for Herbert Morrison to say when introducing the
second reading of the London Passenger Transport
Bill into the House that 'Competition must go; it
stultifies progress, endangers the standard of life of
the workpeople in the industry, and is too
expensive'. It is of interest that the Bill, first
promoted by a Labour administration, was
subsequently enacted by the new 'National'
government.

That Ashfield, as Chairman of the Underground
Group, was in favour of the formation of what

and independent business hands, extending to all
the local passenger transport undertakings within a
widely defined London traffic area'.

Before turning to the London Passenger
Transport Board, the achievements of the
Underground and the Metropolitan should perhaps
be recorded. In 1932, the last full year of their
separate existence, the trains of what was to become
London Transport in popular parlance carried
498 million passengers using 2,951 passenger
vehicles. Table 3 shows how passenger journeys
were spread almost equally between the surface and
the tube lines.

became the LPTB, there can be little doubt. In his
concern at the possible effect of the change in
government, he was reported in Modern Transport
in 1932 as saying that there could be 'no true or
permanent solution of the problems of London
passenger transport without a unification of
ownership, administration and finance, in capable

TABLE 3:			
The Underground in 1932			
Company	No of Locomotives	Passenger Vehicles	No of Passengers (millions)
Metropolitan	57	719	119.7
District	7	564	126.5
London Electric	-	1,295	149.8
City & South London	-	114	61.2
Central London	-	259	41.2
Total	*64*	*2,951*	*498.4*

Note: The Metropolitan totals include the
GN&C; of the company's 57 locomotives, 36 were
steam. The vehicle stock also included 18 parcels
and 544 goods vehicles.

Chapter 4

The London Passenger Transport Board

The London Passenger Transport Board (LPTB) was dominated by Lord Ashfield as Chairman and Frank Pick as Vice Chairman and Chief Executive. With these two men in charge of what was now a public authority, rapid advance was only to be expected. The LPTB's role was set out in ringing terms:

'It shall be the duty of the Board so to exercise their powers under this (1933) Act as to secure the provision of an adequate and properly co-ordinated system of passenger transport for the London Passenger Transport Area, and for that purpose, while avoiding the provision of unnecessary and wasteful competitive services, to take from time to time such steps as they consider necessary for extending and improving the facilities for passenger transport in that area in such manner as to provide most effectively and conveniently for the needs thereof.'

[23 GEO. 5.]   *London Passenger*   [CH. 14.]
           Transport Act, 1933.

CHAPTER 14.

An Act to provide for the establishment of a Passenger Transport Board for an area to be known as the London Passenger Transport Area, which shall comprise certain portions of the London Traffic Area and of the districts adjacent thereto, and for the transfer to that Board of various transport undertakings and interests; to make other provisions with respect to traffic in the said area; and for purposes connected with the matters aforesaid.   [13th April 1933.]

The Board was also under a duty to pay its way.

The London Underground diagram of 1933 saw all pretence at geographical accuracy cease, when a stylised representation took the place of a map. H. C. Beck's original depicted an Underground rather smaller than it is today, with the Central Line for instance stuck at its 1920 size. On the other hand, the eastern ambitions of the District were acknowledged by a box on the edge of the diagram listing the stations beyond Mile End to Upminster '& Southend'. The diagram, today's Journey Planner, was an important symbol of the unity of an undertaking which had been created by statute.

The Metropolitan had fought the formation of the LPTB, and it was here that the Board initially turned their attention. There was the small matter of the Brill branch. By now the train was sometimes quite empty, in which case the crew would often stop and go rabbiting in the woods.

Another practice was the swapping of milk and eggs from nearby farms for lumps of coal from the engine! It was not unusual for the locomotive to derail on the deteriorating track, in which case the occasional passenger had no choice but to walk. So, with fewer than 50 passengers and 20 tons of freight a day, closure was inevitable and took place on   30 November 1935. Locomotive power in later years had been Metropolitan Railway Sharp, Stewart 2-4-0T locomotives, and then the familiar Beyer Peacock 4-4-0Ts were substituted until closure. However, the Aveling & Porter locomotive No 807 was rescued from dereliction by the Industrial Locomotive Society in 1950, and subsequently restored at Neasden. It passed to the National Collection in 1957, and is presently displayed at the Covent Garden museum. The Aylesbury–Verney Junction service followed the Brill branch into oblivion the following summer.

On a more positive note, King's Cross Metropolitan station fell well below the standards which were being achieved elsewhere. To reach it from the main line station or from the tube station meant a long walk; work spanning several years surrounded its closure and replacement by the present station in 1941. It is now adjacent to (but not integrated with) the deep level tube lines, and reached from a separate ticket hall.

At this point, Euston Road runs roughly east and west past the frontages of King's Cross and St Pancras main line stations; 35ft below lies the Metropolitan Line, following the course of the roadway. A tunnel curves out from St Pancras, carrying the tracks of the Widened Lines which meet the Metropolitan and run alongside it to Moorgate. The tunnels connecting with the London & North Eastern then formed a similar junction. West of the point where the tunnels converge, and running parallel to the Metropolitan, was a short length of abandoned tunnel, built in 1868 towards Euston Square but never completed.

To provide for the new Metropolitan station, the eastbound Metropolitan track was diverted into the abandoned tunnel, and a new tunnel was constructed on the south side of the main tunnel. This was to allow the newly redundant portion of the main tunnel to be used partly as an entrance and ticket hall, and partly as a reversing bay, although it was never electrified. Additional space was thus secured for passenger circulation because the main tunnel was generously proportioned to accommodate a double track of the old Great Western broad gauge. In the early 1960s, the reversing bay was filled in, and converted for use as an additional 250ft-long concourse area. This allowed the resiting of the ticket office, and the separation of flows of passengers entering and leaving the station.

Construction exposed both the Underground and St Pancras tunnel lines below, which had to be bridged with girders while keeping the Euston Road traffic moving. Then the 70-year-old abandoned tunnel, wet and layered with accumulated debris, had to be cleaned and waterproofed to fit it for its new use.

A major shortcoming was the capacity limitation represented by the two track section between Baker Street and Finchley Road. What was to prove an abortive scheme had in 1926 resulted in the Metropolitan's enlarging Edgware Road station to two island platforms with a view to constructing a

Top left:
The London Passenger Transport Act, 1933.

Left:
The new and unified London Transport. Pairs of 1938 stock trains on the Bakerloo Line are partnered precisely by trains of CO/CP stock of the same vintage on the Metropolitan Line which flanks them. The scene is just south of Wembley Park; the descending line on the right leads from Neasden depot. The Great Central main lines are on the far right.
London Transport Museum

Above:
World War 2 did not stop all work on the Northern Line extensions and L&NER steam trains continued to run on the High Barnet and Edgware via Mill Hill East branches. Work proceeded apace on the link from Archway to East Finchley, this picture showing the Underground's northbound tunnel mouth. This section was opened to traffic on 3 July 1939.
London Transport Museum U26403

relief line. With the addition of passengers from the 1932 Stanmore branch, the strain was becoming intolerable. The LPTB now determined to construct a new tube line from Baker Street to Finchley Road to enable the Bakerloo Line trains to run to Wembley Park and then over the Metropolitan's branch to Stanmore.

The new scheme involved the building of entirely new double tubes branching off the Bakerloo system at Baker Street and proceeding along and beneath the line of the Metropolitan for 2½ miles to a point approaching Finchley Road, where they had to rise between the Metropolitan tracks. The layout thence to Wembley Park was rearranged to give the Bakerloo trains exclusive use of two of the former lines. As part of the plan, the Metropolitan services were to be speeded up by allowing the trains a clear run of several miles without any stops; tube stations at Swiss Cottage and St John's Wood replaced Lord's, Marlborough Road and Swiss Cottage (Met). Similarly, Metropolitan Line trains were to run non-stop between Finchley Road and Wembley Park, with the intermediate stations served by the

Bakerloo. New island platforms were provided where necessary to allow the (unusual) fast-slow-slow-fast layout of tracks.

At Neasden, new depot facilities were built for both lines, as the workshops element of the Metropolitan's premises was reallocated to Acton. This allowed the Bakerloo's constricted London Road depot site to be reduced in status to stabling sidings. A new diveunder connected Neasden depot to the running lines. The Wembley Park junction for the Stanmore branch had been constructed on the flat, and a burrowing junction north of the station removed the conflict with southbound Metropolitan trains. Further work rearranged the layout at Harrow-on-the-Hill. The Metropolitan crews referred disparagingly to the tube-sized newcomers as toy trains.

At Baker Street the work required a new tube junction and a new southbound tube platform so that Bakerloo trains from both branches could enter the station together. Station rebuilding included the provision of escalators. Step plate junctions, in which successive lining rings in the running tunnels are progressively increased in diameter, were built at the divergences, but Finchley Road provided the major tests of engineering ingenuity. To accommodate the Bakerloo, the northbound Metropolitan Line had to be diverted further west and below the 'North Star' hotel, which itself required underpinning. Only two inches of concrete separated the hotel's cellars from the crown of the new tunnel when it had been finished. The northbound Bakerloo tube then broke surface via the abandoned Metropolitan tunnel. Also at Finchley Road, a 50ft girder supporting the buildings above the trains was found to be partly in

the way of the new ticket hall. It had to have a top section cut away and a strengthening flange welded on while the station was in continuous use.

In the same programme, the rest of the Bakerloo station platforms were lengthened to 377ft to take seven cars instead of six, and at Elephant & Castle terminus a new length of double tube siding was constructed beyond the station to provide two tunnel sidings. They were pointed in the direction of Camberwell, but remain today as completed in 1939. Resignalling enabled extra trains to be run.

The District Line had been extended to Upminster in 1932, but the traffic thus generated only served to increase the passenger volumes to be carried. The major constraint was the series of junctions which form a triangle in the Aldgate area. Before reconstruction, delays occurred through trains already in Aldgate East station fouling the spur line on which Aldgate station stands, and the points controlling it. The other two sides of the triangle were only long enough to accommodate six-car trains. It was to lengthen these sides to take eight-car trains (by utilising the space occupied by the old platforms), as well as to provide better passenger facilities and a larger station, that the work of resiting the station some 500yds further to the east was undertaken.

To get the required headroom for two new ticket halls beneath Whitechapel Road, one at each end of the new station, the tracks had to be lowered by up to 7ft. The work of enlarging the tunnel, which included installing girders up to 68ft in length to support the roadway above, had to allow the continued passage of trains and road traffic, and required extreme care as many of the surface buildings were old and more liable to collapse.

Above:
The same scene on 15 March 1983 shows a 1959 stock train leaving the tunnel with a High Barnet train. The line on the left now only provides access to Highgate depot, seen in the distance. *John Glover*

The fishbelly girders spanning the line and part of the platforms were brought in by road and lowered into the space where the tunnel crown had been demolished. The longer and heavier girders for the work further west, where they were to span the new four-track layout on the old station site, were brought in at night by rail in two halves from opposite ends of the site. They were halted below

their final positions, and swung round on ball races through 90° to straddle both platform and track. Bolted together, the ensemble was then lifted to its resting place.

At the same time, work had been going on below building the new platforms, though the tracks were left more or less at their original level for the time being, supported increasingly on wooden trestles as construction progressed. From the trains, it was possible to peer down to the station taking shape below. Lowering was accomplished by suspending the track from the new roof, dismantling the trestles, and letting down the 1,400ft of double track using blocks and tackle by a maximum of 7ft. This work commenced at 0100 Sunday, and by 0500

Monday the first train ran through on the new alignment. Nine hundred men were employed on the changeover, which also required the demolition of the old platforms, completion of the new ticket hall which had been left unfinished as it would have obstructed the old tracks, and the new signalling installation completed and tested. The new station was opened on 31 October 1938.

Another Metropolitan development was the rebuilding of Uxbridge station on a new site closer to the town centre, completed in 1938. It contains the only stained glass window on the Underground, featuring the coats of arms of the local authorities.

Before work started on these improvements though, the London Passenger Transport Board

Above:
South Tottenham station sees 'new tube stock for the L&NER and LPTB electrification scheme for East London on its way from the carriage works and being towed by a steam engine'. The date is 1 March 1940; it was to be several years before the Central Line extensions were ready.
Fox Photos

Left:
Underground stations, and particularly the eight deep-level stations which were never used for rail services, were pressed into use for accommodation during air raids. They were equipped with wire mesh bunks, snack bars, a sick bay and all the comforts needed. The unrecorded location receives attention from the ARP; the photograph records only the wry comment that the shelters are 'the Last Thing in Luxury'. *Fox Photos*

launched one of its major acts of policy in its five year plan — the New Works Programme, 1935-40. This programme, originally estimated to involve an expenditure of £40 million, and planned for completion by about 1940, was by far the biggest single programme of transport development ever undertaken in the London area.

The need for railway development in London, particularly in the eastern and northeastern sectors where there had been long-standing complaints, had been recognised for many years. But it was only with the creation of the Board in 1933 and the institution of financial pooling agreements with the 'Big Four' main line railways, that it became practicable to consider the needs of London as a whole. The operators wasted no time, and the 1935-40 Programme had as a major feature the projection of tube lines up to the surface and extended over newly electrified main line tracks. In this way, the outer suburbs were to be connected direct to both the West End and the City by tube. The main proposals as they directly affected the LPTB were as follows:

■ Central Line. Extension east from Liverpool Street to Stratford and over L&NER tracks to Leytonstone, Woodford and Ongar. New tube constructed from Leytonstone to Newbury Park, then by L&NER route via Hainault and Woodford. Extension west from North Acton Junction to West Ruislip (later to Denham) over additional tracks laid alongside GWR Birmingham main line.

49

■ Northern Line. Highly complex extensions from Moorgate–Finsbury Park line over L&NER to both Alexandra Palace and East Finchley, meeting at the latter with a new projection of the Archway line. Both were to continue over the L&NER to Finchley Central, branching there both for High Barnet, and Edgware via Mill Hill East. New extension from enlarged Edgware Underground station to Bushey Heath.

Right:
The tube tunnels were at considerable risk from aerial bombing; should the tunnels under the Thames be breached, the whole system would quickly flood and perhaps cause widescale loss of life. This is a view of the floodgate in closed position, installed at the south end of the southbound platform of the Bakerloo Line at Charing Cross.
Modern Transport/Ian Allan Library

Below:
The Underground was not the first railway to use the new Central Line tunnels. A narrow gauge railway (on which passengers were forbidden to ride!) was used to bring materials to and remove the completed work from the work benches.
Naval Systems Ltd

■ Metropolitan Line. Quadrupling of the section Harrow-on-the-Hill–Rickmansworth and extension of electrification from Rickmansworth to Amersham, including the Chesham branch.

While work was quickly put in hand, no extensions of the Central Line were ready for traffic before the war. However, improvement to the original central core, on to which the new tracks were to converge from east and west, was finished by 1938. To enable the standard tube stock to run, the track was renewed and laid on transverse sleepers, and the original third rail electrification converted to the fourth rail London Transport standard. In order to give the required clearances, it was necessary to install the positive conductor rail slightly higher than the standard position, necessitating a modification to the current collection shoes of the rolling stock. Finally, the old station platforms were lengthened to 427ft to take

eight-car trains.

On a level line, these alterations could have been achieved by encircling the running tunnel with the larger sections of station tunnel. But as the tracks were originally constructed to enter and leave each station respectively on rising and falling gradients, some rebuilding of the station approaches was needed. The nearer portions of each gradient had to be brought more nearly level, which meant steepening the remainder of each slope by up to 3ft to gain the extended platforms. All was achieved during night-time engineering occupations. The results of this work remain plainly visible, but Health and Safety at Work requirements would make such enlargements far more complex and costly to carry out today.

With all work in Central London finished, the original Central London Railway was adapted to carry the traffic from the extensions, which was expected to total some 300 trains daily.

The most ambitious of the schemes were the northern extensions of the Northern Line. To begin with, all went well. Archway (formerly Highgate) is a deep-level tube station, from which trains were required to rise to a distinctly higher level at East Finchley. Archway had been constructed as a terminus, and two dead-end siding tunnels projected north for a short distance. One was extended to form a reversing siding with crossover connections, and the other was continued as the

new northbound line. This, with its twin tunnel, rose at 1 in 50 to Highgate, where it was still 80ft below the old L&NER station above. Long escalators were therefore needed to connect the new platforms (which were 480ft long to suit the proposed operation of nine-car trains) with the ticket hall situated immediately below the L&NER platforms.

But the L&NER station was itself built in a cutting between two tunnels, and Archway Road which was the principal access was another 60ft above that. A further escalator was (later) built up the side of the embankment in the open air, to complete the access to the platforms a full 140ft below.

Beyond Highgate the tubes continue to rise, breaking surface one each side of the L&NER tracks at East Finchley, with all four tracks crossing the Great North Road together by bridge. At this point there was some difficulty with the levelling off of the tube, as the tunnel exit had to be high enough for the line to cross the main road, yet as far from Highgate as possible to flatten out the gradient. This brought the tunnel mouth very close to East Finchley station, and as a result the southbound track plunges rather abruptly at 1 in 40 into a tunnel mouth which is slightly lower than its counterpart. This drop was necessary as the southbound tunnel had to pass below the L&NER lines to Finsbury Park above.

There was insufficient width of land at this point

Left:
The 'R' stock trains were formed of seven cars. Vehicles of this type were the first to have body panels of unpainted aluminium in 1953. The last 'R' stock trains were retired from service in 1983. A District Line Wimbledon–Barking service approaches East Putney on 1 March 1980. *John Glover*

completed up to 20 years after the intention, in others, to face eventual abandonment. The replacement of rolling stock came to an end, and a reduction in maintenance programmes, brought about by an acute shortage of labour and materials, had to be accepted. At the same time, with many staff away on active service in the Forces, there was a need to make a contribution to the national effort in aircraft manufacture and war supplies generally. Rolling stock and equipment for such a mundane purpose as providing transport facilities in London were thus maintained in service with great difficulty, while older stock needed a special rehabilitation overhaul after the end of hostilities.

The war formed a test of altogether unprecedented severity for the Underground and its parent organisation. The first concern was to take adequate air raid precautions. The most obvious threat to the Underground in central London was that of flooding. It was well known that if any of the tunnels carrying the tube railways under the Thames were breached, the whole of the tube system would be at risk. Similar consequences might result from a breach of the Embankment's wall paralleling the centre section of the District Line. Certain stations had also to be protected against the possibility of burst water mains, while a breach of Marc Brunel's Thames Tunnel, now carrying the East London Line, might lead to flooding over a wide area.

For traffic reasons, any permanent sealing of the underwater tunnels could not be entertained. At the time of the Munich crisis in 1938 both the Bakerloo and Northern Line tunnels were plugged with concrete, but this was an emergency expedient only. Plans were prepared early in 1939 to install a complete system of electrically operated floodgates on those lines each side of the Thames so that the underwater sections could be isolated from the remainder of the system. Time did not allow the completion of this work by the outbreak of war, and closure of the portions of line affected followed; the last section to be reopened between London Bridge and Moorgate did not do so until May 1940. These construction works represented the most major disruption of the system during the entire war period.

Use of the gates needed care to ensure both continuation of train services and the safety of passengers. Two independent sources of electricity supply were arranged, and hand operation could be resorted to. Manned continuously, closure of all 18 gates followed the receipt of air raid warnings by Leicester Square traffic control office. Track circuit diagrams indicated locally the positions of all trains, and the signalling was interlocked with the gate mechanisms; the gates themselves could be closed in less than a minute. Arrangements were put in hand to work the severed sections separately. As a second line of defence, steel diaphragms were placed nearby in case they were wanted.

The similar works on the District Line were not needed at low tide, and an automatic tide indicator was installed. Acoustic bombs were another hazard, and detection devices were placed on the river bed

---

to enlarge the tunnel entry into the usual bell-mouth, and other means had to be found to minimise the air pressure on trains entering the tunnel. It took the form of a number of pressure relief openings in the top of the tunnel and these were strung out for some distance, gradually spacing out as they went. The intention was to avoid unpleasant 'popping' of the ears by minimising the piston effect as a train dropped into the tunnel at about 35mph; the air ahead of the train is allowed to escape rapidly through the vents, and then less rapidly as the train passes deeper into the tunnel. The pressure thus builds up more gradually, but even so it can be an uncomfortable experience sitting in the front car of a train.

North of East Finchley, the lines converge on two tracks for the long straight run to Finchley Central; had the intended schemes been completed this section might have proved to be a major operational problem with two busy routes diverging at both ends of it. This station was to have been an imposing complex with a pair of island platforms serving four tracks, but no work other than platform lowering was ever carried out, and it remains today a pleasant typically Great Northern station. The (historically) later High Barnet line curves to the right through a cutting to the 'odds and ends' built station of 1933 at West Finchley and further GNR

stations to the terminus. At all the intermediate branch stations, platform heights were left untouched when the Underground took over, and passengers thus stepped down into trains and up out of them.

From Finchley Central the Edgware tracks carried straight on, over the imposing Dollis Brook viaduct which carries the Underground(!) 60ft above ground level to Mill Hill East. Electrification was extended this far on a single line only on 14 March 1941 to serve the barracks — and there matters stuck fast. As for the Metropolitan electrification, only some minor preparatory work was undertaken.

The outbreak of the war brought great changes, not least in the control of the undertaking passing to the Minister of Transport on 1 September 1939. Control of London Transport, as of the main line railway companies, was exercised through the Railway Executive Committee. The Board's traffic, swollen at times by troop movements, was substantially reduced by evacuation, by the blackout, and later by the bombing of London. The population in the area served fell by 2,700,000 so that by late 1944 only 7,147,000 remained. The financial implications were not welcome.

Just as seriously, development work gradually ceased. Uncompleted parts of the New Works Programme were suspended, in some cases to be to record any which posed a threat to the Underground tunnels.

Other less extensive preparatory work included the duplication and paralleling of electricity supply cables, modifying ventilation arrangements to minimise the effects of a poison gas attack, strengthening the structures of essential buildings ranging from generating stations to traffic control offices, and use of disused tube stations as secure accommodation for government and other purposes. The Aldwych branch was closed for the duration and used to store items from the British Museum, including the Elgin Marbles.

The blackout regulations produced major difficulties. As well as all the stations, depots and workshops, every vehicle had to be fitted with special lighting which was the minimum possible to enable the job to be done. Miles of cream netting (which not-so-gradually turned black) covered all but the centre of the windows on underground cars; it adhered so firmly that traces remained on many cars until their final scrapping. Passengers were much tempted to peel it off, and an obnoxious individual called Billy Brown was invented, who by means of car advertisements told the reader:

'I trust you'll pardon my correction
that stuff is there for your protection.'

This invited a reply, such as the addition of:

'We thank you for your information
but want to see the bloody station!'

Signals had to be hooded and dimmed, whilst all kinds of maintenance work became that much more awkward. The strain on passengers and staff alike was great, and many experiments were carried out to see what improvements could be made to illumination levels without incurring unnecessary risks. These met with a fair degree of success.

A major early test was the evacuation. Not only children, but also expectant mothers, mothers with children under five, the blind and the elderly were to be moved out. The plan was to evacuate 1,250,000 persons in the space of four days. In the event, 600,000 were ferried out of inner London by the LPTB and the main line railways. Lack of bombing resulted in many returning, only to be sent on their way again in 1940 and subsequently this was a team effort between public organisations. The police, local authorities and the government departments concerned all had major contributions to make.

Bombing from August 1940 onwards inevitably brought disruption to services, although never to the extent of causing the shutdown of the system as a whole. Most incidents resulted in partial line closures for periods of 10 days or less; those that took longer to repair included the sad destruction at Balham on 14 October 1940 when a bomb pierced the station tunnel roof causing flooding from burst mains and an inrush of gravel and rubbish which half filled both tunnels. Four staff and 68 shelterers died, and the line was closed for three months. Again, at Bank on 11 January 1941, the roadway was penetrated and collapsed, leaving a crater 150ft across. The escalators were wrecked and blast damage was inflicted on trains in the platforms 62ft below street level. Four staff and 53 shelterers lost their lives and two months elapsed before the station reopened.

One of the longest breaks in service was the five-month suspension between King's Cross and Euston Square after the massive air raid of 10 May 1941. Perhaps the worst incident took place at Bethnal Green on 3 March 1943, when a woman carrying a baby tripped and fell down a short staircase only 19 steps long. The press of others behind her seeking shelter during an air raid at the yet unopened station resulted in those behind also falling; within minutes 173 died of suffocation in a space the size of a living room. Over 2,000 incidents relating to damage to railway buildings were recorded, and 1,050 cases of damage to rolling stock. Nineteen railway cars were totally destroyed.

The tube stations made natural shelters from the bombing, and although at first resisted, there proved to be no practicable means of denying people refuge. Indeed, men used crowbars to force the locks on the station entrances, and the authorities quietly capitulated. The first use was on 7 September 1940. Sanitary arrangements were hastily installed, with a drainage system at 81 stations eventually allowing sewage to be pumped to the surface. A refreshment service provided by train or otherwise was feeding 120,000 nightly in late 1940. Most slept on the platforms, although bunks for 22,800 were built. Later, bunk allocations were provided by ticket, and medical posts, washing facilities, storage for bedding and even small libraries eventually made an appearance. The peak night was 27 September 1940 when 177,000 spent the night as guests of the London Underground; thereafter the numbers gradually declined. An oddity was Highgate, still unopened in 1940 because the escalator installation had not been finished, but otherwise complete. The Inner London stations became so crowded as shelters that special trains for shelterers were run to Highgate and unloaded there. The rest of the train service ran non-stop through a brightly lit station full of sleeping people! Some of the uncompleted sections of the Central Line east of Liverpool Street were also used for this purpose, but under the aegis of the local authorities.

Once the principle of using the Underground as shelter accommodation had been accepted, it was natural to consider what else could be done. This resulted in the limited construction of deep-level station platforms below some existing Northern (and Central) Line platforms, in the fond hope that under peacetime conditions they could be utilised as part of an express tube network. Eight shelters were built (out of 10 proposed) at an average depth of 80ft below ground level underneath existing stations. Each shelter had a shaft head at each end with a lift for five persons and a double spiral staircase. Each of the pair of 'station' tunnels was to be 1,400ft long. Their 16ft 6in diameter was divided into two levels with a floor installed at the midway point; at each location around 8,000 bunk beds were installed. There were first aid facilities, kitchens and sanitation, and also connections to the LT station. Although completed from 1942 onwards, the shelters were not used by the public until mid-1944. Their locations were at Belsize Park, Camden Town, Goodge Street, Stockwell, Clapham North, Clapham Common and Clapham South — and at Chancery Lane. Three (Goodge Street, Clapham Common and Chancery Lane) were retained for government use.

After the war, Jamaican immigrants had the misfortune to be housed in Clapham South, which also accommodated detachments from the Royal Navy and Royal Marines for the funeral of King George VI, and were used again during the 1953 Coronation. The last example of their employment as living quarters was at Goodge Street where an Army Transit Camp had been established, but following a fire there in 1956 such use was abandoned.

The section of tunnel between Leytonstone and Gants Hill was turned into an aircraft component factory. The Plessey Company installed the factory in 1942, converting the 2½-mile stretch into a wartime production line employing more than 2,000 workers.

In 1940, Lord Beaverbrook as Minister of Aircraft Production had approached the LPTB about the possibility of using the Underground for the protection of vital production machinery. Construction of the Central Line extension was nearly complete when it was agreed to turn the 300,000sq ft of floor space into a factory, used to make items such as fuel pumps and aero engine starters. Interviewed by *The Times* in 1985, Mr Dennis Barron who at the age of 16, had been paid a mere £1 per week, described working there:

'It was strange, really, like working in a mine, only you could hear the bombing overhead — a terrific bang, and all the lights would shake. Men and women worked side by side; we all liked it because there was such a good group of people working together. We took our work seriously, arrived at 7.30 in the morning and worked until past dinner time and on Saturdays with no overtime pay.'

The tunnels were equipped to handle raw materials inwards and finished parts outwards on a narrow gauge railway, which was also used for taking visiting VIPs on tours of inspection. Other adaptations to the tunnels were the provision of entrances so that no worker had to walk more than

Below:
Wartime use by Plessey of uncompleted Central Line tunnels, 1942.

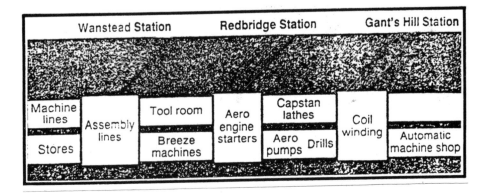

immediate increases in services were possible. Rather did victory bring some embarrassment to the Board, for the general reaction after six years of war manifested itself in a desire for enjoyment and celebration, and heavier loadings were the result.' The focus of all the effort had gone, the staff were exhausted, and the system was run-down and lacking in new equipment.

The longer term scene was influenced by the planners. In 1943, Patrick Abercrombie finished his huge survey of the planning needs of London: it was full of visions of an orderly, beautiful city with fresh air and lively tranquillity to take over after the war. There were to be substantial implications for the railway system. One result was a plan to build new underground railways all over the central area, co-ordinating the efforts of the main line railways and the Underground. Another was to confirm the creation of a 'Green Belt' to surround the capital and limit urban sprawl, which was now seen to be growing at an alarming rate and something to be discouraged. The catch was the complete lack of public money to make any advance towards the goals. These are matters considered further in the next chapter, as are the pressures which determined the fate of the uncompleted parts of the New Works Programme. In fact, the resumption of the Central Line work brought Greenford, Newbury Park and Woodford into the tube network by the end of 1947, and thus within the LPTB era. The development of the trains and the huge influx of new rolling stock during the Board's existence is described in Chapter 6.

Writing their own epitaph in the 1947 Annual Report, the Board recorded that they had 'sought to provide a passenger transport service, by rail and road, worthy of London as a great metropolitan city; at the same time, they have pursued a long-term policy of financial soundness, supported by an appropriate fares structure which could also be justified both by the adequacy of the services and the efficiency of their operation'.

¼ mile — extra ventilation shafts, cloakrooms and sanitation; a canteen for 600 was erected at Redbridge.

Less well known is the use made of the 'Exhibition Subway' at Earl's Court station, where a factory manned by voluntary part-time workers for making aircraft components was established.

The volume of traffic carried reflected the course of the war. Evacuation and the subsequent bombing depressed traffic levels in 1940 and 1941, after which they slowly recovered with the intensification of the war effort and greater movement of HM Forces. Services were also restricted due to coal shortages limiting electricity generation. Although initially the number of passengers carried fell faster than the drop in car miles operated, leading on the whole to easier travelling conditions, the later expansion of demand was met by further

restrictions on the service provided. In 1945, 543 million passenger journeys were catered for by 162 million car miles, a ratio 23% worse than that for 1938/39, and over 60% worse than in 1941. The figures mask any differences in average journey lengths which may have taken place, and do not take account of the way that distribution of traffic over the working day may have changed. Yet here was the genesis of a problem which was to dog the Underground for the next 20 years, when system capacity consistently failed to meet the demands placed upon it.

What sort of a world did the Underground emerge into in 1945 with the cessation of hostilities? Short term, the ending of the strain of wartime operation could not be matched by easier travelling conditions. In the words of the 1945 Annual Report, 'Shortages of staff and fuel remained and no

Chapter 5

The Postwar Years

Nationalisation placed a newly formed London Transport Executive under the British Transport Commission from 1 January 1948. The latter had enough to do in agonising over the affairs of the infant British Railways, and the LTE was deliberately left mainly to its own devices. A minor rash of boundary changes in the Metropolitan Line's area put LT in charge of the section from Harrow-on-the-Hill to south of Aylesbury, the Chesham and the Watford branches. Likewise, British Railways Western Region lost most of the western end of the Central Line, including the uncompleted works on the West Ruislip branch, and the Eastern Region lost the chunks of Great Northern and Great Eastern suburban lines which were in the course of conversion to Underground operation as part of the 1935-40 programme. Other LT acquisitions of the East London Line and east of Whitechapel really only reflected reality in that the providers of the services should be responsible also for the infrastructure. However, these were hardly matters which were fundamental to the running of the Underground; indeed, change was noticeable by its absence. But public expectations were rising, and it was perhaps in these years that London Transport,

as the 1948 nationalisation renamed the undertaking, lost the respect of the public which had been so ably harnessed and demonstrated a long decade ago.

It had been bad luck for the would-be commuters on the Central Line. The New Works programme had promised them great things both east and west of the capital, and a large proportion of the work had been carried out before the war stopped activity. Instead, the hapless passengers along the Eastern Avenue watched the completed tunnels being turned over to war work, and then fitted out with five-mile-long concrete floors — which took a correspondingly long time to remove afterwards. The extension works turned a short inner suburban railway line between Ealing Broadway and Liverpool Street into a veritable railway system of its own, extending miles into the country.

There were two main reasons for the western projection: to balance the workings in the west with those into the Essex borders, and to provide direct West End and City access for the developing areas of Greenford and Ruislip. They also offered a modest measure of relief for the Piccadilly Line.

The first obstacle to be tackled was the total

rebuilding of the inconvenient and makeshift arrangements at Wood Lane, where the original platform on the sharply-curved terminating loop had been supplemented by the through platforms of the Ealing and Shepherd's Bush Railway in 1920. The present westbound Central Line takes a wide sweep around the old site on its way to the replacement station of White City opened in 1947, in the open and just to the west. Built in brick and concrete and in unprepossessing style, it nevertheless gained a Festival of Britain architectural award. The twin island platforms retained the right-hand running inherited from the old layout, giving a curious back-to-front feeling to the station. The

Below:
The turning of Wood Lane into an intermediate station at White City was an extensive undertaking, given that the previous terminal loop resulted in the order of tracks being reversed to right-hand running. The changeover was on 17/18 July 1948; seen here is the first train to pass over the westbound track in its new position on Sunday morning, 18 July.
London Transport Museum U44139

Above:
The modernised but abandoned station at Highgate High Level on the Northern Line extensions was situated between two tunnels. The present tube station is directly below, and steps connect with its ticket office.
John Glover

Left:
A section of line which was abandoned completely without ever becoming part of London Transport proper was the Alexandra Palace branch of the Great Northern. Holden 'N7/1' class 0-6-2T No 69694 departs Crouch End station with the 4.2pm auto-train from Finsbury Park on 10 April 1954. The cable runs for the Underground may be seen at the side of the track. *Brian Morrison*

Above:
The 1935 prototypes for what became the 1938 tube stock were converted to conventional form and saw out the rest of their days on the Epping–Ongar shuttle. A train from Epping enters the North Weald loop on 9 August 1966. *P. H. Groom*

central track, normally used for terminating trains, was flanked by platforms on both sides; access to the depot was retained. Eastbound trains still pass one of the old platform sites in tunnel.

Between Wood Lane and North Acton there were, until 1938, only two Great Western-owned tracks, used by Ealing-bound tube trains and steam-hauled services; quadrupling was undertaken to separate the GW and LT trains. At North Acton, a new burrowing junction was built so that West Ruislip-bound trains could diverge from the Ealing line without crossing its metals.

There was a considerable amount of construction work needed for the new tube to parallel the (now) former Birmingham main line, though none was in tunnel. Much of it was carried on a long succession of bridges and viaducts over roads, railways and waterways. Thus there is a brick viaduct over the River Brent between Hanger Lane and Perivale, followed by three long viaducts in concrete and several bridges or girder spans to carry the line over the east and west forks of the Railtrack line from West Ealing. Beyond Greenford, distinguished by its central bay which accommodates all that remains of BR local services in the area, the tracks multiply at Northolt Junction where the line from Marylebone joins that from Paddington. The result is a great area of land dedicated for railway purposes, but with little traffic other than the tube trains running every 10–15 minutes and a three times an hour Class 165 diesel unit.

At Ruislip Gardens the line passes over West End Lane on a plate girder bridge set very much on the skew, to the extent that the girders have a maximum span of 99ft. On the south side of the line is the extensive Ruislip Depot. This has 16 tracks, each with its own inspection pit 440ft long; together with the carriage sidings, altogether there are 23 parallel lines of track here besides the running lines. West Ruislip is the terminus, the proposed further extension to Denham never having been pursued. From here to Epping is 34 miles and 90min of running time, the longest continuous journey which can be undertaken on the Underground. All the extension works in west London, including the modernistic stations, were built by the GWR, with London Transport being granted running powers. After nationalisation, management and ownership were transferred in stages to London Transport, a process completed in 1963.

Opening of the western extensions by stages in 1947/48 saw the replacement of a modest steam-worked suburban operation, many of the stations served being no more than halts; traffic growth engendered by the new tube railway, although substantial, has never perhaps quite matched expectations. It was a very different matter in the east, where the London & North Eastern Railway was under severe pressure. South West Essex, without a tube railway before, had a splendidly long one when work was completed.

The grand scheme for the area included electrification (at 1,500V dc) of the L&NER suburban service between Liverpool Street and Shenfield, and the extension of the Central Line from Liverpool Street to connect with the L&NER Loughton–Epping–Ongar branch and the Grange Hill loop, which were to be electrified and resignalled.

The extended tube ran from the Central Line platforms at Liverpool Street to a deep-level station at Bethnal Green, afterwards rising to the sub-surface level of the District Line at Mile End through water-bearing ground. The compressed air method of boring could not be employed here because the depth of covering earth was insufficient and the ground too porous to prevent air leakage. The problem was met by chemically treating the earth, both to consolidate it and hold back the water so that tunnelling could proceed. Some complicated engineering was also needed at the station, for the tube emerges on either side of the District Line tracks, and the old station had to be transformed into a new one with a double island platform layout. Mile End is unusual as a tube line station in that it is partly open to daylight on the westbound platform, and access is by stairs only.

For the 1¼ miles between Mile End and Stratford the line had to run beneath several streams that form part of the River Lea system. It was imperative to use compressed air under the east London marshes, and to provide sufficient ground cover, the twin tubes were located beneath the L&NER embankments. At river crossings, however, those embankments ceased, and the tubes were deprived of cover. Beneath the City Mill River only a few feet of waterlogged ballast lay between the tunnel shield and the bed of the river. A 'blow' here would have resulted in disaster, so the ground again had to be artificially consolidated, the injection pipes for forcing the chemical into the ground being driven from pontoons anchored in the river.

Beneath the Carpenters Road L&NER bridge, west of Stratford station, it was impossible to use compressed air, because at this point the tubes were rising to the level of the main line, lying only a little way below the road surface. Here it was necessary to sink two coffer dams (a kind of watertight enclosure), and partly build the tubes within them.

A portion of the tunnel under the roadway had to be made only 7ft in diameter to start with, owing to the presence of a large sewer; after the diversion of the sewer the tunnel was enlarged to 12ft.

At Stratford itself, the tube shared the L&NER station, making cross-platform connections in both directions with the Shenfield electric suburban services provided from 1949, and then dived back into the tube tunnel until it was clear of the extensive railway complex. It rose to the surface in an open cutting to (originally) a junction with the L&NER west of Leyton station. The eastbound tunnel was positioned directly below the Loughton branch signalbox with minimal clearance beneath the ballast; the consolidating chemical treatment was administered from inside the cabin amongst all the levers and locking mechanisms, without interrupting traffic. British Rail continued to operate freight services for a time, and staff trains to Epping ran in the early mornings using diesel multiple-units until 1980. After this, the connection was severed.

At Leytonstone the route forked; some trains continued on former L&NER metals via Woodford, while others entered the new tube, no longer used as a factory, to come to the surface again at Newbury Park. Redbridge station on the extension was built by 'cut and cover' methods, being only 15ft below ground level, but Gants Hill was given a unique treatment. Situated below a roundabout and thus with an underground ticket hall, escalators led down to a concourse between the platforms 150ft long and 20ft high. The domed roof was supported by rows of columns. Some kindly folk compared it

Below:
The Northern Heights project abandoned.

with the monumental stations on the Moscow underground, but while the approach was the same, the execution was mundane. It was reported in *The Times* in 1995 that a twinning arrangement was being sought between Gants Hill and one of the Moscow stations.

At Newbury Park, the tube joined the L&NER tracks from Ilford (later abandoned). Alterations at this station and others on former L&NER lines were carried out by that company; here a huge copper-covered concrete arch shaped like an aircraft hangar and just as draughty was erected alongside to serve as a bus station. For the next 40 years, Hainault station became a terminus for trains from the south, and extensive depot facilities with car washing plant and housing up to 344 cars were built beyond the station.

On the former main line, the LPTB managed to close the level crossings as part of the electrification package. Mostly, alternative facilities were provided, but the severing of Snakes Lane at Woodford station, which required traffic to make a diversion of the best part of a mile, provoked much indignation in local motorists. Loughton station underwent rebuilding, but elsewhere structures were largely preserved then and indeed remain so today. The lines were opened in sections from 1946; it was unfortunate that the L&NER's domestic electrification to Shenfield was delayed, since the tube service immediately attracted more traffic than it could cope with, resulting in questions in the House as early as 1948.

The completion of electrification to Epping on 25 September 1949 would no doubt have been the end of the matter had there not been two further

sections of line to be considered. The loop from Hainault to Woodford passed through the countryside and was incorporated in the electrification programme from the outset. Justified or not, the work was completed in 1948 and the line worked as a shuttle. A contemporary description of the scene north of Grange Hill described 'a tunnel mouth surmounted by a haystack, and a trial train disappearing with much sparking from the newly electrified track, that pleasantly contrasted with cattle munching in the fields'. Little has since changed.

The other section was the wholly rural single track route for the six miles from Epping on to Ongar. The Great Eastern Railway may or may not have had Chelmsford in their sights when pressing out to Ongar, but the line was so patently of a different nature from the Underground system in general that several years elapsed before London Transport could bring themselves to allocate the capital for electrifying it. In the meantime, BR's Eastern Region provided the traditional steam service, but in 1957 electrification was completed and a shuttle service using two electric trains was introduced. These would cross each other in the passing loop at North Weald, and it was said that if each started simultaneously from Epping and Ongar after dark, the lights on the intermediate stations would dim to a dull glow! Thus was the Central Line work completed.

It was even harder luck for the inhabitants of Brockley Hill, Mill Hill and Alexandra Palace. Good progress had been made before work had ceased, yet slowly it all slipped away. Preparations for the extensions beyond Edgware which included the

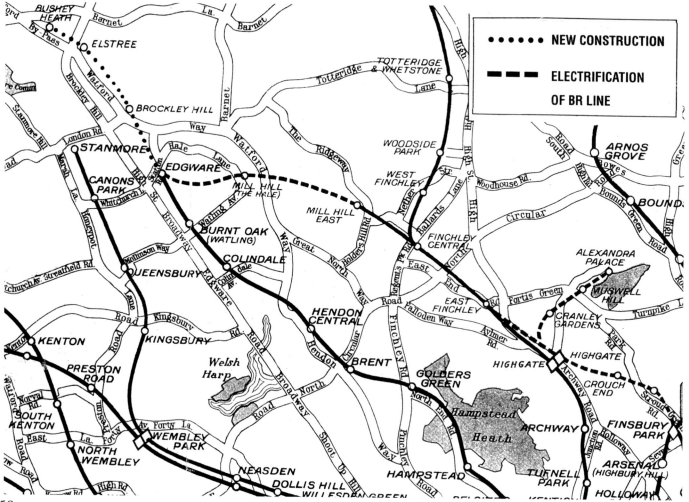

Above:
Electrification to Amersham meant the withdrawal of all London Underground interests north of Amersham. In August 1961, Fairburn 2-6-4T No 42133 waits at Great Missenden, complete with its LT signs, and a train of steam stock. *J. A. Rosser*

commencement of the boring of Elstree tunnel, the building of substations and of Aldenham depot were all to no avail. Aldenham later became the bus overhaul workshops of London Transport, but the rest of the work went to waste.

Further south, the half completed bridge across Seven Sisters Road at Finsbury Park was abandoned. At Drayton Park, where the Great Northern & City Line between Moorgate and Finsbury Park was in the open but at a depth of about 40ft, new running lines were constructed, leaving the old line just north of the station in a 'cut and cover' tunnel. They then emerged through trough-shaped cuttings to the surface, and the intention was that they should continue to rise to a new high level island platform at Finsbury Park. Thence the former flyover curve crossing the L&NER main line tracks was to have been adapted to carry the tube trains on their way to the dizzy heights of Alexandra Palace station, and to East Finchley for onward projection. Work got as far as erecting the London Transport roundels on Highgate high level platforms, but again no further work was carried out once it had stopped in 1941. The only part retained of the new work was the access to the depot at Highgate from East Finchley's centre platforms.

Over the years, the Northern Line extensions have continued to excite the imagination of what might have been, even as the half completed works subsided gently into the undergrowth and were obscured by subsequent building. The following describes an imaginary journey on a non-wartime winter evening:

'The mist was rising, rain was falling, and the wind was blowing cold across Brockley Hill. In the distance I heard a faint "Peep! Peep!" of a 1938 tube stock car; to my right was a wire fence and beyond it I could see lights and LT "Bullseyes" bearing the name Elstree South. I noticed the familiar five-light headcode pattern approaching behind the fence, and the train was bearing the destination "Kennington via East Finchley and City". I fumbled for my Staff Pass and hurried through the barrier to board the train.'

'The train quickly accelerated out of the station, diving almost immediately into a tunnel, but after a

few seconds we began to climb on to an embankment and were soon dazzled by the bright lights of an open-air station — Brockley Hill. Here, we paused for a few seconds. The station was on a viaduct straddling Watford Way. Below was a trolleybus, its long arms stretching up to collect current from wires suspended from the viaduct. Adjacent to the station entrance was a turning circle for route 666, Brockley Hill to Hammersmith, extended from Stanmore Circus to serve the new station.'

'On the train went, over house tops high above the suburbs of Edgware, before diving into a cutting and emerging into a five-platform Edgware station. In another platform, a second 1938 tube stock train waited. The train describer revealed its destination as Moorgate via Finsbury Park, and I changed on to it. We continued our journey, veering to the left after leaving Edgware. Our next stop was Mill Hill (The Hale), and as we waited there, a Midland Compound roared overhead making for St Pancras. On through the cosy suburbs of Mill Hill and Finchley, into the centre platforms at East Finchley. When the train reached the splendid new station at Highgate I alighted. The platform was very icy and I slipped… the next thing I knew I was in Whittington Hospital, and my wife was at my bedside. "I told you that you would come to grief one day, climbing over the wall into that old station" she said. So I had dreamed it… or had I? When I boarded the train at Elstree South, someone had left a ticket on the seat, and I thought I would keep it for my collection. I still have that old ticket which reads Crouch End to any one station on the LT system at a fare of 6d, and dated 23 December 1942. It all goes to show that there are certain things which happen for which no rational explanation can be given.'

One can hardly blame the postwar planners for their refusal to contemplate further continuous urban development. The Underground companies had quite unashamedly capitalised on the drawing power of their services and the consequent suburbanisation of London. Indeed, the Group were proud of their achievements; the Underground's Operating Manager, writing in 1928, had this to say of the extension to Morden, completed two years earlier:

'The surrounding countryside is probably the most undulating and pleasant of any on the outskirts of London, and it is likely that the growth which has taken place at Golders Green, Hendon, and Edgware will be repeated here … The railway, which enables the dweller in this district to reach the City or West End within half an hour, will convert the countryside into a modern suburb and will provide one more incentive to the Londoner to forsake the congested areas for the healthier localities on the outer fringe.'

Expectations were fulfilled, and more. Suburbia was extended by the buses which brought in the passengers from further afield, and who were to be encouraged by the issue of combined bus and

Underground tickets. The identical result was achieved elsewhere, whether at Barking, Ealing, Harrow, Putney or Wembley.

Yet it was all far from plain sailing for the railway companies, and Lord Ashfield's admission that the Underground had never been a profitable enterprise has already been noted. In the 1930s, Frank Pick as Managing Director of the Underground acknowledged gloomily that his problem had no solution: to make the Underground pay he had to stimulate suburban traffic which, when poured into the centre, overloaded the buses and congested the roads.

Part of the problem lay in the nature of passenger transport itself, where the costs and benefits which resulted were distributed on a much wider canvas than the company and its customers. The issues raised by the suburbanisation of Morden *et al* could not be dismissed as a merely private matter between two parties to a commercial transaction, especially in an age which believed in the efficacy of the planned approach.

From the earliest days, entrepreneurs realised that whilst transport facilities might be provided profitably to meet a demand which was already there, the provision of such facilities in themselves could stimulate traffic and increase the values of the surrounding properties. The problem has always been that while the railway interests would benefit from the generated traffic revenues, this was not enough to finance extensions and regeneration of the systems. The gains represented by rises in property values went into the hands of private individual property owners.

One might compare the extensions of the Underground under the New Works Programme 1935-40, which became possible only because of the availability of cheap government loan capital.

Cheap finance, or grants, tended to set the scene; if it was investment in urban railways that was wanted, funding of capital costs would have to be mainly a matter for either central or local government. But what was wanted in the postwar era?

The County of London Plan had spawned various subsidiary work. Even after the more exotic ideas of the Railway (London Plan) Committee of 1944 had been watered down, the British Transport Commission's 1949 Working Party proposals were vast in conception. They suggested a quite remarkable network of new routes lettered from A through to M, crossing London in tunnel. Everything would be electrified.

The Working Party were careful to distinguish between urban tube railways with intensive services and frequent but short stops, and outer suburban railways running in 17ft diameter tunnels taking main line rolling stock but with lower service frequencies, fewer stops and higher average speeds. These do not mix, particularly in the design of rolling stock provided. For a satisfactory outer suburban service, there must be a high seating capacity. In the in-town area, there must be a high overload capacity requiring ample standing space. This can only be obtained at the expense of seats, while the door arrangements need to permit rapid loading and unloading at stations to minimise stop times.

The proposed works may be summarised as follows. It should be noted that the Working Party accepted the need to demolish Blackfriars Bridge, but not Charing Cross or Cannon Street bridges, on planning grounds. (Environment was not a word then in general use.) The new Routes A and B were to have been new underground lines, respectively passenger and freight, linking main line services north and south of the river, which were then using Blackfriars Bridge. Route C was to be a new tube from the Tottenham and Edmonton area via Finsbury Park, King's Cross, Euston, Oxford Circus, Green Park, Victoria, Vauxhall, Stockwell, Brixton, Streatham to East Croydon. Branch lines on the alignment of the Cambridge Road and from Seven Sisters to Walthamstow were 'possibly desirable'.

Route D was the Chingford/Enfield electrification, then via new tube from Hackney Downs to Liverpool Street, Bank, Ludgate Circus, Aldwych and Trafalgar Square to Victoria. A westward extension of this line had lower priority. A low priority Route E would have duplicated the Northern Line south of Kennington with extensions on to the Southern. Route F was the electrification of Marylebone services; again tube projection southwards was of lesser importance. Yet again, Route G, the electrification of Fenchurch Street services, could have resulted eventually in a new westerly tube emerging at Raynes Park.

Route H, the extension of the Bakerloo Line to Camberwell, was authorised but later abandoned; Routes J and K were low priority alternatives taking the Finsbury Park–Moorgate trains into south London. Route L would have taken the Holborn–Aldwych line on to Waterloo, again without priority. The remaining Route M was the electrification of the Liverpool Street–Cambridge main line.

Completion of New Works Programme and certain Southern Region improvements were also marked out for early attention.

The priority tasks identified required 49¼ miles of new tube construction, a total which would have been doubled with the lower priority works added in. With masterly understatement, the Report anticipated that the work would take 20 to 30 years to implement. 'Some regard', the Working Party averred, 'must be paid to the economics of new railways in tunnel across London'.

Of all the new items in the list, the one which clearly had the best claim to an early start was Route C. The 1949 Report comments are of some interest:

'This route covers one of the most important in-town sections for local traffic between Victoria and King's Cross. It is considered that the alignment should be via Green Park and Oxford Circus stations rather than via Hyde Park Corner and Bond Street, since this route is likely to carry a heavier traffic, especially outside the peak hours. Satisfactory cross-platform interchange at Oxford Circus with the Bakerloo Line can be provided, but only if the new route is worked with standard size tube stock, since available space at Oxford Circus is restricted. Besides offering an important new in-town connection, the route will provide additional distribution facilities over the central area from the terminal stations at King's Cross, Euston and Victoria.'

'At its northern end, the route can best be used to

Above:

The Chesham branch train, propelled by Ivatt 2-6-4T No 41284, bears away from the main line on 11 September 1960, the last day of full steam operation. The train is formed of the Ashbury stock, which subsequently found a new life on the Bluebell Railway. *C. R. L. Coles*

give the much needed direct facilities between the Tottenham/Edmonton area and the West End, and will give relief to the overcrowded section of the Piccadilly Line north of King's Cross. It is suggested that the northern terminal must be such that convenient interchange can be provided with the (former Great Eastern) Cambridge main line, which will be electrified. There might possibly be branches on the alignment of the Cambridge Road and from Seven Sisters to Walthamstow. At its southern end, the route proposed via the Brixton Road to Croydon is accepted… no difficulty is anticipated in finding a depot site at the northern end.'

There, in all essence, was the Victoria Line, which opened 20 years later between 1968 and 1972. Why did it take so long?

The major problem turned out to be in persuading government that it was indeed in their best interest to fund its construction. Attitudes in the postwar era to public transport tended to be hostile; capital was scarce to the point of near invisibility for public transport projects. If a commercial rate of return was being sought, then there were other more attractive investments to make. In vain was it argued that it was London (rather than London Transport) which stood to gain. Various learned bodies looked at the project, among them the Chambers Committee of 1955. This was the year in which statutory powers for construction were obtained. By then the argument was bound up with the peak problem generally. Chambers noted the dilemma posed by the imbalance of peak and off-peak traffic:

'We have every sympathy with the view of London Transport that only as a last resort should they be required to incur very heavy expenditure if it is needed only to provide additional comfort during short periods of peak traffic. The alternative of staggering of working hours would be altogether more acceptable…'

So off everybody went in what ultimately turned out to be a wild goose chase, since the staggering of hours had little public appeal.

London Transport thus had a hard time in this period, broken, perhaps briefly, by the Coronation of Her Majesty the Queen in 1953.

In his autobiography, Sir John Elliot as the then Chairman of London Transport recalled how he broke down 'a wall of no' on Route C. First, the plan was put up for approval in principle but without a firm date for construction, and having received it work was slowly carried out at points along the line of route as part of the annual renewals programme. In this way, aerial surveys were completed, 70 exploratory boreholes were sunk, and a mile of experimental tunnelling north of Finsbury Park was excavated and lined by new methods in 1960 'to gain practical experience'. Elliot's other gift to Route C was the bestowal of the name Victoria Line.

In the soft clay soil of the experimental section from Finsbury Park to Tottenham, rotating drum diggers were employed. One was of 14ft external diameter for concrete-lined tunnels, and the other 13ft 1in for tunnels lined with cast-iron segments. Essentially, the diggers consisted of two drums, one within another. The outer 14ft drum had a bevelled cutting edge and was driven into the tunnel face as with the Greathead shield. The inner drum of 7ft 6in diameter was rotated on roller races by hydraulic motors. It had cutting teeth mounted on arms on its outer edge, and cut the area in front of the space between inner and outer drums. The area in front of the inner drum was cut by teeth mounted on an arm across the drum's diameter.

The ram operator was provided with siting guides to enable him to adjust the pressure on the rams to correct any tendency to deviate right or left or up or down from the prescribed direction or gradient. The clay excavated was guided by scoops or paddles to a belt conveyor and subsequently the clay was discharged into skips on rails for eventual hoisting up the working shafts.

When the outer shield reached the end of its thrust, a new ring of tunnel lining was added, the rams pushed against the newly installed ring, and the whole cycle recommenced. The process for the cast-iron-lined tunnels was similar, and with both

Elizabeth R

CORONATION

TUESDAY 2 JUNE 1953

LONDON TRANSPORT

BRITISH RAILWAYS

Left:
The Coronation, 2 June 1953.

cast with convex and concave edges to form knuckle joints, and the rings were finally expanded by wedges, the last being ram-driven home at pressure. The methods of lining, which owed their origin to a water tunnel built for the Central Electricity Generating Board, obviated the need for cement grouting, and were adopted for the construction of the Victoria Line proper.

Drum diggers cannot be used where rocky or otherwise obstructive soil formations are encountered, where the only means of winning a passage is the non-rotating shield, mechanical shovel, or even manual excavation. Larger shields have to be constructed for boring the station tunnels, while pedestrian tunnels within station complexes are excavated with hand tools and pneumatic spades. These tunnels are of short length, and shields to excavate them would be

science of social cost-benefit analysis. Through this it was demonstrated rather than asserted that most of the benefits fell elsewhere, and that road users rather than rail passengers would be the principal beneficiaries. The sum looked as shown in Table 4.

Therefore, the argument went, the gains to the wider community were a sufficient and an acceptable justification for building the line, even though it would be a commercial disaster for London Transport should they have to fulfil a commercial rate of return on their investment. Hence, the go-ahead that was finally forthcoming in 1962 accepted the likely financial consequences for the government.

Although the Victoria Line saga must have sapped the energies of the Executive, as London Transport had become under the BTC, there were other schemes of great importance being undertaken. The District Line services were indirect beneficiaries of the BR Modernisation Plan, which presaged electrification of the London, Tilbury & Southend

TABLE 4:			
Benefits from the Victoria Line			
Groups of Beneficiaries			*% of benefit derived*
Traffic diverted to the Victoria Line			34%
Traffic not diverted: Road users	35%}	52%	
Others	17%}		
Generated traffic			14%
			100%

types of lining a far greater speed of excavation was obtained. Some of this was due to the use of cast-iron segments with flexible joints, the new method allowing for each completed ring of segments to be expanded by jacks against the clay outside, and finally wedged firmly in place when the pressure on the jacks was released. The concrete linings were

uneconomical, as a chamber larger than the shield must necessarily be built in which to erect it. Escalator tunnels are also excavated by hand, as it would be very difficult to control a shield on such a slope as that on which an escalator is built.

The long drawn out struggle to achieve authorisation of the Victoria Line throughout the 1950s eventually turned to the newly developed

Below:
The Moorgate of the past has now been extensively built over. On 1 May 1952, from left to right, were lined up Aldgate–Watford and Moorgate–Watford trains of 'T' stock, Class N2/4 0-6-2T No 69581 with a service to Welwyn Garden City and Fowler Class 3 2-6-2T No 40028 with a train to St Albans City.
R. E. Vincent

61

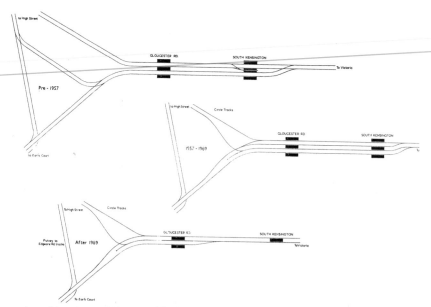

lines. Hitherto, Underground trains had been part of the general maelstrom of services, each vying for priority. Of the flat junctions for three routes east of Barking station used by 700 trains daily, it was admitted candidly that they caused many delays. So, in the expansive manner of the times, a complex series of flyovers and diveunders was constructed to provide physical separation of conflicting movements. The plan entailed the complete segregation of services at all points; thus the crossovers from the Tilbury line to the District at Campbell Road Junction, Bow, and the North London Junction at Bromley were also removed.

Down the line at Upminster a new Underground depot was constructed with all mod cons. District Line facilities had never been entirely satisfactory, and the new 34-train-capacity depot replaced the inadequate installation at East Ham. Two of the reception roads were given washing machines so that all trains could be washed as they came out of service. All nine roads in the car examination shed were given pits. Overhead conductors, carrying small trolleys with jumper cables to provide power to trains, ran the full length of the pits, as no conductor rails can be installed in such areas. The conductors on the jumper cables are inserted into receptacle boxes on the cars when power is required; this is standard London Transport practice. There was also a small lifting shop.

At that time, it was usual for shunters to hand-operate points and hand signal the trains from the ground. A new method adopted at Upminster provided for all points to be power-operated and controlled from the tower. One shunter in the tower would give instructions to drivers via loudspeakers by the trackside, the position of the trains being determined by reference to a track circuit diagram.

Drivers were given the right to reply with a 'talk back' facility. After giving an instruction to a driver, the loudspeaker automatically switched functions to become a microphone so that the driver could lean out of his cab and respond. All speaker/micro-phones could be controlled individually by the shunter on duty, but in case of total confusion a panic button was installed to display a red light and, hopefully, to stop everything.

The erection of the West London Air Terminal gave London Transport the excuse they needed to sort out the confusion abounding in the Earl's Court–High Street Kensington–South Kensington triangle. The layout, which stemmed from the separate ownership and operation of the previous century had the fundamental disadvantage of a conflict between eastbound District Line and westbound Circle Line trains at the flat junction east of South Kensington station where four tracks merged into two. By removing the crossing to a new site west of Gloucester Road and reversing the running direction of the two inner tracks, it became possible to hold a westbound Circle Line train without it delaying District Line services behind it. Furthermore, eastbound passengers who had a choice of two platforms at which to wait would only have one, the most northerly. At that time, non-stopping of trains was still in vogue, and these used the inner of the two eastbound tracks. The revised layout was brought into use in 1957.

It did not, however, last. The abandon-ment of non-stopping meant that there was little purpose served by maintaining two eastbound tracks, while

the westbound junction could be moved further west with no adverse effects. In 1969, eight platform faces were reduced to five, and South Kensington became one ultra-wide island platform. A new connection west of Gloucester Road allowed all westbound trains to use the former Circle Line platform during less busy periods.

In 1959, a practically new station was brought into use at Notting Hill Gate. Previously there were two stations, one each side of the busy highway. These served the

Central and the District/Circle Lines respectively, and some 2,000,000 passengers changed between them each year. A sub-surface ticket hall provided access to the two lines, with interchange available by subways at a low level. The eastbound Central Line platform here is 100ft below surface, the westbound partly above it and to one side, while the Circle Line platforms are some distance away but only 27ft below ground level. The work was therefore somewhat complex! The old shafts for lifts and stairs were used subsequently for ventilation purposes.

The District Line suffered from some platforms being of sub-standard length, and the end cars could be reached only by narrow catwalks. Work at Blackfriars involved lengthening the platforms by 74ft; the task included the demolition of the existing running tunnel and the construction of a wider covered way for the platforms. It also involved the bridging of the Fleet River, reduced many years previously from the status of a navigable

waterway to an underground sewer, but still carrying a considerable volume of water, and the section-by-section replacement of the roadway above.

The soil along the Thames Embankment is very largely made up ground and mud. When the line was built, as much as 24ft of ruins dating back 2,000 years or so had to be cut through, and the original foundations carried down to 13ft below rail level. The general construction then was of brick walls and an arch with a concrete invert, made wider at the stations with girders to support buildings. The rebuilding method used was to excavate trenches outside the existing tunnel walls from street level, and sink piles through the trenches to support concrete bases for the new structure. These bases in turn formed the support for new pre-cast concrete columns, the spaces between which were filled with wall slabs and concrete. Opening the roadway then allowed a pair of cranes to lower the nine new roof beams on to the columns; the placing of each beam was an entire night's work. A concrete slab subsequently formed the base of the new roadway.

Over the Fleet sewer the vertical columns were carried on two reinforced concrete beams. A further complication was the presence of both a pedestrian and a pipe subway in the area.

With the new walls and roof completed, the old

tunnel inside was demolished except for the lower sections of the brick walls, which were then used to form the base of the platform extensions. The work was completed in 1962; similar platform extensions were also undertaken at Westminster.

The last of the 1935-40 projects was the Metropolitan Line's main line rebuilding. Whereas the prewar scheme had envisaged the conversion of 'steam' stock to electric multiple unit use, galloping dilapidation coupled with the growing demand which was apparent by the mid-1950s secured authorisation using new stock in 1956. Work was thus started on the four-tracking and electrification of the Metropolitan Line north of Harrow. The scheme was allowed to proceed, as it extended way beyond the Green Belt to areas where development was to be encouraged.

The postwar Metropolitan system was badly in need of relief. By 1955, peak problems were acute; on the main line services from the City through Baker Street and Finchley Road, 18 train sets and three electric locomotives only were required in the off-peak, but this rose to 50 train sets and nine locomotives at peak times. Peak operation provided many difficult problems; between 17.00 and 18.00, 27 trains carrying 15,000 passengers needed to be dispatched from Baker Street. During this hour, 34 trains approached Baker Street from the Aldgate direction. Of these, 18 were for the main line, and had to cross the paths of 16 eastbound trains from Edgware Road at the flat junction. In addition, 14 trains left the main line platforms for the City,

Below:
Peak services on the Metropolitan at Baker Street, 1955.

Right:
The Amersham electrification: track plan 1962.

complications arose at the City termini, with the Moorgate and Liverpool Street terminating workings all having to cross the westbound tracks. At the latter station, terminus of the locomotive-hauled trains from Aylesbury and Chesham, a spare locomotive was needed to haul the trains out again.

The original modernisation proposals had envisaged the four tracks extending through to the far side of Rickmansworth, but reappraisal cut this back to Watford South Junction, a little to the north of Moor Park station. Similarly, it was decided that platforms need not be provided at intermediate stations on what became the new fast lines. The existing locomotive-hauled stock and the venerable multiple-units would all be replaced with a brand new design which was to provide for all service requirements on the Metropolitan main line. Physical site work started in 1958, and the changeover to total multiple unit working was on 11 September 1961. The widening scheme was not completed until mid-1962.

The traditional pattern of working was of six-car trains of 'steam' stock hauled by one of the Metropolitan Railway's Metrovick Bo-Bos to Rickmansworth, where locomotives would be changed. A British Railways ex-LMS Class 4 2-6-4T then took over for the steady climb to Amersham and beyond. At Chalfont & Latimer, the branch connection to Chesham in the bay platform would be formed of an Ivatt 2-6-2T, propelling one of the ancient three-car push-pull sets created out of the 'Ashbury' stock built in Manchester between 1898 and 1900. Other services to Watford and Rickmansworth were formed of the T stock multiple-units. All of these trains were traditional compartment stock, and the transition to saloons with air-operated doors and loss of seating capacity raised howls of protest in Metro-Land. In reality, saloon vehicles were inevitable, as the Railway

compromises are, but especially in view of some of the products bought by British Railways in this period, the Metropolitan Line commuter did rather well. As London Transport said brightly, the A stock 'affords comfort for long distance passengers as all seating is transverse, but the wide vestibules with air-operated doors in which shorter distance passengers can stand in reasonable comfort, give the best of both worlds in which this stock has to run'. In all fairness, the A stock was very well conceived.

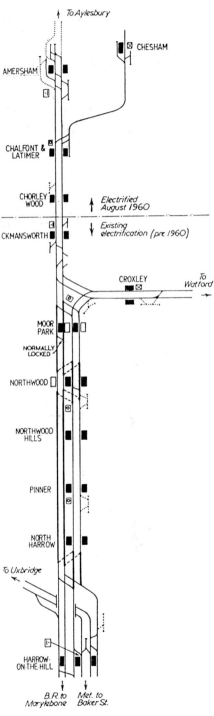

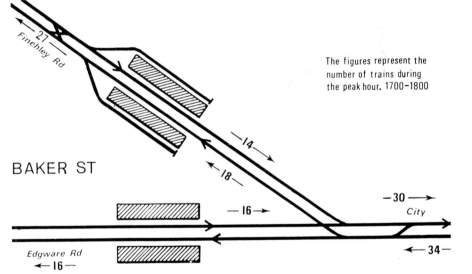

The figures represent the number of trains during the peak hour. 1700-1800

making 30 eastbound in total. Parallel working over the junction was thus used whenever possible. The remaining nine trains on the main line northwards originated at Baker Street, for Harrow, Watford or Uxbridge.

Station allowances were varied according to train and station. On the Circle the time was generally 20sec, but at Baker Street this was increased to anything between 30sec and 2min to suit the crowded conditions east of the junction. Further

Inspectorate was not prepared to sanction new stock without emergency exits through the ends of the cars; the constraint was the single line tunnels between Baker Street and Finchley Road. Nor were slam doors to be permitted. Experimental rebuilding on two T stock trailer underframes took place in 1946/7, in what turned out to be very preliminary work.

The familiar A stock is described elsewhere. It was not welcomed universally as indeed few

The track widening scheme placed the fast tracks alongside the slow lines, rather than one each side as had been adopted earlier south of Harrow. At North Harrow, Pinner and Northwood Hills the additional tracks were built clear of the existing platforms, but at Northwood land was not available on the west side of the existing station so that total reconstruction here, and at Moor Park which became a four platformed station, was needed. Amersham gained an extra platform, since it was now to be the terminus of all London Transport operations. On the Chesham branch, a bay was let into the (lengthened) terminus platform and a siding was also electrified. The signalbox at Chesham was retained and although certain signals,

particularly the down home and up starting signals were replaced by colour lights, most of the semaphores and mechanical points remained in use.

There were numerous bridge rebuildings. Resignalling was carried out as part of the project, and this provided for standard BR four aspect signalling on the fast lines (where speeds of up to 70mph were permitted) and through to Amersham, due to the dual use with BR trains to and from Marylebone. Standard LT two aspects sufficed elsewhere, although the occasional provision of repeater signals on the same post gave the appearance of four aspects. Following completion of the electrification, London Transport surrendered

all interests beyond Amersham or, to be precise, at Mantles Wood, north of a point close to Railtrack milepost 25¼, and designated with a boundary marker.

The end of 1962 saw the demise of the London Transport Executive, and its replacement with the London Transport Board, which was a fully fledged nationalised industry in its own right and responsible direct to the Minister. The separation from British Railways was all but complete; there were now no revenue pooling arrangements between the two. The Act paid lip service to the need to continue co-ordination with British Railways, but the reality was that each would henceforth go its own way.

Above:
A pristine 'A60' stock train runs into Northwood Hills, *en route* for Watford. Four-car working off-peak was still in vogue at this time; only later was it decided that it caused as many problems as it solved. The A60 Cravens cars, albeit wide by Underground standards, are each only 53ft long. This compares with 57ft or 64ft for contemporary BR passenger rolling stock. *J. A. Rosser*

Right:
As part of the Barbican redevelopment in the City of London in 1963–64, the Metropolitan and the Widened Lines were diverted further south between Aldersgate and Moorgate and placed in a concrete box. The new alignment was subsequently built over, the railway having taken up a new, straighter, alignment. This was the view looking east towards Moorgate.
London Transport Museum

Chapter 6

Development of the Underground Train

It is perhaps now time to consider the trains themselves.

The electric motor as applied to trains for traction purposes has always been of direct current series type, and commonly mounted on the axle. Stopping has been effected by the friction of the brake shoes on the wheel treads, operated by a compressed air supply. Collector shoes which rubbed on the conductor rails picked up the traction current, which was then fed to the motors and controlled on the multiple unit principle. All the systems had to be sufficiently developed for the whole to work, but once the nut of multiple unit control had been cracked, the electric train was able to come into its own. Thereafter, the locomotive had no place in purely urban transit systems. Sprague's invention had enabled two or more motor cars in a train to be controlled from a master controller with only a small current passing through it and along the train. Each power car picked up its own current from the live rail, and fire and insulation hazards were avoided. The tube railways used electro-magnetic contactor (switch) control energised by control wires utilising the 600V dc supply on the British Thomson-Houston system; the Metropolitan used the electro-pneumatic form

developed by Westinghouse, with low voltage electro-magnetic valves controlling air pressure to cylinders, and the pistons working the main switches.

In operation, the driver is not faced with a mass of relays, cut-outs or resistances. Just as the driver of a steam locomotive had an ultimate control in the regulator, so the driver of an electric train is concerned only with a single master controller. When he operates the handle or 'winds it up', the following sequence in a traditional installation takes place.

The contactors connect the motors to the current supply, at first in series through starting resistances, where surplus electrical energy which the motors are unable to assimilate is dissipated as heat. As the train gathers speed, an accelerating relay cuts out the starting resistance in a number of steps by the automatic closing of contactors. When all the resistance has been cut, each motor is working on only half the voltage of the power supply, but is sufficiently accelerated to start absorbing the full line voltage. The next phase is therefore the regrouping of the motor circuits in parallel, with the starting resistances again in operation. They are cut out in steps as before, until finally the motors are in

full parallel; that is, they are receiving the full voltage, being connected directly across the power supply. In the improved type of Pneumatic Camshaft Motor (PCM) control, introduced in 1936, the more sensitive pneumatic accelerator, basically a small air-oil engine operating contacts, replaced the old individual contactors. The stages are as before, but at the intermediate stage a valve operating on the engine forces air against the oil, which in turn moves a piston and camshaft and cuts out resistances. The third, parallel, stage is reached with resistance automatically restored, but at this point the engine operates in reverse and allows the motors full voltage by cutting out resistances. It should be appreciated that these movements, although appearing lengthy and involved when described, take place in the few seconds in which the train is getting under way.

When the driver cuts the power and the train coasts, a 'no-volt' relay in the circuit comes into operation. Its purpose is to prevent the full voltage being suddenly fed to the motors after power is restored, by ensuring that the equipment is returned to its original starting condition and with the complete sequence of operations to follow. The driver may move his controller freely through

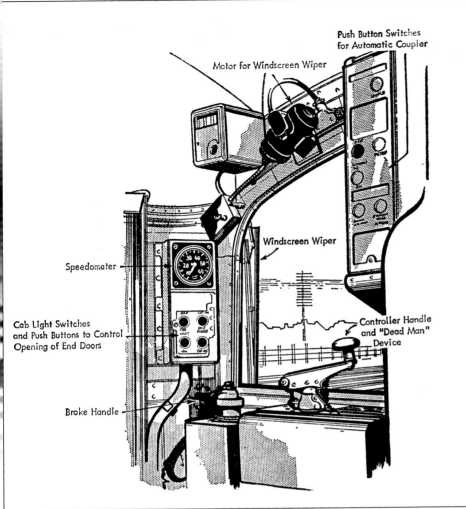

Push Button Switches
for Automatic Coupler

Motor for Windscreen Wiper

Windscreen Wiper

Speedometer

Cab Light Switches
and Push Buttons to Control
Opening of End Doors

Controller Handle
and "Dead Man"
Device

Brake Handle

Far left:
The Bakerloo was a Yerkes line; Piccadilly Circus is unusual in that the end of a reversing crossover occupies part of the station tunnel. A northbound train of that stalwart of the tube lines, the 1938 stock, is arriving on 13 April 1983.
John Glover

Above:
Tube stock cab interior.

Left:
BTH traction equipment advertisement, with 1938 stock, 1952.
Author's collection

several accelerating positions or notches, but the accelerating relay ensures that the proper sequence is traversed. Should he lift his hand off the controller handle, the main supply to the controller is broken, current is cut off, and the brakes are applied. This is the safety device introduced in 1906/07 and fitted to all rolling stock to guard against a driver's personal mishap, be it illness or collapse. The colloquial name for this part of the master controller is the 'dead man's handle'.

Braking of trains followed the Westinghouse developments, whereby movement of the operating handle to induce a fall in pressure in the system would result in the brakes being applied. Full exhaustion as a result of the release of the dead man's handle, the operation of the passenger emergency alarms or the activation of the trip cock all resulted in a full emergency brake application. The problem with the Westinghouse brake was the time delay inherent in it and the sequential operation along the length of the train as the brake pipe pressure fell. The electro-pneumatic (EP) brake installed from 1930 used electrically-operated valves to apply the brake in each car simultaneously; the valves allowed compressed air from the main air pipe to enter and leave the brake cylinders. This was henceforth used for service operation, but the Westinghouse brake was retained for safety purposes. The 'Standard' or 'pre-1938' tube stock was all fitted with the EP brake, but only later builds had it supplied as from new.

The use of gatemen to control entry and exit from the trains was very labour intensive, and this hastened the search for some method of door provision and operation which could be controlled remotely. This was found in the sliding door which, when open, was recessed into a pocket in the body side. Operation was either by hand (as for many years on the surface lines) or by compressed air engine, one to each door leaf, controlled through electro-pneumatic valves. Opening and closing was overseen by the guard, and a mechanical interlock detected whether the door was properly closed. Later interlocks consisted of a glass bottle, part filled with mercury, and containing a pair of electrical contacts. Every sliding door on a train operates one of these devices, tilting the glass bottle when all the doors are closed, so that the mercury bridges the contacts and the door closed circuit is complete, and which then lights the guard's pilot light. The interlocks are extremely reliable, which is just as well seeing that there are more than three million interlock operations every day on the Underground. Only when the doors were all proved shut could the starting signal be given to the driver by means of a bell. One Person Operation (OPO), of course, came rather later.

Various additional safety devices have been tried. The original air-operated doors had a pressure sensitive edge, which if obstructed caused the door to reopen. This negated the secondary objective, which was to reduce station stop times. The 'sensitive' aspect was quickly abandoned, although a determined foot can still hold a door open indefinitely. To release an item of clothing or a case, one door of a pair when shut can be forced back about four inches. A further innovation was passenger door control, which conserved heat in the open air sections that were rapidly increasing as the Underground spread out to the suburbs. Initially, this was not sufficiently reliable, and was dropped until recent years. Indicators which alerted staff to the location of door problems proved

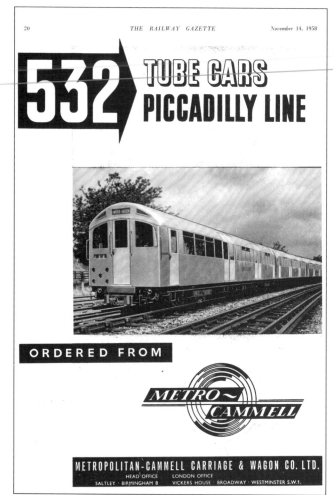

Left:
Metro-Cammell advertisement, with 1956 stock, 1958.
Author's collection

Below:
The interior of the 1938 stock, in all its essentials, has in many respects been repeated in many other rolling stock types. This 1938 car, No 4927, was still in London Underground service in 1995. *John Glover*

Opposite top:
The Waterloo & City Line of the Southern Railway obtained new English Electric-built trains in 1940. A five-car formation, when new, is seen above ground.
Ian Allan Library

Opposite below:
Compared with the contemporaneous Underground stock, the Southern Railway cars looked decidedly dowdy. This is a 1940 picture, taken before they entered service. *Southern Railway*

difficult to achieve, a problem later solved by the placing of fault detection lights on the roof of each car.

The robustness of some of the early cars was well illustrated by the two cars from the original fleet of 1906 delivered to the Great Northern, Piccadilly & Brompton Railway. This pair of cars was in use for no less than 50 years, finishing their passenger carrying careers on the not-too-demanding Holborn–Aldwych shuttle. Converted to air door operation in the 1920s, they were further modified in 1930 to work as single units. They were allowed a five year break during the 1939–45 war when the branch was closed, to be resuscitated afterwards and fitted with electro-pneumatic brakes. They left the Aldwych branch in 1948 to be used as pilot cars, their last duty being with a flat wagon as a stores train between Acton Works and Northfields depot. Final withdrawal was in 1956.

This though was exceptional, and when the initial batches of electric multiple-unit stock needed replacement or supplementation, it was possible to incorporate a number of improvements. The all-steel clerestory roofed 'pre-1938' stock for the tube lines was built in several batches from 1922 to 1934 to a grand total of 1,466 cars, and was the work of half a dozen different builders. Batches built up to 1930 were replacements for the original stock on the Yerkes tubes; the rest for the Piccadilly extensions. Despite the name 'Standard', it was not all operationally compatible for some years. Three basic types were produced, consisting of (driving) motors (M), trailers (T), and control trailers (CT). Trailer cars lacked traction motors and compressors, but seated 48 passengers or so, unlike the driving motors which lost one third of their seating potential in the equipment compartment behind

the cab. However, it did make life much easier for the fitter, who could carry out an inspection from both inside and outside, the latter by raising louvred panels in the coachwork. The frames of these motor cars were upswept at the driving end to give clearance for the motor bogie with its 3ft diameter wheels (all the rest were 2ft 8in in diameter). The control trailers were provided with cabs and driving gear but were underused, and several were converted to ordinary trailers.

The final orders for the Piccadilly incorporated several improvements. Faster trains were needed, and weak field control was used. This allowed higher speeds of 50mph or so on the long open stretches of line, albeit at the expense of additional current consumption. Seven-car trains with three motor cars replaced six-car trains with two. Weight was kept to a minimum by the use of aluminium alloy wherever possible, and by building the steel superstructure of light pressings. External surfaces of the coachwork were rounded off to permit a smoother passage through the car washing apparatus. Inside rearrangement resulted in the guard's control panels in motor cars being built into the end walls, and the addition of power-operated single leaf doors at each end.

Formations of seven cars became general, made up M-T-T-M and used thus off-peak, with an additional CT-T-M added at peak. Pairs of four-car sets were used on the Central Line to which these trains gravitated later, but their last outpost on the Northern City Line saw a slack hour formation of M-CT, supplemented with CT-T-T-M at peak. The best known variation was the nine-car experiment on the Northern Line from February 1938. As a response to complaints of severe overcrowding on the Edgware branch, some platform lengthening was carried out and in the peaks trains were made up M-T-M+T-T-T+M-T-M. The guard rode in the seventh vehicle. Elaborate arrangements were made, with the two rear cars on southbound journeys stopping in tunnel and hence not available for entry or exit between Golders Green and Tottenham Court Road. At the latter station the first two cars stopped in tunnel. The guard had to isolate the door mechanisms as necessary. Perhaps surprisingly, the scheme was said to have worked well, but it was discontinued at the outbreak of war and was not revived subsequently. However, the new fleet of 1938 stock was ordered in the expectation that it would continue, which led to a major reshuffling of the fleet later on.

The pre-1938 stock survived in London Transport revenue-earning service until 1966, but a handful of cars saw further use with British Rail on the Isle of Wight until 1989. Five of these cars have returned to London Underground, where they have been united with pre-1938 cars which latterly were part of the engineering fleet. There are hopes that one day some may be restored to form a vintage train.

The 1935 experimental stock, some of which was delivered with streamlined front ends, was a precursor to the huge 1938 stock fleet. Including the conversions of the 1935 prototypes, and the similar 1949 additions, the fleet totalled eventually 1,230 cars. As in the experimental sets, all control and traction equipment was removed from its traditional home to new positions beneath the floor, thus providing extra passenger space. These were also the first production tube trains to use low voltage electrical supplies for lighting and other equipment instead of the earlier system of direct supply from the current rails. Motor cars now seated 42 passengers, and additional doors were provided. Introduced for the first time was the non-driving motor car (NDM). The seven car formations were made up in two semi-permanent sets of M-NDM-T-M+M-T-M.

The presence of five motored cars out of seven was a recognition that multiple unit working could also give superior performance characteristics if motors could be distributed intermediately along the length of the train to increase speed and acceleration. Such stock also had the same power/weight ratio irrespective of train length, which could thus be varied to suit the traffic offering without altering operational performance.

Braking performance was improved. To prevent rates of braking which might produce wheel lock and skidding (and hence wear 'flats' on the wheels), a retardation controller was added. Two tubular rings of glass containing mercury were so mounted that when a certain braking rate had been reached the mercury flowed up one of the tubes and indirectly cut off further supplies of air to the brake cylinder. Should the braking approach a severity sufficient to lock the wheels, the forward surge of the train caused a similar displacement of mercury in the second tube, which released air from the brake cylinder and eased the brakes. The result was that a train could be brought smoothly to a standstill. This was a relatively crude but effective means of compensating for the different weights of empty and heavily loaded trains.

Compared with the pre-1938 stock, the body design had all external corners rounded off, and it was given a semi-streamlined appearance. To each bogie of the motor cars were fitted 168hp nose-suspended motors, giving a creditable 1,680hp over the whole train. Automatic coupling between sets made possible the instantaneous connection of the mechanical, electrical and pneumatic mechanism, no longer needed in what then became the middle of the train. A new car type appeared after the war, the Uncoupling Non-Driving Motor (UNDM). This took the place of the normal motor car at the 'coupling up' end of a three-car set and was fitted with simplified driving equipment in a cabinet behind the panelling at the car end. For shunting purposes, the end window in the communicating door was adequate for the use of the driver. Seventy were built new in 1951, with a further 22 conversions following the scrapping of the nine-car train experiment. Given the large size of the fleet, variations were remarkably few. They included a car with glass extended into the upper portion of the doors and which allowed better vision for standing passengers. At one time the 1938 stock formed all trains on the Northern and Bakerloo Lines (supplemented with 58 1927 stock trailers in the case of the latter), and provided a few trains for the Piccadilly. With their life prolonged by traffic growth, the final trains ran in Underground service in 1988. Probably the most comfortable of trains that have ever run on the Underground, a number were refurbished and reduced to two-car sets. They are now in service on the Isle of Wight, where they displaced their even more elderly cousins.

The 1938 stock was all built by Metropolitan Cammell or Birmingham RCW, but with the tube stock which followed, BR Derby took the place of Birmingham. Following construction of prototypes in 1956, the aluminium bodied car with rubber suspension and fluorescent lighting became standard. Underframes remained in steel, as aluminium versions would need to be designed too large to fit the restricted space if they were to have adequate strength. A prominent feature was the illuminated roller destination blind, high up on the front of the train so that passengers could see it above the heads of others as the train entered the station. Mass produced as seven-car trains for (initially) the Piccadilly (1959 stock) and as eight-car trains for the Central (1962 stock), these cars otherwise followed closely the 1938 design. It had

been intended to equip the Central Line with new stock based on the 1960 Cravens design but in the event only 12 motor cars were constructed. Some were used for the Automatic Train Operation (ATO) installation on the Woodford–Hainault line, converted to conventional One Person Operation (OPO) in 1986. These units were notable for a new type of Wedglock coupler. Unlike previous stock where an 'A' end motor could only be coupled to a 'D' end motor, these cars could be coupled either way. However, this was achieved at the expense of duplicating all the electrical connections.

The Victoria Line trains of 1967 stock began running on trial in 1964, and their ATO equipment is described later. The driver closes the doors, presses the twin start buttons and the train does the rest. The aluminium alloy car bodies have a distinctive wrap-round windscreen without corner pillars. The cars' primary springing is rubber, but the secondary suspension incorporates hydraulic units. Tractive power is provided by 80hp motors driving on all four axles of the driving motor cars. Rheostatic braking is incorporated; this uses the traction motors as generators, dissipating the energy in rheostats and thus exerting a retarding force. Braking combines two systems acting in three stages — rheostatic braking on motored wheels only, rheostatic braking on motored wheels and air braking on trailer wheels, and both rheostatic and air braking on motored wheels and air braking on

trailer wheels, all operating in conjunction with mercury retardation control.

For the first time headlights, as opposed to marker lights, were fitted from new. These illuminate the tunnel in front, giving the train operator some idea of the train's movement in the absence of colour light signals, of which there are few. The 1967 stock was also the first to be equipped with public address.

Also built by Metro-Cammell were the very similar 1972 Mk I and Mk II designs sent originally to the Northern and Jubilee Lines, and designed for crew operation. The Mk II stock was built with red painted doors, a first attempt to brighten up the appearance of ageing and pitted aluminium then becoming apparent on the oldest cars. Cars of both types have been exhibited in the Lord Mayor's Show in 1981 and 1984, though only on the second occasion did the Mk I driving motor manage to get round the course!

The 87½ new trains of 1973 tube stock delivered for the Piccadilly Line made provision for extra floor space to accommodate passengers and their luggage travelling to Heathrow; this was achieved by setting back the screens at the doors to offer enlarged vestibules. Car length was also increased, with the six-car train at 350ft being about 17ft less than the seven-car 1959 stock trains replaced and which were a little too long for the underground platforms. This had the benefit of paving the way for

One Person Operation, and saved the weight and expense of a seventh set of running gear. Fortunately, the curves on the Piccadilly are not such as to make train-to-platform gaps unacceptable with longer cars. A selective close facility for the doors was provided, to enable most of the doors in each car to remain closed at terminals to keep the train warm in winter.

Technically, the Westinghouse air brake was finally omitted, and replaced by the Westcode electro-pneumatic brake. The guard's controls were repositioned from the rear saloon to the rear cab. Fault finding was to be made easier by the installation of a Train Equipment Panel, but this was apparently more trouble than it was worth. Only 21 three-car units with driving motor cars at each end were provided; the rest had UNDMs at one end. Since the completion of the Heathrow loop, trains are turned in service, and care has to be taken that 'A' ends are always coupled to 'D' ends.

Experiments were also carried out with thyristor control on the Experimental Tube Train (ETT) of 1973 stock. It is also known as 'chopper' control because its action in regulating current employs a chopper movement. Very basically, the thyristor can be likened to an electronic one-way valve providing an instantaneous current limiter. In this case the control smooths acceleration and reduces electrical losses through that function. Also, the kinetic energy of a train during braking is converted back

into electric current, available for use by other trains during their acceleration. However, this works only when such trains are in the same electrical section as the train regenerating the current, since electricity cannot be stored.

The 1983 tube stock was ordered at a time when Underground fortunes were at a low ebb, to the extent that only 15 six-car trains were to be purchased. Subsequent revival led to a decision to re-equip the whole of the Jubilee Line with these units, and builders Metro-Cammell constructed another 16½ trains. These entered service in 1987–88.

In many ways, the 1983 stock is a diminutive version of the 'D' stock on the District Line, with passenger door control, single leaf doors and cab arrangements to a similar specification. Interiors are finished in bright colours, contrasting with what are now seen as the dull greys and blues in the units of 25 years ago. This was the last fleet of conventional trains.

The 1986 stock designs were intended as a real advance in technology, just as the 1935 experimental stock had been a half century earlier.

There was a shopping list of items which at least needed examination to see whether change could be supported. Could the costly and heavy underframe be replaced with welded aluminium,

and offer revised internal layouts? Was thyristor 'chopper' control yet an economic possibility? Could electric braking which needed all axles to be motored be justified on the basis of cleanliness, if not on performance? What improvements could be made to ride quality, ventilation and noise levels to match rising expectations? Was full automation worth considering?

Some experiments were carried out on service cars of 1972 Mk I stock. Steerable bogies to keep both axles parallel to the rails when negotiating curves and thus reduce flange wear were fitted to one car, but were not judged satisfactory. Another had bogies of a new type with the motors mounted on the frame instead of being axle-hung, and these were adopted. Thyristor

control was a feature of the 1973 stock Experimental Tube Train, since disbanded. Disc brakes were also tried on a 1973 car. The 1986 stock proper though consisted of three four-car prototypes, two of which were built by Metro-

Cammell, and one by BREL (now ABB Transportation Ltd) of Derby. Electrically, GEC, Brown Boveri and Brush provided equipments. Each prototype train was made up of a pair of two-car units with a cab at one end; they could be coupled in any combination to make a train of up to eight cars. Doors were mounted externally to the welded (as opposed to riveted) aluminium body shells, and thus no longer slid into a pocket within the body sides when opened. Doors could be both opened and closed by passengers, and an audible signal warned when they were to be closed by the driver. The cab ends were moulded in glass reinforced plastic. Thyristor control and electric braking was provided.

Both types of bogies mentioned above featured

be set back and thus create wider central aisles for standing. Seating capacity, at 34 per car and 292 for an eight-car set, is 17% less than the 328 of the 1962 stock trains which they replace. This calculation does, though, ignore the small 'perch' seats at the car ends. The car interior layout allows the possible rearrangement (or even removal) of seats in the centre section of the cars at some future date.

Flooring is of rubber. The heating and ventilation systems are designed to maintain a temperature of 20°C. The ends of the cars have windows to enhance passenger security, and wider interconnecting doors to speed train evacuation in tunnels. Announcements are made by somewhat

in the prototype cars. These had 700mm diameter wheels. Unfortunately, attempts to design for the use of 600mm diameter wheels, which would have allowed the car floors to be completely flat, were unsuccessful.

In appearance terms trains were given either a red, blue or green prevailing colour scheme for easy identification. The internal design tended to provide more standing space and fewer seats, with a decided 'new look', occasioned no doubt by the employment of design consultants from an early stage. The trains were displayed to the Press in 1987, and provided experimental service as six-car formations on the Jubilee Line in 1988/9.

They have been stored out of service since 1989.

For the Central Line proper, 85 x 8-car trains were ordered from ABB; these were delivered between 1992 and 1995. A further 20 cars were ordered for (what was then) Network SouthEast's Waterloo & City Line. There are three types of car: type A driving motor with cab and shoegear, type B non-driving motor with neither cab nor shoegear, and type C (similar to type A) but without a cab. It will be noted that all car types are powered; indeed, every axle is motored. Types B and C are also fitted with shunting control cabinets for depot movements. The capital cost was around £4 million per train.

Cars are semi-permanently coupled in pairs A+B

(175 sets) or B+C (165 sets); all types of car have automatic couplers at what might be termed the exposed end of each pair. As a further minor variation, 32 of the cars are fitted with de-icing equipment. Since Central Line trains are regularly reversed via the Hainault loop, operators are no doubt pleased that all types of two-car unit are fully reversible.

The trains feature extensive painted surfaces and bigger curved windows, with each pair of doors 314mm wider than the 1962 stock and push button operated. Doors are hung externally to the body; together with banishing under-seat equipment elsewhere (except for the wheels towards the ends of the cars), this allows the all-longitudinal seats to

irritating digitised speech recordings, in female voice mode. Maximum speed is 65mph and there is a chevron primary and pneumatic secondary suspension system for ride quality.

Technically, there is a monocoque extruded aluminium body shell, which acts effectively as a beam suspended between two bogies. The latter are of welded box-section and of Japanese origin; the suspension system is designed so that the car floor height remains constant relative to the platforms, whatever the passenger load. This is an important feature for access by the mobility impaired, but minimising the height variations helps everybody.

All axles are motored, and thyristor (chopper) control with regenerative braking fitted. Trains have

Automatic Train Control and Automatic Train Protection (ATC/ATP), and are capable of being both operated automatically during the peaks and driver operated at other times. This has been described as the ultimate development of the Victoria Line system. CCTV is fitted in the cabs, and enables the driver to see the station platform as he approaches and before he departs. The latter is an additional safeguard against anyone being trapped in a door. The PA system allows the line controller to speak to the passengers as well as the driver, and a 'talk back' facility for passenger use is provided. These are 'clever' trains, with on-board performance monitoring and fault diagnostics. All aspects of the new trains are high-tech, and will no doubt bring high-tech problems in their wake, but pre-planning should minimise or at least contain the effects of this.

It is now time to examine the surface stock story from the early electric days.

In about 1923, the Metropolitan Railway converted some of their steam stock into motor coaches and regrouped the trailers into multiple unit trains. The conversion was carried out by Metropolitan Vickers, and the motor cars were equipped with 200hp motors. Subsequently, two of the trains were fitted with larger experimental motors of 275hp, and the successful results led to the introduction of the new T stock.

The first batch appeared in 1927, and the 12 motor cars each had two 275hp motors in each of the two bogies. These cars were coupled to existing trailers and control trailers to form trains for service on the Watford line. The control equipment was situated in a separate compartment behind the cab and not placed underfloor. A second batch of 30 motor cars, 15 trailers and 10 control trailers was delivered in 1930, and a final delivery was made in 1933 of 18 motor cars, 33 trailers and 14 control trailers. They differed from earlier stock by virtue of their steel panelled bodies and roller bearing axleboxes. Latterly, the T stock also worked to Amersham, made up into six-car and eight-car trains, with two motor cars in each case. A special three car formation was used for operating the Chesham branch shuttle after electrification but before delivery of the A stock.

A remarkable series of 100 all-steel cars was built for the District by the Metropolitan Carriage & Wagon Co in 1920/21. Known as the F stock but nicknamed 'Tanks', these high performance trains had three pairs of hand-operated double doors on each bodyside, and were adept at clearing huge crowds. In appearance, the 'Tanks' differed from previous and subsequent offerings, for they were fitted with elliptical roofs capped with six large ventilators and two oval shaped windows placed at each end of all cars. At 9ft 7in, the bodies were 11in wider than previous trains, as a result of which there was an inward slope of the body above the waistline. Incompatibility with other stock kept the F class apart during its 40 years of service; in the 1950s the class found a new home on the Metropolitan services out to Uxbridge which were able to exploit their power. During their life, the 'Tanks' became a test-bed for electro-pneumatic braking systems, and were fitted with air doors. Final withdrawal took place in 1963.

Apart from the F trains, the characteristic American appearance of District Line stock was perpetuated, particularly the clerestory and the straight sided bodies with large windows. Latterly

running under the generic name of Q stock, this class was built as separate sub-groups lettered G, K, L, M and N between 1923 and 1935. In total 172 motor cars, each with two 240hp motors, and 77 trailers were built, although 36 motor cars were subsequently demoted to trailer status. The cars were built with sliding doors, originally hand-operated on the earlier types, but all fitted for compressed air operation by 1939.

The G cars had a boxy look; this was replaced by a softer appearance with the longer K class cars which had the ends of the clerestory rounded off. A destination indicator was also built in. The L cars offered two class travel in the trailers, the First Class being separated by a glazed screen and a door from the Third; a further division within the First was the separation between smoking and non-smoking accommodation. The M class of 14 motors and 14 trailers was run initially as four six-car sets on the Hammersmith & City; they were the first surface trains to be delivered with air doors, and incorporated passenger door control for the first time on the Underground. They were kept in sets initially due to their incompatibility with other stock, which included their electro-pneumatic brakes. The N cars were all but identical, but came from another manufacturer.

Two G class cars, one to work and one as a spare, were converted to single cars to operate the Acton Town to South Acton shuttle from 1939 until the line closed in 1959. This was the first application of One Person Operation on the Underground, albeit in very specialist circumstances. Extra precautions were taken in that traction control could only be obtained after the driver had shut himself in the cab, and telephone wires were installed along the trackside as in tunnel sections so that the driver could cut off the current without leaving the train. Alterations to the control circuits limited the speeds which could be attained on the short run. The rest of the Q stock was withdrawn by the end of the 1960s, its final appearance being on the East London Line.

The 1935 re-equipment programme enabled the replacement of elderly surface as well as tube stock. Three classes of basically similar specification were purchased: O stock cars for the Hammersmith & City, P stock for the Metropolitan, and Q38 stock for the District. A total of 573 cars was ordered from the Gloucester and Birmingham companies, of which 287 were motor cars. However, the trailers were built with conversion to motor cars in mind should

the installation of extra power be considered worthwhile later.

The new stock again broke new ground. The elliptical roofs, flush fitting windows and flared body panels, the latter to prevent passengers leaping on the non-existent footboards and attempting to open the air-operated doors on departing trains, gave the cars an extremely sleek appearance. Fittings varied according to the line on which the stock was to be used, and were dictated mainly by compatibility considerations with existing stock.

All motor cars were equipped with two motors rated at 152hp each, one to each bogie. Car bodies were 51ft 1¼in long, and seated 40 passengers. The trailers followed the motor cars, but the O and P types were reclassified OP as being interchangeable. Trailers had a driving cab door fitted but locked out of use. Most of the conversion to motor cars that took place was in connection with the subsequent R stock, but three conversions of P trailers were undertaken as a result of war damage. Another intriguing reconstruction was of P stock motor car No 14233, which was spliced with Q38 stock trailer No 03167 after both had suffered war damage, to be returned to service after rebuilding in 1941. This car has survived to be preserved.

Unit formations were M-T-M and M-M, and five-, six- or eight-car trains were run.

Dealing first with the motor cars, the O and P stocks were fitted with Wedglock automatic couplers, incorporating mechanical, electrical and pneumatic supplies in one single connection; in cars of the O stock the guard's control panel was in the driver's cab, whereas in the P stock it was in the passenger saloon. Both types were fitted with Metadyne control machines which used a rotary transformer. The Metadyne system offered smoother acceleration and regenerative braking — the feeding back of the energy dissipated in braking to the power supply system for other trains to use. It was not an unqualified success, and after one train had been fitted with spare PCM type equipments of the 1938 tube stock type in 1955, the whole fleet was converted. The cars were reclassified CO and CP, the trailers COP.

It would be tedious to relate the problems which resulted from a nearly-but-not-quite compatibility, the 'handing' of cars, and changing ideas on the length of trains and to which lines they might best be allocated. The CO/CP stock had a long life, the last examples being withdrawn in 1981.

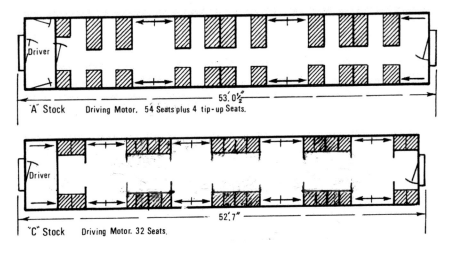

Right:
Seating arrangements compared: the A stock and the refurbished C stock.

Left:
The Circle Line in the late 1940s had to struggle on with increasingly elderly rolling stock. At South Kensington, a mixture of 1913 and 1921 stock forms an inner-rail service.
J. A. Rosser collection

Below:
The 'C69/77' stock has now completed its half-life refurbishment. Externally, the most noticeable result is the new London Underground corporate livery. An inner-rail Circle Line service arrives at Farringdon on 13 March 1995, passing an outer-rail service.
John Glover

Right:
An A stock train on the East London Line shows a tangible reminder of the contribution London Docklands Development Corporation made towards its refurbishment
John Glover

The Q38 stock was built for use with the rest of the Q fleet on the District, and the 25 motor cars had resistance and contactor control similar to the existing District cars. Likewise, they were fitted with Ward couplers. However, the rest of the Q fleet needed replacement at the end of the war, and the new R stock was born. Similar in general appearance to the Q38 stock, the new cars were all powered with a single 110hp nose-suspended traction motor in each of their two bogies. There were thus no trailers.

Although there were four sub-classes within the R stock fleet, all cars had features in common. Fluorescent lighting was fitted throughout, the 110V ac supply coming from a motor generator fitted one to each pair of cars. A detector light pinpointed door problems, while a roller blind indicator was displayed above the driver's cab window.

The R38 cars were all driving cars converted from 125 of the 183 Q38 trailers, as had been anticipated when they were built. The motors for the converted cars were installed in the original bogies, after modification, at Acton Works; the car bodies were sent to Gloucester where the body conversion, which included the fitting of a driver's cab, was carried out. The bogies were refitted at Ealing Common depot. The first batch of 82 cars was converted in 1949-51 to run with the R47 stock; this was followed by a further conversion of 43 cars to run with the R49 stock. In all, 79 were eastward facing cars with Wedglock couplers at the outer end and semi-permanent bar couplers at the inner end. The other 46 cars were westbound driving cars, not normally required to couple at their driving ends and thus only fitted at this end with a Ward coupler for emergency use.

The R47 cars comprised a batch of 143 non-driving motor cars of steel construction built by Birmingham (89 cars) and Gloucester (54 cars), delivered from 1949.

The 90 R49 vehicles were built by Metro-Cammell in 1952/53 and were lightweight aluminium cars, the first to be built in quantity in Britain. The weight saved was in the order of 5.9 tons per car, and comparative tests carried out between Acton Town and South Ealing confirmed that the increased capital cost was sufficiently offset by reduced current consumption, particularly during acceleration. Included in this batch were six driving cars, so that some all-aluminium formations could be made up. Fearful of public opposition, London Transport left only one car, and then only one of the lightweight trains unpainted, apart from a thin red band at waist level and with a speed whisker on the cab. However, consideration of the then cost of external painting which was saved eventually won the day.

A further 20 cars were placed in service in 1959. These consisted of seven more Q38 trailer conversions and 13 new non-driving aluminium motors from Metro-Cammell. These last were styled R59 cars. The steel cars were painted silver to match the new cars, and gradually all R stock was turned out in silver, though without the red band.

One of the R59 cars, No 23584, was sent to an exhibition of aluminium stock in Strasbourg in 1960. This was the first time that an Underground car had travelled abroad on business, although many had been built on the Continent.

The R stock survived until 1983.

All the surface stock remaining to be considered is still in service, and has been made suitable for OPO. The A stock was delivered in two batches from 1961, to provide a complete replacement for what

was by then decidedly elderly rolling stock of multiple-unit, electric and steam locomotive-hauled types. This programme was carried out in conjunction with the electrification to Amersham and the cessation of London Transport interests beyond that point. Built by Cravens of Sheffield, the A60 order was for 248 cars in four-car units, followed by an order for 216 identical A62 cars for the Uxbridge services. Two driving motor cars sandwiched two trailers, and the performance was specified to match that of the previous stock. This meant that the traction motors were controlled to either a high or low acceleration rate but with a low balancing speed and suitable for in-town station spacing of 0.5 miles or so, or a lower rate with a different motor field strength to take full advantage of the longer outer sections beyond Baker Street with 60mph running.

The A stock was built to the maximum width possible of 9ft 8in (thus barring it from most of the Circle Line), and this made 3+2 seating each side of a central gangway possible. The width allowed for each seat was 17½in. The standard eight car formation seated 464 plus 916 standing (total 1,380); eight cars of T stock seated 600 at five-a-side in 60 compartments. An extra five in each compartment was judged to be the limit, but highly uncomfortable for everybody. To overcome the loss of heat as the doors opened up in the Chilterns on a frosty morning, the saloons were provided with extra powerful heaters.

Bearing in mind the Rickmansworth curve which would turn trains round, automatic couplers were fitted providing full reversibility.

Conversion to OPO was completed in 1986. This work comprised the relocation of the guard's panels in the driving cabs, the fitting of public address, train radio, new windscreen wipers and toughened

glass in cabs, and twin headlights. As there is no call for four-car trains other than on the Chesham shuttle and the East London Line, only 24 units have had both cabs converted. This has left the inner cabs on most of the eight-car trains unusable, resulting in some loss of flexibility.

The C stock was again built in two batches. The C69 series of 35⅓ trains of six cars each was for the Hammersmith & City and Circle; ordered in 1968 from Metro-Cammell, it was delivered 1970/71. The second batch, designated C77 and consisting of 11 trains for the Edgware Road–Wimbledon service, appeared in 1977.

Designed for quick loading and unloading, these cars featured no less than four pairs of double doors along each side of a car body only 49ft long. This has meant that, as built, there were only 32 transverse seats, arranged 2+2 in each car. Unusually, all passenger accommodation is identical; the cab in the driving motor cars merely adds an extra 3ft 7in to their length. Bogie centres were adjusted to minimise overhang on curves for both car designs.

Evaluation of the options suggested that maximum flexibility would be achieved by constructing two car units (M+T) with one cab, three of which would form a service train. This gave the opportunity (never exploited) to run 8-car formations also, but in any case Hammersmith depot lifting shop could only hold two cars on a road. Automatic couplers are fitted at all unit outer ends. Among their new features was rheostatic braking as on the contemporary 1967 stock tube cars, a secondary suspension system of rubber-air springing units, and thermostat-controlled blower-heater fans mounted in the roof. A selective door close facility enables all but one pair of doors in each car to be kept closed at terminals in cold weather. These trains pioneered manual, as opposed to automatic, One Person Operation on the Underground in 1984/85.

Service experience has been satisfactory, apart from poor riding qualities blamed on track condition. As built, the trains also offered a low degree of passenger comfort for journeys of any length.

Only three main unit types now provide the whole of the surface stock requirements for the District and Metropolitan Lines. The 75 six-car all-aluminium D stock trains made their début in 1980. As with the Piccadilly 1973 trains, six longer cars replaced seven shorter ones, greatly simplifying formation problems. A total of 65 eastward facing and 65 westward facing three-car single cab units were built (DM-T-UNDM), together with 20 double cab units with automatic couplers at both ends (DM-T-DM).

Four doors on each car side were again provided, but this time of single leaf only and thus 3ft 6in wide as opposed to the 4ft 6in or so with double doors. Door opening is by passenger controls, released from the cab. Any door which fails to close properly can be reopened individually, and all doors can be remotely opened from the cab if necessary. Innovations included coil spring suspension supported by rubber cushions, and motor and wheelset interchangeability with the 1973 tube stock. Traction brake controls were also new, comprising a right hand 'fore and aft' vertical lever incorporating the dead man device, instead of the previous left hand rotary operated controller.

Seating is mainly longitudinal. In the ceilings are concealed fans. These were boosted by additional fans after experience, and this measure coupled with the installation of opening quarterlights cured the trouble of excessive heat in summer. Modifications have also included the fitting of additional grab handles. These small matters apart, Metro-Cammell's D stock has proved to be most successful.

The allocation of cars to lines is not constant. The East London Line has had more changes than most over the last 30 years; being self contained, only a relatively small fleet of trains is needed, and the conditions are not such that any particular type of train is required for traffic reasons. Hence, the F stock which had enjoyed a 10-year reign gave way to Q stock in 1963, which lasted a year until it was displaced by CP stock. In 1965 the Q stock was back again for six years, to be followed in 1971 by CO/CP stock. The year 1974 saw the surprise appearance of 1938 tube stock, which lasted until the summer of 1977, after which the A stock from the Metropolitan main line put in an appearance. D stock ran the service from 1985 until 1987, after which the A stock reappeared, this time in OPO guise.

Rolling stock refurbishment has become a main occupation of the 1990s. There are two main reasons for this.

First, safety: in the aftermath of the King's Cross fire, a general review disclosed a number of changes which were desirable. These included:

- elimination of non-essential use of combustible materials in car interiors or in equipment;

- revising the emergency brake alarm system to alert the driver, but not to cause an automatic brake application between stations;

- speed control after a driver has had to pass a signal at danger (under the Rules), whether because of signal failure or other reason;

- fitting public address to all rolling stock;

- fitting high intensity headlights to make trains more visible to staff on the track; and

- 'correct side door enable' or, to interpret, a transmission/reception device between the lineside and the driving cab which allows the driver to open a train's doors only on the platform side.

The second reason is image. Underground trains have a long life, sometimes almost unbelievably so. Seating layouts for what became the Metropolitan A stock were being tried out as a works mock-up in 1939 and as a series of in-service experiments from 1946. The A stock entered service between 1961 and 1963, and refurbishment of what are basically sound vehicles may require them to remain in service well into the 21st century. Who today drives a car with that sort of pedigree?

It is hardly surprising if aesthetic tastes have changed over time. Also, it is sad to note, have perceptions of personal safety, whether this is justified or not. Research on test refurbishments has shown much support for providing windows in the car ends to improve visibility through the train, lighting enhancements, a reworking of seating and handrail positions, and a new design of upholstery.

The painting of the East London Line trains was begun in 1988, at a cost of £5,000 per vehicle. The first A stock trains to be treated featured red fronts, blue doors and grey panels. As the repaint was sponsored by the London Docklands Development Corporation, they carried the LDDC logo. Several livery variations have been tried on the A stock, the C stock and the 1967-72 family of tube stock. The hope is that the new corporate livery will offer a much improved appearance over pitted aluminium, and be easier to clean if, or perhaps when, it is attacked by the spray can. The new external finishes complement the interior refurbishment programmes.

Putting this all together results in a substantial workload. However, if a train is to last 30 years or more in service, a comprehensive updating at around half-life is surely justifiable. To carry out all the required work on each unit at the same time has its attractions; work on the more deserving types of rolling stock is now substantially complete. It is also effective. It can be illuminating to listen to conversations between passengers, many of whom are deceived into thinking that the refurbished sets really are new. However, the reality is also that the credit is given for the 'image' elements, with none for safety-related work.

Although not then forming part of the system owned by London Underground, developments on the Waterloo & City tube line are recorded here for the sake of completeness. When the original rolling stock became due for renewal in 1940, English Electric supplied 12 Motor Open Brake Thirds with 40 seats and 16 Trailer Open Thirds with 52 seats. These vehicles were only 47ft long and 8ft 73/4 in wide. Maximum speed was 40mph on the 5min journey between the two stations. Motor coaches were fitted with two 190hp totally enclosed traction motors and weighed 28 tons; the trailers weighed 19 tons. The normal formation was two motor cars sandwiching three trailers, but single car working was envisaged during off-peak hours and the motor cars were accordingly provided with cabs at each end. Their drab appearance was markedly improved by the application of Network SouthEast livery.

Internally, the motor car floors were on two levels, to provide space below for the switchgear and larger diameter than normal motor bogie wheels. Seating was a mixture of unidirectional transverse in the centre and raised longitudinal at the ends of the cars. Current supplies were altered to the standard Southern Railway outside third, which enabled the cars to run unaided on Southern tracks to and from main depots or workshops, although day-to-day attention was carried out at the line's Waterloo depot. Car access from the surface was available only via the Armstrong hydraulic lift situated alongside the main line station, with access below gained from the up line (towards Bank) beyond the end of the platform. The dimensions of the lift precluded the use of any longer stock, though the tunnel dimensions at 12ft 1½in diameter are marginally greater than the standard tube tunnel. By a considerable margin, the Class 487 cars were the oldest operational trains in the London area at the time of their withdrawal in 1993.

They were replaced by 20 cars of a minor variant of the 1992 Central Line stock, from which five four-car trains can be made up. The line was also converted from third to fourth rail electrification. The whole line passed to London Underground in April 1994.

Although a propulsion system based on the use of bogie-mounted linear induction motors operating in conjunction with a reaction rail laid between the running rails was considered, this option was not pursued.

TABLE 5:
Principal allocations of car types to lines, 1995

Tube stock

1959/62	Northern
1967	Victoria
1972 MkI	Northern
1972 MkII	Bakerloo
1973	Piccadilly
1983	Jubilee
1992	Central, Waterloo & City

Surface stock

A	Metropolitan, East London
C	Circle, Hammersmith & City, District Edgware Road and Wimbledon
D	District (all other services)

Chapter 7

The Underground Station

Northern and Central Lines into the suburbs. Most of these stations are now in London Underground ownership, but there are exceptions. Upminster and New Cross are two of the 21 stations managed by British Rail out of a total of 269 served currently by the Underground. It must be admitted that the total of Underground stations is a little elastic; does the Waterloo & City Line station at Bank make the LUL total there now two, and what about Paddington? The Bakerloo and District/Circle Lines share the nowadays combined station in Praed Street, while the Hammersmith & City platforms are a hike of 250yd or so along Railtrack's platforms and over a bridge at Bishop's Road.

Station design and construction and, frequently, subsequent modification has to accommodate the varying traffic needs of the individual locations. Whether the architecture is homely or functional, neo-Georgian or the Underground's own style evolved by Pick and his consultant architect Charles Holden, the station has a necessary operational function to perform. If it fails in this it fails completely. The simplest arrangement is a single platform, found today in seven locations: Chesham, Kensington (Olympia), Mill Hill East, New Cross, New Cross Gate, Shoreditch, and the 1986-built Heathrow Terminal 4. This last is placed on the terminal loop of the Piccadilly Line, and is served by trains in the one (clockwise) direction only.

At the other end of the scale, the busiest stations are Victoria, Oxford Circus, Liverpool Street, King's Cross, Waterloo and Piccadilly Circus, each of which sees between 30 million and 60 million passengers joining or alighting there each year. As such, they compare with the 50 million annual usage of Heathrow Airport. These stations serve up to five lines, and with only four platforms in the case of Victoria. They are large premises: Oxford Circus has 14 escalators, 25 stairways, and $5\frac{1}{2}$ miles of platforms and subways. As many as 10 platforms are in use at Baker Street, solely for Underground trains, but the total is inflated due to two platforms being used only for terminating the Metropolitan main line services. Moorgate can also boast 10 platforms, but here four are for the exclusive use of British Rail.

What are the operational elements in station design at a busy location? On the passenger side, conflicting flows of incoming, interchanging and outgoing passengers must be kept separated as far as possible, while it is desirable to maintain as many entrances and exits from the premises consistent with acceptable staffing levels. There must be space for people to buy tickets, and ticket queues in stations at main line termini where many have heavy luggage move noticeably slower than city stations where the majority have Travelcards. Barriers, passages, circulating areas and escalators must have roughly equivalent capacity if bottlenecks are not to form; the inability to clear an area into which an escalator disgorges is a particular danger. Similarly, there must be a means to shut off platforms if the train service is delayed and the platform becomes overcrowded. Closed circuit television controlled from an operations room can be useful for surveillance, while public address is helpful. Station platforms on the Victoria Line were built straight or nearly so, to enable the driver to look back down the length of the train, and forwards from the back by the use of closed circuit television. Older stations have had to be adapted for One Person Operation, using mirrors and as many television monitors as necessary for the driver to be able to view the

Previous page:
The substantial Metropolitan Railway station at Ruislip was a fitting gateway to 'London's Healthiest Suburb', and dates from 1904. This 1982 picture shows the somewhat severe exterior. *John Glover*

Top:
At the unmistakable Underground station of Rayners Lane, 1938, the pedestrian entrances are on the direct line of the pavement; there is no way in from the conventional 'front'. This is also a 1982 picture. *Les Bertram*

Above:
The former Great Northern Railway ownership is apparent at the three-platformed Finchley Central, seen here with a Kennington via Charing Cross train of 1972 MkI stock arriving from the Mill Hill East branch on 5 August 1976. *John Glover*

For the passenger, the station ranks in importance along with the train in which he or she travels, since it is here that he or she gains access to and exits from the system, as well as changing trains. Possibly more so than any other railway in the world, the London Underground can demonstrate a range of styles of building and architectural treatment over its century and a quarter of history which is truly breathtaking in its diversity.

The first stations served by the Underground were those on the Metropolitan's initial system, of which none remain today in their original form. However, the chronology is not as straightforward as it might at first appear. Many stations served today by the Underground were built originally by the main line railway companies with services that they themselves operated; among the more notable examples are the East London Line stations (first served by Underground trains in the 1880s), and those on the long extensions of what are today the

outside of the whole train properly.

Good clear directional information to passengers
is most important, and coloured lights over the
escalators (follow red for Paddington etc) were a
feature for many years. Underground platforms
usually carry a comprehensive notice of stations
served directly opposite where a passenger arrives
on the platform, line diagrams are everywhere, and
illuminated signs referring to exits, as opposed to
interchanges, are colour coded in yellow.
Destination indicators which show the subsequent
train or trains are of great value to passengers,
especially on lines where there are a number of
divergent routes. At Earl's Court westbound District
Line platforms for instance, trains may be bound for
any one of four branches on the lines to Ealing
Broadway, Richmond, Wimbledon or Kensington
(Olympia), and it is imperative to know where the
train is going. However, the only variation possible
on the eastbound Piccadilly Line at the same station
is whether the train is going the whole length of the
route, and the information is of much less value.
Passengers do like to know how long they will have
to wait, and the electronic dot-matrix indicators
now widely installed show the next three trains and
their estimated arrival times. These indicators
consist of a matrix of light emitting diodes which are

illuminated in any combination to show letters,
figures or diagrams, so that a wide variety of
information and messages can be displayed. Good
information brings user confidence, provided it is
also accurate.

In a system as old as the Underground, there is
rarely an opportunity to start from first principles.
New lines have to be meshed in with the existing as
best they can, and designed to facilitate
arrangements for interchange between lines where
this is expected to be heavy. Sometimes, changing
from one line to another is a minor marathon; one
can walk a long way around Charing Cross (it was
once two stations, Strand and Trafalgar Square),
while Monument (District & Circle) and Bank
(Central) are separated by the full length of the
Northern Line platforms as well as stairs and
escalators. Bank (Waterloo & City) platforms are
also a long subway walk from the Northern Line,
but in a quite different direction, while the
Docklands Light Railway is at deeper level still
below the Northern Line.

Many stations have been reconstructed or built
anew on a different site. This work entails the most
complicated of all Underground engineering when
such things as subways, sewers, mains and even
tunnels may have to be stopped up, diverted or
otherwise accommodated. Engineers have not only
these things to consider, but they must always make
provision in their plans for the continuing daily
traffic.

For the operators, time taken at station stops is
non-productive time during which the train is

cluttering up the system and not earning revenue;
the shorter the stopping period the better. There is
a caveat though, as ideally all station stops are of the
same length. If trains consistently spend a longer
than average time at only one station due to the
numbers of passengers joining and alighting, this
has the result of bunching up the service and
ultimately restricting the frequency at which they
can be operated. Dwell times will vary from a
minimum of 15sec off-peak and 20sec peak to
20–30sec at busier locations. Overall speeds also
depend on the number of station stops; it was to
reduce end-to-end journey times and make more
productive use of trains and crews that the 'non-
stopping' of trains was in vogue during the inter-war
period.

A limiting factor in the early days was the method
of telling the driver when it was safe to start. Before
the ubiquitous door interlocks and bell signals were
invented for use with the now universal sliding
doors, a train starting device more elegant than a
guard's whistle was introduced. A pair of bare wires
insulated from each other was suspended from the
roof at one end of each platform. By shorting these
wires together with the metal handle of his flag, the
guard caused a letter 'S' to appear in lights under
the starting signal. A 'reminder' bell near the
driver's cab was also set ringing. This arrangement
was installed on the District and Metropolitan, and
lasted on parts of the latter until the electrification
of 1960 finally allowed the withdrawal of the slam
door compartment stock.

The track layout at terminals is of especial

Above:
The escalators at Earl's Court leading to the Exhibition Hall have been restored using the original lighting columns, as could once have been seen throughout the system. Although space is available for three escalators, the centre portion contains a fixed stairway only.
John Glover

Below:
The pair of travelators at Bank station were completed in 1960; with the transfer of ownership of the Waterloo & City Line in 1994, they are the only ones on London Underground. This 1995 view is from the bottom landing in the evening peak, looking up, with home-bound commuters returning.
John Glover

significance, since trains spend longer than average at such locations. At an intermediate station, the provision of a central bay as at Putney Bridge (with platform) or Marble Arch (without) keeps the terminating train clear of the running lines, and it does not foul any other train movements when

moving to or from that position. The disadvantage of the siding beyond the platform arrangement is that it takes time to detrain all passengers and close the doors before the train can proceed, by which time another train can be waiting behind. The provision of a mere crossover to reverse trains, as on the Bakerloo Line at Piccadilly Circus (southbound to northbound) is too restrictive for general use, while a crossover requiring trains to reverse in tunnel on a running line as at Hampstead is even worse!

At terminals, the usual choice in tunnel is an island with crossovers (Walthamstow Central), or on the surface a three-track multiple platform arrangement (Uxbridge). Platforms both sides of a track can be useful in separating arriving and departing passengers by judicious use of the door opening/door closing sequence. It can, though, make for cold trains in the winter months. If it is necessary to speed up the turnround of trains, step-back crews can be employed. By having staff positioned ready to take the train out again after it has arrived, the minimum turnround is not affected by the time taken by the incoming crew to change ends. Terminal loops as at Kennington are not

favoured; while there is no need to change ends, neither can layover time be provided as the train cannot be sidetracked. The Heathrow loop is a little different, as there are two platforms available at Terminals 1,2,3. Loops also introduce the coupling problems of stock reversal which would otherwise be avoided on both the Northern and Piccadilly Lines.

Other determinants of the capacity of lines are the performance of trains, junction conflicts, signal spacing, gradients and curvature. On a railway, the capacity is determined by the most restrictive element; thus Bakerloo Line capacity was increased by eliminating the use of the Stanmore branch junction at Baker Street when the Jubilee Line was opened. The capacity was then constrained by the ability of the signalling system to cope with a frequency increase. Beyond that, it might be the speed restriction on the curve north of Charing Cross, which at less than five chains radius is one of the sharpest on the system. Nevertheless, a service frequency of 30 trains per hour should be achievable on most parts of the Underground system.

Access to what became known as the surface Underground lines was by stairs, and since the platforms were no more than 5m or so below street level, this caused little difficulty. Even today, Sloane Square is distinctly unusual in having up escalators installed on both platforms. The building of the deep-level tube lines, however, meant that some form of mechanically assisted access became essential. Initially this meant lifts.

The simplest means was used to build the shafts, by assembling the lining segment rings on the surface, undermining them, and letting the whole sink under its own weight. The City & South London Railway used Armstrong's hydraulic lifts, the power from the piston being translated into the movement of the cage by a system of ropes and pulleys. More common were electrically operated lifts, by the Sprague and Otis companies. Lift shafts were commonly built to accommodate two or more lifts, to allow for traffic growth as well as escape from one to another in the case of failure. Lifts were thus not immediately installed in all of them, and some never received their full complement. By 1907 there were 249 lifts on the growing Underground system.

Initially, all lifts were manually controlled by staff, but the first semi-automatic lifts appeared at Warren Street in 1928. It was then but a short step to the fully automatic variety, first seen at Earl's Court four years later.

The capacity of a transport system can be increased by speeding up the vehicles, and this is just as applicable to vertical movement. Initially, lifts travelled at 100 to 120ft/min, but speeds of 290ft/min were reached at Angel and Leicester Square in 1924/25. A speed of 600ft/min was attained at Goodge Street in 1937 while Hampstead, the deepest Underground station with a 181ft deep lift shaft, had 800ft/min lifts installed in 1954. These took a mere 18sec for the journey. In these later installations, time switches controlled movement to provide an evenly spaced service.

Lift safety measures incorporate door contacts so that the lift cannot be started until the doors are properly closed. Speeds are regulated by a governor and an automatic brake to ensure that plunges to the bottom of the shaft are prevented. If a lift becomes stalled in transit, passengers are

transferred to another lift brought alongside using connecting doors; as a last resort the slow process of hand winching may be resorted to. A separate staircase, usually spiral, is always provided for emergency use. At school in Hampstead, the author was forbidden to race the lifts; this was only possible when the high speed versions were not working, as was not unusual.

Although a few of the original lift installations survived until the 1990s at lightly used stations (such as the 1907 Otis manually controlled installation at Mornington Crescent), replacement with escalators or new lifts has been general. Lift renewal is a complex process. First, the old lift has to be dismantled and removed, and new lift guides built for the car to be assembled *in situ*. The machine rooms and landings have to be rebuilt to match the new equipment, following which the ropes and wiring are installed prior to acceptance tests. Physically, the work takes nine months or maybe much more; in

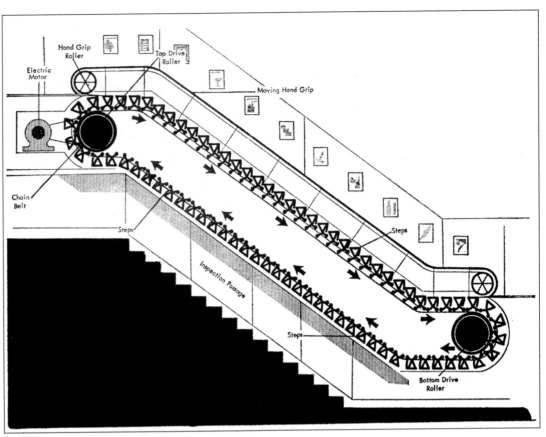

the interim passengers often have to resort to the emergency stairs or the station may even be closed while the work is carried out. In 1994, 60 lifts remained in service at a total of 25 stations.

The word 'escalator' is an American term dating from 1904. Just as the elevator was used to elevate the passenger, so the new invention 'escaladed' him.

For some time, the limitations of lifts had been apparent. Apart from, at that time, the need to staff them, the interruption of the flow of passengers was irksome and could lead to long waiting times. The aim was to find a conveyance which could deal

economically with a steady trickle of passengers, and yet could absorb a surge at peak hours without becoming overloaded or causing congestion. Hence the search for some form of continuous movement, first patented by a Mr Reno. His first moving stairway (albeit without steps!) was installed at Coney Island in New York in 1894, and was moved to Brooklyn Bridge the following year. By 1900, he had gained sufficient experience to build a three-mile-long moving walkway at the Paris Exposition. In London, Reno constructed a pair of concentric spiral moving stairways in a lift shaft at Holloway Road in 1906. They never entered public service, as the Board of Trade was not convinced as to their

Above:
Escalator mechanism.

Below:
The oldest form of vertical transport is the lift; it is still valuable at deep stations where escalator shafts would be costly to build and the time taken to descend or ascend relatively great. This picture shows the high-speed lifts installed at Hampstead in 1954, complete with a member of staff. It is far from clear as to what task he is performing.
London Transport Museum U5218

safety. So it was that the Otis Seeberger design became the first to appear on the Underground system at Earl's Court in 1911.

Being first in the field meant that precedents did not exist, and being a run-on order from elsewhere, nobody objected to the highly original gradient of 26° 23' 16½"! These escalators were of the 'shunt' type, whereby passengers stepped off them sideways. Such was public unfamiliarity, that the company hired a man with a wooden leg known as 'Bumper' Harris whose sole purpose in life was to ride up and down and demonstrate how to use it.

Lifts still had their place at the deeper stations, since with a vertical rise of more than about 90ft two flights of escalators with an intermediate landing are needed. But such was the escalator's general superiority with two escalators being reckoned to do the work of five lifts, that new lift installations stopped altogether after a couple of years. Raised cleats on the steps, which ended in a 'comb' at the landings to trap debris, became universal after Otis bought out Reno and his patents. The first cleat/comb escalator was installed

passengers actually reduced the capacity. Since then, the maximum speed has been set at 145ft/min, and this can handle 10,000 passengers an hour comfortably. Lesser speeds to conserve energy at times of light traffic may also be set.

Safety devices include the obvious plungers for emergency use, and these will stop the escalator in about 4ft; these activate the brakes, which will also operate if the electricity supply fails. Detectors are also installed to stop the machine should a drive chain break.

During the 1920s an extensive programme of station improvement and modernisation was undertaken, and this often included the replacement of lifts by escalators. The problem was that the slope required by an escalator shaft would not join the existing ticket office with the existing below ground passages. Typically, the remedy was to construct a new surface ticket hall underneath a road intersection. Escalator shafts from there lead to landings above tube level since the tracks are generally too closely spaced to allow direct access to platforms. A short stairway joins the two. Since then, few stations in the central area have had more than a series of subway entrances to mark their presence. This kind of work is tremendously expensive; replacing the four lifts at Angel with two sets of three escalators (with an intermediate landing in between) cost £25 million.

Escalators, too, need renewal, and a prolonged major effort has restored escalator availability to a much higher level than that experienced generally in recent years.

The water table under London is rising, and with it comes the increased risk of flooding of the system. Exceptional rainfall or the breaching of water supply or sewerage pipes can also result in the discharge of water into the Underground system — where it is not welcomed. Without a satisfactory means of dealing with water, the Underground would quickly resemble one massive sump.

About 700 pumps are installed at 350 sites throughout the system. This includes a key installation next to the westbound Circle and District Line platform at Victoria, which deals with up to 1.2 million gallons of water in a 24hr period. One of the biggest tests of the maintenance men came in July 1987 with the rupture of a 42in Thames Water Authority main at Euston. An estimated 18 million gallons of water poured into the BR car park and on into the Underground. The torrent surged across the booking hall and cascaded down the eight escalators, rendering them instantly unserviceable. Water filled the lower machine

at Clapham Common in 1924. All 'shunts' were then removed.

A 30° gradient became the standard. A great variety of machines was constructed, later substituting aluminium for much of the woodwork used originally and, much later, shown to be a fire hazard. Indeed, the 1936 Moorgate installation made a virtue of its use of wood panels veneered with samples from trees growing all over the British Empire. For the record, the greatest vertical rise can now be found at Angel (90ft). The shortest is at

Chancery Lane (15ft). The maximum number in any one shaft is four (at Holborn). In the western suburb of Greenford is the oddity of an escalator up from surface ticket halls to platform on viaduct. There was a similar installation at Alperton, the escalator itself having been obtained from the 1951 Festival of Britain site.

Experiments over the years have sought to determine the optimum speed. This rose rapidly from the 90ft/min until 180ft/min was reached, but it was found that understandable hesitancy by some

chambers, ran on to all six platforms, spilling on to the track and into the tunnel, filling the track inverts. According to the track gradients, it then followed the tunnels; on the Victoria Line, it was quickly demonstrated that it is downhill to Warren Street! The pumping out operation, which took three days, was at one stage removing more than 1,000 gallons/min from the station to the car park and into the sewer.

Such incidents which involve prolonged suspension of services are exceptional, but it is only constant attention that keeps the Underground as remarkably dry as it is.

A problem as old as Underground railways is that of ventilating the tunnels adequately with economy, and without causing discomfort to passengers or creating nuisance for residents near ventilation shafts. It was an insoluble problem in steam days, but there were so many other inconveniences associated with horse-drawn surface travel that many were resigned to the smoke and dirt. The problem was much reduced with the end of steam traction, but even so the residual difficulties have taken many years of research to overcome. The

Below:
A bank of three passenger-operated ticket machines at South Kensington, now all displaced by the introduction of the Underground Ticketing System.
John Glover

Central London Railway installed 'ozonisers' which were meant to purify the air, and some of the ducts at stations can still be spotted. The ozonisers certainly sucked air into the stations, but apparently the tang clung about the person for some time afterwards, and finally condemned the experiment.

Modern practice is to exhaust spent and heated air from the tunnels by means of powerful fans discharging into special ducts, and to admit fresh air through the natural channels of station entrances and escalator shafts. To augment this incoming flow, fresh air is also pumped through shafts enclosed in staircase wells, or through shafts sunk specially for the purpose.

An earlier method, still employed, works on the exhaust fan principle. Between Bounds Green and Finsbury Park three of the numerous shafts used during construction were retained to act as air extraction ducts. Below ground, two galleries and headings connected the shafts to the running tunnels. A later example is at Notting Hill Gate where a stairway shaft, no longer used, was extended to the roof level of an office block over the station site. All this adaptation and new construction has proved worthwhile, and the experience of having positively to force one's way against the rushes of air in passageways as fast moving trains approached a station is now forgotten.

A further aim has been to keep the air temperatures in the Underground at a reasonable

level, since heat is created faster than it is dissipated through the tunnel segments and into the surrounding clay. With the help of over 100 fans, the temperature underground is kept to an annual average in the region of 23°C.

Most of the Underground's stations are on the surface, but even so it is not the most obvious organisation to run a garden competition. An event of long standing, it was early justified 'by adding greatly to the cheerfulness of the railway', to the extent that management were prepared to pay for five shillings' (25p) worth of seed at each location. In spite of all the obvious difficulties, a challenge cup is awarded annually, with the gardens being judged on visual impact, health and vigour, choice and care of plants, design, and site problems overcome. Theft, vandalism and sheer thoughtlessness are problems to be coped with, but the efforts are appreciated by many.

A ticket represents the means by which an acknowledgment is given by the railway for a fare tendered, and confers on the passenger an authority to travel within the terms of the contract which has thus been made. It follows that the ticket and the means of obtaining it are all important parts of the organisation. Besides being a more-or-less foolproof way of collecting revenue, tickets provide a record of where a passenger entered the system. Without a ticket it is not possible to charge fares graduated by distance, which is a severe limitation. In London, the best known examples of flat fares were the L&SWR's Waterloo & City (which had only two stations anyway), and the Central London Railway which opened its doors in 1900 with the commercial policy which gave it the popular nickname of 'The Twopenny Tube'. However, most of the other tube lines also opened with a flat fare.

Until recent years, the issuing methods used were almost entirely traditional, save for a little relatively unsophisticated mechanisation (none the worse for that, one might add), and some ill-fated experiments. Even the Underground Official Handbook of 1988 admitted that most of the previous attempts to improve the issue and control of tickets, coupled with an effort to reduce fraud and increase ticket office security, had been unsuccessful. Before examining current developments, though, it is useful to consider the history.

Thomas Edmondson invented his system of preprinted and numbered card tickets, dating press and numbered card tickets, dating press and storage rack in 1836, and this was universally adopted by British railway companies. When the Metropolitan Railway commenced operations in 1863 it saw no reason to differ, but the tube railways in this as in other matters had more allegiance to North American transit operations in their more individual approach. Besides flat fares collected at turnstiles, Bell Punch tickets were issued by conductors, and the use of roll tickets of various colours was commonplace. On the CLR, tickets bought at the office were surrendered on entering the system. Edmondson tickets were a rarity.

By 1907 however, competition from buses was beginning to bite, and this forced the Underground companies into ever more complex ticketing. Flat fares were too easily undercut: 2d (0.8p) was probably less than some were prepared to pay for the six miles from Shepherd's Bush to Bank, but it looked distinctly expensive for what the advertising industry in a later generation called 'short hops'.

Tickets

The City & South London Railway had tried to help its ticket collectors by matching the ticket colour to the destination station, of which it had 15 by 1907. That the company was hard pushed to find sufficient means of distinguishing the Edmondson cards is evident, with red, reddish-brown, pink, lilac and purple all being used. Return tickets were even more colourful, as each half was coloured according to its correct code! Others used various overprints, but the complexity was beginning to get out of hand.

What did distinguish the Underground from the main line railways was the sheer volume of journeys made. In 1875, with less than 10 route miles of track, the Metropolitan was calculated as issuing 20% more tickets than the whole of the Great Western Railway. With the proliferation of through booked tickets which ensued after 1907, the situation quickly became unsustainable, given also the number of stations on the network and the possibility of different classes of travel on the Metropolitan and District railways. This culminated in the gradual introduction of so-called 'scheme' tickets from 1911, when all stations available at a given fare were listed on the back of the ticket instead of requiring separate prints for each. This facility only applied to stations within the group, and through tickets to any railways not included in the Conference still retained separate issues. The reason was as much to do with the apportionment of receipts between companies as anything else, but the range of bookings which were (and were not) available always contained many idiosyncrasies, and has persisted thus ever since. Even then, there were a number of different ticket types to be contended with, and among the less obvious nowadays were workmen's tickets, those for the military and police, to say nothing of 'Dogs and Folding Mailcarts'.

Mechanisation of ticket issue was of high priority, and by the time the 'Rapidprinter' machines which printed, dated, guillotined and ejected a ticket on the press of a button by the ticket clerk arrived in the late 1920s, the Underground Group was issuing something in the order of 270 million tickets a year. Other mechanical help took the form of change-giving machines, and various dispensing devices for office use containing preprinted tickets. However, most clerks became sufficiently skilled at their work that they could usually work quicker than the customer whom, it may be said, also benefited from research. A new design of brass plate with an upward curve was introduced, to make it easier for passengers to scoop up their tickets and change. A test at an (unidentified) Underground station in 1930 revealed that 663 tickets could be issued by a clerk from a single window in the half hour period from 0700 to 0730, at a rate of 22.1 tickets per minute — or 2.7sec each. Such dexterity was an indication both of traffic volumes and the speeds which passenger-operated ticket machines would have to match.

The earliest slot machines of the 'pull bar' variety appeared in 1904, dispensing preprinted tickets,

And although the physical interchange between lines was far less satisfactory than it was later made, the lesson for the companies was clear: they had to make the system a lot more attractive to the user. This move was linked to the establishment of the London Passenger Traffic Conference, and the later coining of the word 'Underground' to market the companies. Graduated fares and through ticketing between the lines were introduced and, with them, Mr Edmondson's familiar product.

but free-standing electric machines did not appear until 1937. By then the problems of change giving had been solved, and machines of the period also sorted mixed coinage placed in them by means of the 'bunch hopper'. They were installed at all the principal stations, and covered the main fare denominations. At the busiest locations, they accounted for up to 70% of ticket issues, or 30% systemwide since small stations had none. The fare for each machine was shown on an illuminated panel, which also contained the names of all the destination stations covered by that fare. Tickets were printed from a roll of blank card in similar fashion to the 'Rapidprinters' and the simpler 'Miniprinters' in the ticket offices. The machines had to be filled with ticket rolls and change, and emptied of cash, as well as having the date adjusted and the meters read each night. The sound of mountains of loose coin cascading into the collecting boxes wielded by the late shift clerks is one which now belongs to the past.

The 1950s saw the introduction of the 'Station of Origin' ticket, which conferred the right to travel for any journey from the originating station to any other where the fare was that shown on the face of the ticket. There matters stagnated until the automation phase of the 1960s as embodied by the Victoria Line. For there was a lot wrong with the ticketing system. Barrier checks were cursory, particularly for ingoing passengers, adequate staffing became ever more difficult, and it became clear that a large amount of revenue was being lost by fraud. What could be done to automate the process?

So began the installation of mechanical barriers,

Below:
Underground ticket types used with UTS.
Author's collection

through which all passengers would have to pass both to gain entry to and exit from the system. Special yellow tickets with an oxide backing were issued to operate the barriers, and all machines had to be adapted to encode the tickets on issue. A contemporary account described how the Automatic Fare Collection (AFC) system was used:

'The four-door gate has two sets of twin doors. When the passenger inserts his ticket into a slot, the first pair of doors opens, allowing him to step through, and as he does so, the second pair of doors opens and the first pair closes behind him. The whole process can be carried out at normal walking speed, and if there is a continuous stream of passengers inserting valid tickets one after another, the door will remain open, giving an unimpeded flow. The (alternative) tripod gate has a three-armed turnstile which is released by the insertion of a valid ticket and allows one passenger at a time to pass through. At inwards barriers the ticket is returned to the passenger, but at outwards barriers, at the end of the journey, the ticket is retained in the gate. Both types of gate are operated by tickets with a magnetic oxide backing on which the journey details are electronically encoded. When passengers place their tickets in the slot, these details are read by electronic equipment in the gates, which open only if the ticket is valid.'
Annual Report, 1968

But it quickly became clear that the system aspects had not been thought through. If manual barriers were to be dispensed with, all passengers had to have encoded tickets, and this included those issued at the smallest stations on the Underground system as well as the large numbers of BR stations from which barrier-free transfer was available. What sort of costs might be incurred in a comprehensive installation? In 1977, the cost of

adapting and enlarging the ticket hall at Bank station for AFC was put at around £1 million, compared with £5,000–£10,000 for a small suburban station. In the meantime, few of the public could be bothered to use the barriers, especially if they were carrying luggage. With technical problems to contend with as well as several changes of plan, the vision faded and the outward barriers, followed by the inward, fell into gradual disuse.

The adoption of decimal currency on 15 February 1971 posed a few problems for London Transport, which had favoured the £ Sterling being halved in value and divided into 100 pence — what today might be termed a '50p pound'. With their extensive use of coin operated machines, the Board took strong exception to the proposed introduction of $\frac{1}{2}$p coins, the lack of any coin between 2p and 5p, and the lack of a close relationship of old values and coins with the new. It was all too difficult for them, and it was indeed at London Transport's behest that the $2\frac{1}{2}$p (sixpence) was retained in the coinage for the time being.

Rebirth of automatic ticketing came in the 1980s, with the Underground Ticketing System (UTS). The objective had now expanded to improve the control and issue of tickets and security for the staff. It also represented a return to first principles; the previous systems had developed gradually from the early days, and modernisation had always been piecemeal. The main features of the new system are:

- Self service ticket machines which issue a wide range of daily tickets and give change.
- Automatic ticket checking on entry and exit at Central London (Zone 1) stations, in which 80% of all journeys start or finish.
- Creation of 'open' no-barrier suburban

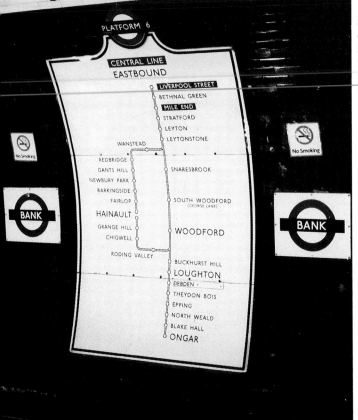

stations without regular ticket checks, but with more roving inspectors able to levy penalty fares.

■ Secure 'wall' ticket offices for staff. All machines can be serviced without leaving the office.

■ Data capture to provide centralised accounting reports and management information.

A credit-card sized ticket was adopted as standard, with a magnetic strip on the back for encoded data. Encoding takes place on issue, together with visual printing of station at which issued, fare paid and other details.

The design of the automatic gates installed in the central zone uses a 'paddle' system, in which the paddles are kept closed electro-pneumatically. Tickets have to be inserted and collected from another slot before the gates will open; photo-electric cells detect the presence of a passenger so that the gates remain open while the passenger passes through. The gates open automatically in the event of power failure, or by the operation of emergency buttons. The minimum number of gates at any one station is one inward, one outward and one reversible gate. At busy stations such as Oxford Circus as many as 26 gates have been installed, replacing a maximum of 10 manned booths.

Each station is controlled by its own computer, and linked to a mainframe installation at Baker Street. Stations are also daisy-chained together so that they are not cut off by a failure of the main link. Through this interconnection, the control centre can update the fares at individual stations. Data on fares and usage is extracted by the control centre. Installation was completed in 1989, and linked to the compatible British Rail system. UTS features many enhancements over what had been intended previously, such are the advances in micro-electronics. It takes less than a second for gates to perform 64 checks and rewrite the magnetic stripe. Thus the new ticket readers are able to detect irregularities in ticket use through time, history, geography and price tests. The acid test though was its acceptance by the public and the staff who had to use and run the system respectively. This has been achieved and the number of stations with UTS is slowly being increased.

One of the most well-known manifestations of the Underground is the map, diagram of lines, journey planner or what you will. Since 1933 the map has appeared regularly, having twice undergone major redesign at the hands of new cartographers, and with minor (or occasionally major) adjustments made at each reprinting. It has always been available in a poster edition as displayed on station platforms, and as a pocket edition, but it has also appeared on T-shirts, mugs and carrier bags, on postcards and in diaries, as a jigsaw and as a tea towel. Recognised all over the world as an icon of London, it also happens to be a useful guide for those wanting to use the system!

As time went by, firm proposals for extensions were incorporated and shown by dashed lines as 'under construction' or 'to be electrified'. This was fine, as long as the work was eventually completed, but the Northern Line became less extensive with every edition during the postwar years until it regressed to the position reached in 1941.

In 1955 a grid was superimposed and keyed to an index of the 272 stations then extant. Little changes continued, such as an improvement in the typography, the indication of which stations had car parks, and the closure of the South Acton branch. By this time Beck's map with its curved transitions from horizontal to vertical and limited use of the diagonal was judged passé and Harold F. Hutchinson's 1960/61 map took its place. In contrast, this used lines at 45° wherever possible, and eschewed all curvature. Perhaps it was meant to reflect the spirit of the times, but in truth it was heartily disliked. When Paul Garbutt, the LTE's Chief Secretary, doodled a more rounded replacement in a fit of boredom after a good Christmas lunch, his ideas were enthusiastically taken up. The first Garbutt map appeared in 1964, and its descendants which have had to cope with the Victoria, Jubilee and Docklands lines are still with us. Only one physical feature has ever been shown: the River Thames, which over the years has been twisted this way and that.

There have always been major trouble spots for would-be designers, the City being the most intractable. Hutchinson's design was weak here, with the main problem being the need to enlarge the area significantly to get all the lines in without unbalancing either the appearance or distorting relationships. Interchange between lines presents problems for which compromise is often inevitable, and a couple of examples are examined here.

Hammersmith consists of two completely separate stations on different sites, the walk between them requiring the use of a public subway to cross the road. Should they be shown separately, or as an interchange? The present convention is interchange, but it has not always been so.

Branch lines may be shown as divergences from their main lines or as separate lines from their junction station. Today, the distinction depends on the way in which the service is operated: if the line is always self contained (Waterloo–Bank) interchange is shown; if through trains are operated as part of the basic service (Finchley Central–Mill Hill East) it is a divergence from the main line; if sometimes one, sometimes the other (Chalfont & Latimer–Chesham) it is shown as interchange but with a broken line connection indicating, in this case, 'peak hours only'.

Many other conundrums have had to be resolved over the passage of time. How many of Railtrack's lines should be shown? To what extent should weekend station closures and peak hour only operations be covered? Does the walk between Fenchurch Street and Tower Hill count as interchange? What about one-way working as on the Heathrow terminal loop? Is it helpful to anticipate future events such as additions to the system, or does it serve only to confuse? An answer has to be found to all such questions.

Finally, on the question of colour, the last word must go to a letter to *The Times*. In response to a report that some changes to the line colours were being contemplated (in reality only changes of shade to make each line as distinctive as possible), Adrian Room of Petersfield protested:

'One of the delights of consulting the map has always been the aptness of the colours. The green District Line, for example, extends from the green trees of Richmond Park in the west and the green lawn tennis courts of Wimbledon in the south to the green fields of Essex in the east, while the red Central Line is the main artery through the city.'

'Similarly the black Northern Line represents the more built-up (formerly sooty and smoky) area of the capital, and off this trunk line extends the brown trunk of the Bakerloo Line. The blue Victoria Line too, crosses the Thames, while the yellow Circle Line runs round continuously through many bright and busy centres and mainline stations.'

'LRT can hardly improve on this, and I hope they will think hard before changing the colours on our map!'

Developments have occurred with the adoption of line management, and in 1990 the East London Line was recoloured orange, and the Hammersmith & City salmon pink. The acquisition of the Waterloo & City Line has led to the introduction of another new colour on the journey planner: turquoise. However, the basic colours remain very familiar.

Chapter 8

Operations and Control

Above:
The Underground prided itself in rising to the occasion when large numbers presented themselves for travelling. This entirely hatted crowd is waiting to be taken home from the RAF pageant at Colindale c1927.
Author's collection

Many regarded the prewar London Transport as reaching a high point which has never been attained since. Indeed, as folklore would have it: declining traffics, staff shortages and unreliability were wholly phenomena of the 1950s onwards. But what was the London Underground capable of 60 years ago? One of their largest tasks was the transport arrangements for the Coronation of King George VI on Wednesday 12 May 1937. It is perhaps worth looking at this operation in detail.

In those far-off days with no television and few cars, there was little alternative to public transport. The success or otherwise of such an operation depended upon the adequacy of the planning and operation by the transport providers. There had been some recent experience of major Royal

occasions, notably the Silver Jubilee of 1935, but even so these could not match the intensity of movement in the first part of May 1937 around the West End. This started with Cup Final day on 1 May. Subsequently traffic rose daily; the last of three dawn rehearsals of the procession on 9 May had over a million spectators.

Pre-planning decided that there was a need to operate all-night trains on the Tuesday night on all lines; for Coronation day itself some stations on the processional route would be closed or partially closed to assist in crowd control. Some stations in the outer areas were also closed, but in these cases to economise on running time. It was not just the procession, attraction that it was; crowds of sightseers were expected to throng the streets to view the decorations and illuminations. At key stations, a special system of barrier control was instituted, with bell signals or telephones between platforms, ticket halls and subway entrances. Gates were erected to enable the passenger flows between platforms to be regulated to match accommodation available. This required substantial augmentation of

staff, and the 6,000 employees were supplemented by no fewer than 1,319 'extras'. Some were recently retired staff, but all had to be instructed in their duties and perhaps receive some training. Over 600 regular staff received temporary promotion.

When the Underground opened for business on the Tuesday morning, it was to run continuously for 46hr. At Charing Cross (now Embankment) alone, 6,530 trains worked through the station, which handled 467,000 passengers. These were part of the 5,669,000 carried in this exhausting traffic day. Not having overnight breaks in service avoided huge influxes at the start of operations, and the peak was reached, incredibly, at 05.30. This perhaps indicated the success of warnings to the public to be in good time, seeing that the procession did not arrive at Westminster Abbey until 11.00! The police request to close some stations partially backfired as it merely put undue strain on the rest. Nevertheless, a continuous 30 trains/hr was successfully maintained during this time on all lines. Included in this were 17 specials run for 10,000 schoolchildren, 1,000 troops and 2,000 dignitaries.

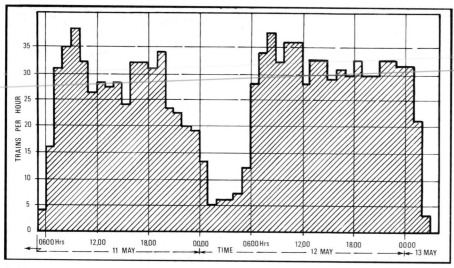

inter-station distances, with an addition for station stop times. These need to be adjusted according to whether the period is the peak or off-peak, or whether the stop is in the central area or the suburbs. Too long an allowance and the train waits time, which results in a slow and inefficient operation; too tight, and chronic unpunctuality quickly ensues. The number of trains required to operate the service is determined by taking the round trip time plus the layover at each terminus and dividing it by the service frequency.

In putting a timetable together, the requirements at the different times of the day need to be blended with each other. It is obviously undesirable to

Weather always plays an important part. May 1937 was cold and foggy, with some rain. Consequently, return journeys tended to be earlier than anticipated, and by 16.15 queues totalling 630yd long had formed outside St James's Park station. Traffic levels fell away after 01.00 on the Thursday morning, the service finally ceasing at 02.15. The respite was brief; over three million passengers were carried on each of the following three traffic days, which was approaching twice normal levels. There are numerous statistics to illustrate the magnitude of what was achieved, including the 12-ton weight of tickets issued during the week. Operationally, it would seem that a state of near perfection was achieved, with no instances of failure causing appreciable delay or inconvenience to passengers on Coronation Day itself. Minor problems only were encountered on other days.

Whatever the cost, it was excellent public relations. 'The manner in which the (Underground workers) have carried out their task must excite universal admiration', enthused The Morning Post (now The Daily Telegraph). 'When it was inevitable that human beings should be packed like sardines, the sardines have at least been made to feel that the packers regretted unfortunate necessity along with them.' The editorial went on to suggest that if the Underground could cope with such a massive influx of passengers, the nation would do well to develop the network further as a solution to London's ever-growing traffic problems. This support for the public network was all the more encouraging as, although the trams and trolleybuses were running, the buses were absent at the time due to a strike.

Few travellers on the Underground need to give any thought to the timetable, most probably assuming that trains run on some sort of continuous basis. In reality, the timetable is constructed carefully to extract the maximum out of the resources which are available. Any railway service can only be as good as its timetable, and given the things that can go wrong, the performance

is usually a little below what has been planned. Arguments have raged over whether timetable compilation is an art or a science; the consensus seems to be that it is a science, but one in which the art of the specialist gives the result the final polish.

The timetable is the written expression of the formal plan of action, which confirms what is being offered to the passenger and summarises what the organisation expects of its staff. It also indirectly commits the resources which are necessary to provide the service advertised. Before the timetable compilation is attempted, therefore, the volume and pattern of traffic must be known or assumed, and the resources available must be assessed.

The decision to revise a timetable may stem from a number of reasons as well as shifts in the pattern of demand sufficient to affect the service levels to be provided. Technical changes involving the trains, track layouts or signalling, and the availability of staff, are all matters to which the compiler may need to address his skills. A thorough knowledge of the physical characteristics of the line, and the performance capability of rolling stock are also needed.

The journey time is the summation of the individual point-to-point timings for the

proceed directly from a 10min off-peak service to a peak frequency of perhaps 2min between trains. Given also differential running times, the trickiest part of the job is to achieve a gradual change in frequency without causing large service gaps.

The Underground lines are unequal in their resource requirements and Table 6 shows how many trains are needed to operate the maximum timetabled service, by line:

TABLE 6:
Maximum number of trains needed to provide timetabled peak services, 1994

Line	Trains
Bakerloo	28
Central	71
Circle	14
District	74
East London	5
Hammersmith & City	15
Jubilee	24
Metropolitan	42
Northern	82
Piccadilly	69
Victoria	34
Waterloo & City	4
Total	**462**

Above:
The first safety rule is not to start anything which cannot be stopped. Most trains are driven manually with the driver observing the colour light signals, but if a train should pass a signal at danger the raised train stop will engage the trip cock on the train and apply the brakes automatically. The trip cock can only be reset by the driver descending to track level. In the event of any failure, the trip cock becomes and remains raised.
John Glover

Right:
East London Line: trains per hour by section of line, day of week and time of day, 1990.

All trains are formed of six, seven or eight cars according to line, the only exceptions now being the self-contained services on the East London Line, the Waterloo & City Line and the Chesham branch of the Metropolitan. On these, four cars are deemed sufficient.

There is also a great difference in the service required at different times of the day, as an analysis of the East London Line 1990 timetable shows. The ability to supplement or reduce the service level depends on the physical constraints; the diagram shows that trains can be extended to Shoreditch, as they are in the Monday to Friday peaks and also for the Sunday morning market. It also indicates how four trains can provide either a Shoreditch service or a higher frequency south of Whitechapel, but not both. However, the Shoreditch, New Cross and New Cross Gate stubs are all single tracked, which does place a practical limitation on the service variations which can be achieved. The additional driver required for the Monday to Friday peak service is a direct result of the turnround time at Shoreditch being a mere 2min. Thus each incoming driver 'steps back' to the following train, to ensure that the timetable is achieved. It might be added that the end-to-end journey times on the East London Line are 12min to either destination, over a distance of under four miles.

A basic principle is that trains should run at even intervals. This service is split equally between New Cross and New Cross Gate, thus offering each of them half the basic service frequency. The addition of a third southern branch to East Dulwich,

discussed in Chapter 13, would further complicate matters.

The alternatives then for the East London Line would be:

■ to give each branch one third of the total service, so that an even interval service, if relatively infrequent, is maintained to each; or

■ to split the total service in some other proportions, as traffic levels may suggest, in which case train intervals on the branches will be irregular; or

■ to concentrate through services on two (or even one) of the branches, with the other(s) served by a shuttle service from Surrey Quays and all through passengers having to change.

To these sorts of problems, which are repeated in one form or another all over railway systems, there are no perfect solutions. The difficulties, however, are those of mathematics rather than unresponsive or reluctant management. It might also be added that physical limitations at junctions, and the availability of a terminal bay at the interchange station (or the possibilities of providing one), must also be taken into account. The best single answer, which is only feasible if the business justifies it, is to run an intensive service. One third of a 30tph service is still 10tph, or a train every 6min.

Timetables also determine service connectional possibilities, and obvious problems arise if the services to be connected do not run at similar intervals. Sometimes it is only possible to make one set of connections; thus it may have to be decided if the Chesham shuttle from Chalfont & Latimer is sufficiently important for the whole of the Metropolitan main line timetable to be constructed around connections into and out of both up and down trains at Chalfont.

The timetable also has to return the trains at the end of the day to where they will be wanted the following morning. This is not necessarily back to their starting points, since outbased trains stabling in sidings overnight have to return to depots for periodic routine examination. At intervals, they also require both internal and external cleaning.

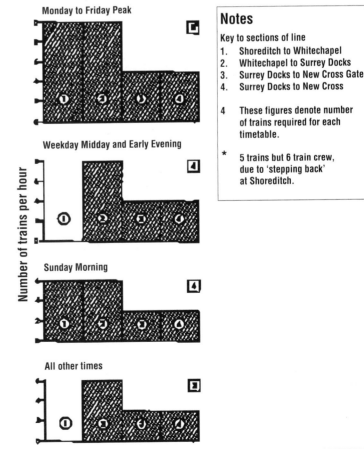

East London Line: trains per hour by section of line, day of week and time of day, 1990

Monday to Friday Peak

Weekday Midday and Early Evening

Sunday Morning

All other times

Number of trains per hour

Notes

Key to sections of line
1. **Shoreditch to Whitechapel**
2. **Whitechapel to Surrey Docks**
3. **Surrey Docks to New Cross Gate**
4. **Surrey Docks to New Cross**

4 **These figures denote number of trains required for each timetable.**

* **5 trains but 6 train crew, due to 'stepping back' at Shoreditch.**

end in the late 1950s, was discontinued because:

- it tended to confuse the public (and, sometimes, the staff);
- it made service regulation difficult, in that trains which were nominally 'non-stopping' were in practice often held up by the previous 'stopping' train; and
- service frequency at the omitted stations fell unacceptably low in the evenings and on Sundays.

Today, there are only some sections of line which close early, eg Woodford–Hainault at 20.00, and some stations which are closed at certain times, eg Cannon Street at weekends.

Twenty million passengers daily entrust themselves to the care of the Underground, and the 17,500 staff require training in their own tasks and the work of the railway in general. In 1963, London Transport opened its new railway training centre at White City on a site formerly occupied by the rolling stock shed of the Central London Railway. The centre replaced the outdated and outmoded 1920 establishment at Lambeth North.

The courses were aimed mainly at new entrants and those seeking promotion. Instruction covered the duties of operating apprentices, stationmen and stationwomen, booking clerks, station foremen, and guards; all entrants to these grades received background and theoretical training in the school, with practical work at stations and on trains. To enable suitable staff to qualify as ticket collectors, guards, motormen, signalmen, station foremen and station supervisors, there were promotional training courses, varying in length from four days for ticket collectors to 36 days for station supervisors. From time to time, special courses were organised also to train railway instructors, traffic controllers, divisional inspectors and other senior staff. The centre had 11 teaching staff.

The White City school was claimed to be the most comprehensively equipped railway training centre in the country, with an intake of 3,500 students each year. The facilities were designed so that practically all out of course incidents and failures likely to be encountered in day-to-day operation could be reproduced with either replicas or models of prototype equipment. These arrangements were aimed particularly at control grades, since it meant

Generally, operational control can be made more effective if services are self-contained between specific terminals where possible, such as running Arnos Grove–Rayners Lane and Cockfosters–Heathrow on the Piccadilly Line. All trains though should pass common crew change points.

The above summarises the main constraints and methods, but in addition special timetables need to be devised for sporting and other events. Junction working can produce parallel movements which do not interfere with each other, or conflicting ones. Trains on several lines can get themselves reversed as on the Northern Line's Kennington Loop, which can lead to stock marshalling difficulties. Uncoupling to run shorter trains during the off-peak is no longer practised, but when it was a feature of Underground operation a major difficulty was that, on splitting, there would be two trains but only one train crew.

'Non-stopping' of Underground services through lesser used stations used to be quite widespread practice. Nowadays it really exists only on the Metropolitan Line north of Finchley Road, where the Underground takes on more of the attributes of a 'proper' railway.

The practice of non-stopping, which came to an

that they could be set to unravel, practically, a number of difficult situations which could otherwise only be reproduced on the railway itself — which was hardly practicable for the majority!

One room contained a full size section of an Underground station, with running track, platform, tunnel entrance and various ancillary equipment. Incidents could thus be simulated to demonstrate the application of the rules, while the 'passengers' were kept informed by public address. A 600V traction supply was laid on, and a device to reproduce current arcing was installed. Elsewhere, there were working electro-pneumatic and Westinghouse brake mechanisms as fitted to Underground trains, and electrical control apparatus and automatic couplers. A cutaway 1938 stock tube car demonstrated the air-operated door mechanisms and the guard's panel, and also the Drico (Driver-Controller) communication equipment. Lift and escalators were not forgotten, while a fully fledged booking office was fitted with ticket issuing and change-giving machines.

The model railway had 175ft of track, and was fully signalled and controlled from miniature lever frames with illuminated track diagrams or push button signalling. Eleven trains could be accommodated at one time and, needless to say, the instructor was able to introduce a wide range of 'failures'.

The use of video enabled consideration of historic accidents and their effects on current practice, and provision of a record of an actual operating incident, enabling the class to construct alternative courses of action and their likely effects. It was also useful for recording and subsequent analysis of role playing incidents which could be staged on the mock platform. Over 4,000 staff currently attend courses every year.

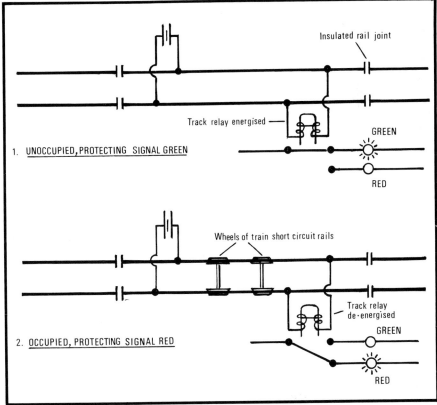

Signalling is the means of enabling the railway to run frequent trains at speed on potentially conflicting courses, but with safety of operation. The complexity of the signalling system is related to what is expected of it; thus the capacity of a line is

Above:
Simplified diagram of a track circuit, showing at top unoccupied, protecting signal green, below occupied, protecting signal red.

dependent in part on the signal spacing, which determines the minimum gap between succeeding trains. As a safety back-up, additional devices come into play, should either the human element or mechanical defect supervene. The most important advance in safety was the adoption of automatic signalling, whereby each train alternately protects itself and clears the road behind by completing and breaking certain electrical circuits in its passage.

The traditional 'block' system with the 'blocks' being defined as the distances between the stations and with one train only allowed in each at any one time sufficed for a while with steam traction. Semaphore signals were quickly supplanted by colour lights (although the last semaphores used by

Underground trains survived at Richmond BR until 1980), but early tunnel signals were operated electro-mechanically, having moving spectacles illuminated from behind with an oil lamp! Growing weights of traffic and electric traction required a more flexible approach to signalling which was not conditioned by the station spacing.

Automatic signalling is no new invention, since it was adopted by the Metropolitan and London Electric Railways in 1905 and 1907 respectively, and earlier still on some of the main line railways. The system works as follows (see diagram P 93). The running rails are divided into lengths which are insulated from each other electrically. The signal current passes along the rails on one side of a section of track, through a track relay, and then back through the rails on the other side. When current is flowing through the relay, its contacts are closed, and this completes the circuit for the control of the signal and causes it to show a proceed aspect.

When a train passes the starting signal and thus enters the track circuit section which the signal protects, the wheels and axles bridge the running rails and short circuit the signal current. This de-energises the signal relay which causes the signal to show a red aspect. When the train clears the track circuit section by passing another signal plus a further short section or overlap beyond that, the short circuit is removed. The signal relay is re-energised, and the normal green aspect of an automatic signal is restored, allowing the following

train to proceed. The length of the overlap is designed to be sufficient to enable a train travelling at maximum permitted speed to stop short of any obstruction using an emergency brake application. With several automatic sections between two signalboxes which retain non-automatic control as at junctions, trains can follow each other safely without further intervention. As all trains on the Underground system are now of multiple-unit stock, the variation of acceleration and braking characteristics as found on an all-purpose railway is missing, and the signalling can be specified and designed that much more precisely.

The track circuit depends upon the presence of a train to short circuit the running rails, but on little used sidings or crossovers a build up of rust could prevent this from happening. This is dealt with in two ways: 'rusty rail' workings are deliberately introduced into the working timetable so that as many lines as possible see a train during the normal course of events, and secondly a narrow wavy band of stainless steel is welded to the head of the rails. This ensures that rust does not prevent electrical continuity being maintained.

Should a driver ignore the signal aspects, a second line of protection is brought into play. The automatic train stop apparatus alongside the rails will apply the brakes, taking control out of the driver's hands. Normally, the arm on the train stop lies clear of the trains, but it is raised automatically

by air pressure when the signal turns to a danger aspect. In this position, the arm position is pre-set to make contact with a trip cock on the train, and if contact is made the cock will open and release the compressed air supply in the train pipe and apply the brakes, causing the train to stop within the overlap distance. The raising of the train stop is detected by the preceding stop signal which will remain at danger until the fault is rectified; this 'fail safe' approach is always apparent in railway signalling matters, and it will be realised that a loss of current in the track circuiting device already described will always cause the signal to display a red aspect.

On the Underground system, two aspect red/green signals are sufficient for most purposes; yellow is used as a repeater for a red aspect in advance where the sighting distance is limited. Exceptions include the sections where Underground and British Rail trains use the same tracks as happens north of Harrow-on-the-Hill, where four aspect Railtrack signals provide additional braking distance.

Automatic signals cannot cope with junctions, and here semi-automatic signals are installed which have to be cleared each time for the route selected, although they will restore themselves to danger automatically after the train has passed. It follows that they normally display a red aspect. Usually, such signals can be set to full automatic operation when all trains are to take the same route. Junction signals will normally feature the 'lunar' lights, a series of three white lights placed at an angle above the signal head as a visual indication to the driver of the route setting. Lack of any indication indicates that the 'normal' route is set.

For slow speed operation, the theatre type indicator is used. This can display various numbers, each of which indicates a separate route, through the illumination of a pattern of light bulbs. It will usually be found above a ground or shunt signal controlling the entrance to sidings.

Signalling may also be used to control train speeds rather more directly than just displaying large numerals to denote speed restriction signs at the side of the track. A specific problem was the southbound run from East Finchley on the Northern Line. From entering the tunnel, the gradient falls steadily at 1 in 50 for the two miles to Archway station, outside which there is a sharp and

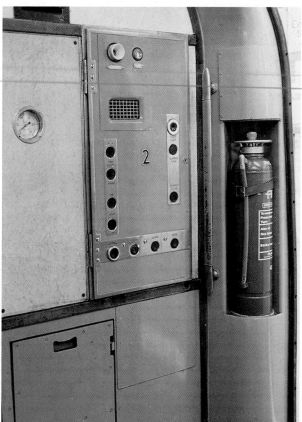

therefore speed restricted curve. Two timing points were therefore arranged on the section. The first controls a signal about 200yd beyond it, which will not clear if the train exceeds 40mph over the timing length. The second section controls a signal about 100yd beyond it and 250yd from the curve, which will not clear to any train exceeding 30mph over the second length. In this way, the speed has been reduced so that the curve cannot be taken too fast, since if a speeding driver should attempt to do so, the automatic train stop will come into action.

Later refinements but with a similar end in mind

have been applied to approach control systems, where the speed of an approaching train is assessed by the current it generates in coils situated with magnets under the rail. The detector now consists of a 12ft length of dummy positive current rail adjacent to the home signal, with a stainless steel surface; beneath it are 12 permanent magnets and coils, in which a current is induced by the positive shoes of the train making contact with the inductor. This causes a small alternating current to be generated in the coil, its frequency proportional to the speed of the train. A related relay responding only to alternating current below a given frequency is connected, and only when the relay operates does the signal clear. Measurements correct to 0.5mph are said to have been achieved, the advantage being that the detector makes constant checks as the decelerating train's pick-up shoes pass over the inductors. Speed control of this nature allows trains to enter platforms where the signalling would normally demand that they be detained in the running tunnels as, of course, the time taken in the platforms will allow the next train in front to proceed further. Another application is in the approach to dead end platform tunnels underground, following the disastrous accident at Moorgate in 1975. Here, for reasons never fully established, the driver of the train failed to stop in the platform. Instead, he carried on and the train hit the end of the tunnel with the loss of 42 lives.

It is always easy to be wise after the event, and railway safety has had a century and a half in which

to develop. This has led to rail becoming one of the safest forms of transport available, since the whole operation takes place in a strictly controlled environment. Yet one must never lose sight of the purpose of the railway, which in the case of the Underground is mass movement. Safety is important, but there is a cost involved, and the standards must be consistent with the fulfillment of the basic *raison d'être* of the organisation. One problem that has raised its head several times is the procedure to be followed when a driver encounters a signal at red and which resolutely refuses to change to a proceed aspect. In order to keep the traffic moving, the stop and proceed rule was devised which, after a 1min interval, allows the driver to 'trip' past it and, after resetting the trip cock on the train, to proceed at a speed consistent with stopping short of any obstruction that he may encounter or at the next signal. The obstruction may be no more than a failed train stop which, as noted, will cause the signal behind to remain at red. However, it may be a failed train, in which case the normal procedure would be to push it until such time as it can be diverted to siding or depot. So far, so good, and any other arrangement would be far more disruptive.

Nevertheless, the safety of this operation depends upon the driver of the second train continuing with care and attention to what he is doing. On 8 April 1953, this did not happen. A damaged train stop caused a signal between Stratford and Leyton on the Central Line to display a permanent red aspect. Eleven trains passed the signal according to the rules; the twelfth was in the process of doing so when it was struck heavily in the rear. The Inspecting Officer commented on the damage, 'which greatly exceeded that ever experienced in any previous damage to tube stock. The leading driving cab of the first car (of the rear train) was wrecked and the headstock was forced down with such violence that the whole end of the car was lifted and became jammed between the track and the roof of the tube, buckling itself in the process. This had two results — firstly, the whole of the energy of the train was dissipated at that point instead of some, at least, being expended on pushing (the preceding) train further forwards; and secondly, the lifting of the front end caused the rear end to be lowered, enabling the buffer of the second car to ride over that of the first car and to telescope into it for a distance of six feet'. The accident took place during the rush hour and was, at that time, the only really serious accident in the history of the Underground. The accident caused 12 deaths, with the cause being a lack of care or misjudgement by the driver. There have been a number of other accidents from the same basic cause both before and since, but none with such devastating results. In the last analysis, no safety device can replace the skill and vigilance of the staff.

The railwayman deserves all the help he can get, and an anticipated hazard concerned the two major types of rolling stock. Those for surface and tube operation respectively have totally different cross-sections, and the extensions of the 1930s and the years following brought with them increased opportunities for both types to share the same tracks. Sometimes, this sharing also encompassed the main line railways, whose goods trains continued to run long after the passenger services had been ceded to London Transport. The risk thus arose of a surface or main line train being diverted in error towards a tube tunnel of 12ft diameter, against which the signalling would not provide

protection. The solution was to first detect surface trains and then to stop them.

The method chosen was to suspend a series of three mercury-filled glass tubes from an overhead gantry, clear of tube stock but obstructing larger trains. Breakage of the tubes returned the signals in advance to danger, with their associated tripcock mechanisms. The first installation was at Hammersmith in 1932, to prevent District Line trains entering the eastbound Piccadilly Line tunnels at Barons Court. Other detection methods have also been used. On the Central Line eastward extensions, it was necessary to distinguish between electric tube trains and BR services, and electric trains were required to 'prove' their presence through the pick-up shoes making contact with a length of specially installed conductor rail on the opposite side of the track to the positive rail. Traditionally, each junction location was controlled by its own signalbox, featuring a miniature lever frame. This mirrored main line practice, with each lever controlling a separate set of points or a signal. The first was installed at the present Acton Town station in 1905, and the following describes the Aldgate box which controlled the triple triangular junction at the eastern extremity of the Circle Line:

'In the cabin a long power frame of miniature levers is worked by signalmen who handle at peak periods as many as 120 trains per hour.'

'Above the frame an illuminated diagram gives a picture of the various tracks and the position of trains moving over them. Trains are advised to the cabin on a train describer panel, and are described on a transmitter as they are dispatched away from the controlled area. Signalmen receive trains by "pulling off" a signal after setting the road where necessary. These signals are of the semi-automatic type, and are restored to danger by the passage of the trains past them. The signal cannot clear again until the signalman has restored his lever to normal and "restroked", or reversed it. The levers have both electrical and mechanical locking as safeguards against irregular movement.'

'Back-locking relay apparatus prevents a signalman from inadvertently replacing a lever and resetting a road once a train has accepted the signal, and mechanical locks block the movement of any lever, other than the one pulled, that could set up a conflicting movement. Below the cabin is a room housing 266 relays in glass-fronted covers to protect them from dust and damp. More than 50 miles of wire was needed to complete the circuiting in this room when the equipment was installed.'

The first change was to consolidate the movement of a number of levers, so that each performed a series of functions and set up an entire route. Local control remained possible, through the expedient of switching the box back into the system. Next, remote control of the levers from an adjacent

location by push-button was introduced, using compressed air to activate them. Push-buttons conferred a number of advantages, not the least of which was that the signalman could remain seated. Routes no longer needed to be reset after use, and it became possible to pre-select the following route which was required and which would then be set up automatically. The status of each route, whether it was clear, pre-selected or at danger was shown by panel lights. The first of these installations was commissioned at Ealing Broadway in 1952.

Hitherto, the signalman had initiated the movements, albeit over a wide area; the next step was to use the trains themselves through the working timetable to set up their own routes. At simple facing junctions, the automatic train describers can be used to control the junction points; at trailing junctions, signals can be arranged to pass trains on a first come-first served basis.

In 1955 the first programme machine, or 'pianola' was installed experimentally at the complex Camden Town junctions on the Northern Line. This contemporary description nowadays reads like a combination of a primeval computer and the music rolls used by steam-driven fairground organs! But this is not to mock the real advance which the development represented:

'The programme machine carries a plastic roll about 8ft long and 8in wide, on which is recorded the day's train service in terms of the train time, the reporting numbers, and their destination. Each

entry is in the form of punched holes in the roll which forms a unique code. Feeler arms on the machine press against the roll, and as the roll advances the holes come into position and make various contacts.'

'These are sufficient to initiate the setting up of the route for each train. As each train proceeds, the programme machine roll is automatically stepped to the next entry. Checks ensure that the train being described is that which should be approaching according to the timetable, in which case the route will be set at the correct time. (This could involve the much troubled "Positive Train Identification" system, whereby each train confirmed its identity automatically.) If a train is late by more than a pre-set time, the machine may "ask" for a supervisor to decide on the course of action or, if trains arrive at a converging junction out of order the machine may automatically step forward to deal with the train that has arrived first, storing the route details in its memory until the missing train arrives. It should perhaps be noted that the programme machines do not directly operate points and signals, which is

carried out as previously; there is thus no safety connotation. The machine takes the place of the signalman in his decision as to what action to initiate next.'

The inevitable move into computerisation of such tasks is proceeding concurrently with resignalling schemes. The first use of computers was for track circuits, and allowed the elimination of the insulation joints in running rails. These could be replaced by impedance bonds, the track circuit being tuned to a particular computer detector. Trials began with electronic versions of the programme machine at Watford in the 1970s, subsequent installations covered Heathrow and the northern part of the Piccadilly Line. The Metropolitan and Jubilee Lines followed.

With increasing sophistication, the need for signalmen to be able to identify trains on sight disappeared. Consequently, the headcode was also phased out, and from the 1959 tube stock build onwards, marker or headlights only were carried. Underground codes were related to destinations, and the juxtaposition of which out of three, four or five lights (according to type of stock) formed the code. The Metropolitan's electric locomotives had three locations only.

Early headcodes were provided by positioning oil lamps, an anachronism on an electrified railway. Amazingly, though, oil tail lamps continued to be carried by the CO/CP and R stocks into the 1980s, as only one fuse was fitted to the electric tail lamps.

Although signalling was originally carried out locally, centralisation has gradually concentrated the task into the hands of train regulators in single locations. But regulators, signalmen and programme machines alike require supervision from some kind of control organisation, which is in a position to take a broader view of what is happening on the network.

Control offices can be traced back to the early days of the District Railway, when the telegraph office at Earl's Court was notified of breakdowns and failures, following which orders were issued to maintenance chargehands standing by at various key points. Signal fitters at Aldgate East, electrical linesmen at Victoria, and locomotive foremen could thus be summoned to deal with any emergency, whilst a chief inspector stationed at Earl's Court was responsible for train working throughout the District system.

Complex track layouts may offer some flexibility, but in general they are a curse on the operators. The 'keep it simple' school of thought, based on the maxim that the more there is to go right, the more there is to go wrong, has something to commend it. With a high degree of service interaction, even a quite trivial delay at one location can have consequential effects out of all proportion to its inherent significance. The problems are clearly worse when lines are being run at or near their capacity.

The example of Earl's Court on the surface lines shows some of the problems. In the peak hour, the westbound District Line at Earl's Court has to deal with services from Embankment in the east and High Street Kensington in the north, bound for four separate destinations west of the station. In addition, there is a need to mesh in with the Circle Line services in both directions. Most of the junctions are grade separated and there are two westbound platforms available at Earl's Court itself as well as two terminal platforms at High Street Kensington. Nevertheless, given also the interfaces elsewhere with the Hammersmith & City and the Metropolitan Lines, the huge scope for out of course running is apparent.

Problems which fall to the controllers to deal with include those which local management has been unable to resolve, such as no driver being

available to take over a train when it arrives at a crew changeover point. This can be doubly disruptive to the operation, since not only is there a potential gap in the service, but there is also a train without a driver holding up the system. Other commonplace events include train, signal and track failures, or actions by passengers or staff. The job of the controllers, who are organised on a line basis, is to keep an eye on all that is happening, and to anticipate and to minimise the effects of unwanted events on the train service. The principle is that of intervention when needed; if everything is running perfectly, the controller has nothing to do.

To undertake the control task effectively, a flow of incoming information is required, together with an intimate knowledge of the track layout, rolling stock characteristics, station facilities, the timetable and traction and other current supplies. The objective is to minimise the causes of delay and to contain such delays as cannot be prevented to the smallest possible geographical area.

In the event of disruption, the controller has to decide on the appropriate action. This may include turning trains short of destination, ensuring train crews are available, reducing the service interval, organising a replacement bus service, calling out engineering staff and, of course, restoring the service to normal. The controller has an information assistant who can use the selective public address facility to inform passengers of operational problems, whether they be irregular running or the non-availability of lifts at a particular station. It has to be said that such public announcements are not always audible, and often seem to be largely irrelevant.

At all times, the safety of staff and passengers alike must take top priority. For major incidents, the line controller can turn to the Headquarters Controller, who would normally summon the public emergency services.

Effective control depends upon effective communication, and the telephone, useful as it is, has serious drawbacks — notably that it cannot be used to or from a moving train. Along the walls of all tunnel sections may be seen two bare copper wires. Their primary function is to discharge the traction current, which is carried out by pinching the two wires together to make contact. This is essentially an emergency measure, to counteract any fusing or arcing which may arise. Right from the earliest days of tube railways, drivers were also provided with a telephone which could be clipped to the wires, which has the same discharging effect. It also enables the driver to talk to the substation control room and pass messages through those staff to the line controller. Unless instructed otherwise, the traction current will be reconnected by the substation control after a short interval. This can be overridden by the driver in emergency, and always if passengers are to be detrained and walked to a station, by placing short circuiting bars on the rails. Detraining is to be avoided if at all possible, as it can take a long time for passengers to be led through the entire train and out through one of the cab doors and then along the track to the nearest means of exit. At the very least, there are likely to be some bills presented for dry-cleaning! Tunnel emergency lighting is automatically switched on.

Such communication is really for emergency use only, and the Drico system dating from the 1950s allows direct speech communication through speakers in the cab and the control room. Contact is made through attachment to the same tunnel wires; again the train must be stationary, and there is no facility for control to call the driver.

For the Victoria Line, which was built for Automatic Train Operation (ATO), carrier wave contact through the conductor rails was used to transmit messages between the driver and the regulator. While this system could be used while the train was in motion, it suffered from interference and could not be used if short circuiting devices had been put down after the current had been discharged. It was thus likely to be useless in the event of a real emergency when communications were most needed. The 1967 Victoria Line stock was the first to be built with a public address facility.

With Driver Only Operation in mind, train radio was developed to overcome this rather unsatisfactory state of affairs. Train radio allows communication while the train is moving, unlike the previous cumbersome system which required the driver to stop and attach the telephone handset. Priority has been given to train radio since it benefits the whole operation of the railway, and a high premium is attached to its reliability, providing as it does the front line communication between train and control.

Train radio is operated by means of a continuous leaky-feeder cable through the running tunnels, transmitting to and receiving from fixed on-train equipment. Radio also allows contact with supervisory and management staff, who are out and about on the system. Station staff also benefit, and principal tunnel stations now have radio contact with the surface. These personal sets are effective on trains or immediately adjacent to the track. Initially, development was hampered by the allocation of an insufficient number of radio frequencies.

The provision of direct contact at all times is one of the prerequisites for driver-only operation. STORNO train radio is fitted to all DOO trains, which has now almost allowed the Drico equipment to be dispensed with.

Chapter 9

Engineering Support

Without the engineering function, there could be no Underground. This chapter takes a look at some of the many areas in which the engineers contribute to the operation of the system.

The first stage of Acton Works, for many years the central railway overhaul workshops in west London, was opened in 1922. As such, it was responsible for the cars of the District, both Bakerloo branches and the Piccadilly Lines. The overhaul capacity was in the order of 16 cars/week, and motor cars were expected to put in an appearance about every 50,000 miles; this equated roughly to their annual mileage. The overhaul requirement for trailers was less, at 70,000 miles.

Subsequent expansion was intended to increase the throughput to 60 cars per week and add body repair and painting to the tasks undertaken. The works was also to cater for all the lines, though not at that stage the Metropolitan which was then a separate concern.

At its maximum extent, Acton Works occupied a 50-acre site to the south of Acton Town station and provided facilities for heavy overhaul and reconditioning of all London Transport's railway rolling stock as well as supplying reconditioned wheels and other components to the running depots. Acton Works is no more, the site is now being used for much more modest purposes; this description by Howson of the progress of

Underground cars through the complex at its zenith has been retained for its interest.

'The works are arranged so that cars for overhaul are first drawn up at a platform alongside the trimming shop, where the seats are removed. The seats are either washed or retrimmed and then stored ready to go back to the cars after overhaul. Cars can then proceed to the lifting shop, where the car body is lifted off its service bogies or trucks by means of a 30-ton overhead traversing crane and placed on special accommodation bogies, which are old bogies built up with raised transverse beams so that the body sits much higher off the track than usual, giving additional working space beneath.'

'After the car bodies are lifted on to accommodation bogies, the service trucks have their traction motors and current collection equipment removed and are drawn by chain into the truck shop. Down one side of this large building is the dismantling track or road, along which the trucks are slowly moved and progressively stripped down to the bare frames.'

'On the far side of the shop is the truck assembly line and across the wide space between pass all the various components on a series of conveyors. On their journey across the shop, the components are cleaned, inspected and reconditioned or renewed as necessary.'

'The truck frames themselves are now removed

from the line and come under close scrutiny for defects, such as rivets working loose, which may occur under the stress of continued running.

'All that is now left of the service trucks on the dismantling road are the pairs of wheels and axles and these are moved to the extreme end of the truck shop, known as the wheel area. Here the wheel assemblies, comprising either wheels with gear drive mounted directly on the axle, or plain wheels and axles, are subject to very close examination for wear and faults. Wheel axles, approximately 5in in diameter, sometimes reveal faults during a special testing process. If so, they are tested on an ultrasonic flaw detector. Should there be any suspicion of a crack on an axle, the wheels are pressed off and subjected to a test on a magnetic particle tester. In this, fluorescent ink containing particles is sprayed on to the axle, which is then electrified. The particles are thus attracted magnetically to the opposite poles of any crack, which thereupon reveals itself as a black hair line. Overhauled wheel assemblies are conveyed to the assembly line, and then begins the building up of

Below:
The virtual demise of Acton Works required much more work to be undertaken in line depots. This is Neasden in 1983 with 1971 MkII rolling stock.
John Glover

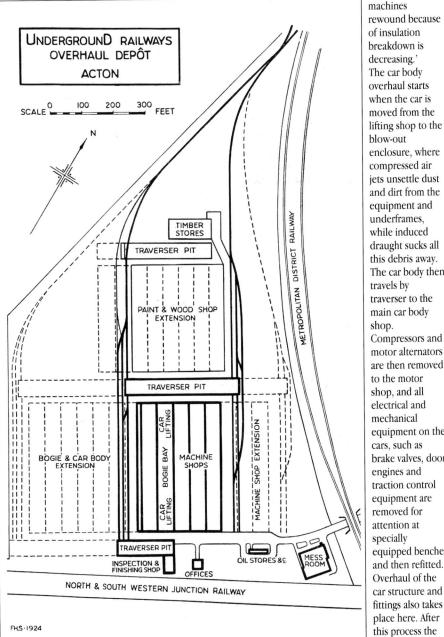

UNDERGROUND RAILWAYS OVERHAUL DEPÔT ACTON

SCALE 0 100 200 300 FEET

N

TIMBER STORES

TRAVERSER PIT

PAINT & WOOD SHOP EXTENSION

METROPOLITAN DISTRICT RAILWAY

TRAVERSER PIT

BOGIE & CAR BODY EXTENSION

CAR LIFTING · BOGIE BAY · CAR LIFTING

MACHINE SHOPS

MACHINE SHOP EXTENSION

TRAVERSER PIT

INSPECTION & FINISHING SHOP

OFFICES

OIL STORES &c

MESS ROOM

NORTH & SOUTH WESTERN JUNCTION RAILWAY

FHS·1924

Above:
Layout of Acton Works, when opened in 1924.
Author's collection

the bogie, which continues as the bogie slowly moves along the line in the reverse direction to that in which it entered. The completed trucks are now ready to return to the lifting shop.'

'The motor shop overhauls traction motors, compressors, alternators and a variety of other machines such as lift and escalator motors. Motor overhaul is a specialised business and can vary from superficial attention and cleaning to complete rebuilding from the shaft upwards. Three of the processes involved are the stoving of reconditioned armatures to drive out moisture and ensure good insulation, the banding of armatures to prevent the copper bars from rising due to the high rotating motor speeds, and the armature insulation tests at 2,000V — or double if the armature is rebuilt. These high tension tests are carried out within a special raised enclosure to keep out unauthorised personnel during testing. Modern traction motors use better insulating materials, so the number of

machines rewound because of insulation breakdown is decreasing.'
The car body overhaul starts when the car is moved from the lifting shop to the blow-out enclosure, where compressed air jets unsettle dust and dirt from the equipment and underframes, while induced draught sucks all this debris away. The car body then travels by traverser to the main car body shop. Compressors and motor alternators are then removed to the motor shop, and all electrical and mechanical equipment on the cars, such as brake valves, door engines and traction control equipment are removed for attention at specially equipped benches and then refitted. Overhaul of the car structure and fittings also takes place here. After this process the car body is sent through the paint

shop and then returns to the lifting shop where it is lowered on to its service trucks. Roads with pit facilities are provided for inspection and testing on completed cars. The cars are then coupled into unit formation, the seats refitted, and a final test run performed.'

Even in this description, the seeds of change can be detected. Maintenance requirements overall were decreasing, and further economies were foreseen. For example, if the vehicle bodies needed to lifted from their bogies less frequently, this would be of little value if the lifting was still needed to remove the wheelsets so that they could be machined periodically to restore their correct profile. Underfloor wheel lathes to re-machine the wheels, but without removing them from the vehicles, were first introduced in 1947. These lathes dealt with the flanges only, but in 1961 a new machine was put into service at Northfields depot which could machine the entire profile. This used rollers pressed against the inner faces of the wheels to rotate them, while hydraulic jacks supported the axleboxes and hence the vehicle's weight. The

copying tool to cut away the surplus metal was then moved across the wheel flange and tread, following a master profile. Using this method, it was not even necessary to uncouple the vehicles, and a complete four-car set would be drawn progressively across the lathe by winch.

Armature rewinding was being replaced with the use of better insulation techniques. Painting of aluminium cars with plastic faced interiors was not necessary. Wheel changes were being extended from one year to every four years, and heavy overhauls from every four to every nine years. Heavy mechanical work was being replaced with increasing requirements for electrical and electronic work. For modern rolling stock with nine years adopted as the basis for heavy overhauls, the half-life overhaul at 18 years has similar work content to previous half-life overhauls. However, the nine and 27 year overhauls are much lighter, with some items removed for repair but most equipment being subjected only to a clean-up and test. For example, the cars in a train no longer need to be separated, let alone have the bodies lifted off the bogies.

Given the age of much of the equipment at Acton, the upshot was the decision in 1985 to transfer all car overhauls to the line depots, with equipment removed from the vehicles maintained at a new facility at Acton or by outside contractors. The new Acton unit concentrates on seat retrimming, wheel main-tenance, sub-assembly work, electrical and electronic maintenance and machining. None of these required a rail connection, since the plan was to bring the parts for overhaul in by road. Meanwhile, Acton was allowed to tender for other work, such as the conversion of the Metropolitan Line A stock to One Person Operation.

Golders Green was the first of the line depots to take on this work in 1986, and has been quickly followed by others. These main depots have always dealt with day-to-day cleaning, inspection and maintenance. A lifting facility and inspection pits both beneath and at the side of the cars were also part of the standard provision, and do of course aid the new tasks. One should not assume that the facilities are always new; Hammersmith depot still remains largely as built by the Great Western Railway on a very restricted site. This does limit the work which can be undertaken there.

Requirements vary according to type (and age) of train; at Ealing Common on the District Line, each train receives every 24hr a check of the safety systems. Then, every 14 days, a thorough examination is made of the braking systems, the door operating mechanisms and the current collecting equipment. A more detailed examination of all equipment is carried out at 30 weeks; more extensive overhaul work is performed at 4–4½ year intervals.

There are 245 route miles served by Underground trains, of which 20 miles are in 'cut and cover' tunnels, 88 miles are in tube tunnels, and 137 miles are in the open. In 1971/72, mileages were officially remeasured in kilometres; while the location of the zero point for the system is really academic, the choice of the now defunct Ongar sand drag for this honour seemed a little quaint.

The track is the literal foundation of the railway: it has to be strong and resilient enough to withstand the weight, speed and frequency of rail traffic to be run upon it, sufficiently stable to offset the worst that climate and weather can do, and to wear well and minimise the requirements for maintenance and, ultimately, renewal. For the sake of good

relations with the surrounding property owners, it must also offer reasonably unobtrusive running.

Early days saw much experience being gained the hard way. On the Bakerloo, it was decided to lower the rails into the tunnels down vertical shafts, turning them at the bottom to reach the trackbed. This meant that 36ft was the longest length that could be accommodated. The Central London Railway opted for 44-ton locomotives to haul their trains. These 28 machines were built by the General Electric Company of America, and were of the double-bogie type, with a centrally placed cab and sloping front and rear ends. They were quickly blamed for vibration in the properties above. Investigation narrowed the problem down to a relatively flimsy track construction combined with a high proportion of unsprung locomotive weight. Rebuilding of the locomotives reduced the nuisance, but the solution was the adoption of multiple-unit operation. Recommendations which

followed from this incident included enlarged tunnel clearances in future construction, and deeper rail sections to give added stiffness.

The corrugation of running rails was also discovered as a source of noise nuisance for passengers, and the 'roaring rails' phenomenon can still be found occasionally. Part of the solution in this case was the introduction of regular rail grinding to restore the rail profile to a smooth surface. In any event, Underground travel tends to be noisy as the tunnels reflect the noise back into

the train. Experimental use of asbestos sprayed on tunnel walls in the 1930s was thankfully found too costly for general adoption, since it had to be expensively removed in recent years for health reasons. Relief was eventually forthcoming by the installation of sound-absorbent screens at below car body level, and the introduction of rail welding to reduce the number of joints. Eventually, track construction and electrification systems were standardised.

Interestingly, the old problem of environmental

noise from trains has yet to be completely solved. The lack of 'give' in the track construction on the Docklands Light Railway has led to sound baffles being installed, and rail corrugation has had to be removed by grinding.

For many years, the standard running rail on the Underground system was of 95lb/yd bull-headed section in 60ft lengths, secured by oak or steel keys to chairs in which the rail was seated, which were coach-screwed to the sleepers. Conductor rails were of 130lb/yd rectangular section in tube tunnels, and 150lb/yd flat-bottomed section elsewhere. The outer conductor rail carries the positive traction current, and will be found on the side furthest from the station platform wherever possible; the centre conductor is the return. Both are, of necessity, supported on insulators.

Wooden sleepers have many attributes, among them the relative ease of handling compared with the heavy concrete variety. Jarrah wood, a costly hardwood imported from Australia was universally used in tunnel sections, with sleeper ends held in concrete to prevent track movement. Track 'creep' could, if not prevented, lead to clearances between trains and tunnels being fouled. In the open sections, creosoted fir or similar wood sleepers at rather closer intervals was the standard.

The weakest part of the rail is at the joint with the adjoining rail, and this is always supported by closer spacing of the sleepers. However, rails become worn and are subject to cracking at joints, and moves were made to extend rail lengths. Standard rails are welded into 300ft lengths at the Permanent Way Depot, and transported to site on trains of bogie bolster wagons. Once on site, the wagons are withdrawn and longer lengths are then welded together. Constraints to the process include the allowance needed for rail expansion, (of little import in the tunnels as the temperature remains

fairly constant), and the insulating joints giving electrical separation within each running rail, required for signalling purposes. For the rails themselves, flat bottom section is now standard, although some locations have been thus equipped for many years.

Much of the trackwork now needs thorough renewal from the foundations upwards, and studies are under way as to how this might best be achieved. Track fires in tunnels need to be eliminated, and involve more people than just the Civil Engineer. Work under consideration includes screeding all ballast, use of non-flammable rail lubricants, eliminating the hydraulic handbrake on trains and its propensity to drip oil, train-mounted transponders to detect conductor rail gaps and cut the current without sparking, thermo-energy cameras on trains to

measure temperature changes and, perhaps in the long term, laying fibre optic cables in the tunnels able to detect to the nearest metre local rises in temperature of 2°C.

What is permissible in terms of track geometry will affect the speeds attainable and the type of rolling stock which can be run; furthermore, it is the most restrictive of the curves or junction layouts on a railway which is the determining factor. One of the advantages of a light rail system is its greater ability to accept these constraints, but for the Underground a maximum gradient of 1 in 30, and curves of not less than 20 chains radius are desirable. At junctions, curvature is eased as far as possible, but space constraints in older tunnels frequently result in less than ideal situations. In any event, trains need to clear junctions as quickly as possible to keep the throughput of traffic moving, and in this sense 'clearance' is what the signalling system will accept.

Points and crossings all receive heavy wear, as the wheels passing over them deliver a series of blows. The tougher manganese steel is used in busier locations, since it is not only the capital cost but also the disruption caused by replacement or by welding repairs which justify its use. Wearing of all rails, particularly on sharp curves, may also be eased by the use of rail lubricators which use the wheels of passing trains to spread a film of grease for distances of up to half a mile.

Points are operated by compressed air. Movements actuated by the signalling apparatus complete a number of electrical circuits, one of which opens a valve to admit compressed air to the cylinder of an air engine placed alongside the points, and the ensuing thrust of the piston moves the point blades across. This gives rise to the characteristic 'hiss — crash', which can be observed when points are changed. Air supplies are contained in the piping which is present on the walls of all running tunnels. Facing points, that is where the approaching train has the choice of route, must be locked in position to prevent their

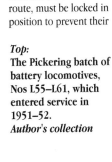
Top:
The Pickering batch of battery locomotives, Nos L55–L61, which entered service in 1951–52.
Author's collection

Left:
Night Watch, 1949. This was one of several advertisements keeping readers informed of the work of London Transport.
Author's collection

movement during the passage of the train, but those which are always trailing to the direction of traffic may be unworked, with the blades being pushed across by the leading wheels. Some electrically-operated points are now being installed.

Track mechanisation and maintenance are nowadays highly mechanised, and the depot for the whole of the Underground system is at Lillie Bridge, west of Earl's Court. Despite its space limitations, it is well situated at the geographical centre of the system which minimises the valuable time taken to run works trains in non-traffic hours, though it is no longer connected to the Railtrack system via the West London line.

Recent remodelling of the premises has provided a new points and crossings workshop, a new railway track layout to separate road and rail movements in the depot, the rationalisation of storage facilities and the installation of a new maintenance area for battery locomotives. Part of the depot has been covered by an elevated raft supporting a new exhibition hall for Earl's Court.

Rail welding is carried out at Ruislip. Flash butt welding consists of placing the rail butts, or ends, together, and passing high tension current through them. The rails are drawn apart slightly during the operation to create an arc, and when this has been done a few times the butt becomes so hot and soft that when pressed tightly together they fuse into one.

A fleet of wagons for track maintenance purposes is retained. These include ballast hoppers and flat wagons for carrying pre-assembled sections of track. Of interest are the specialist vehicles, which include four cranes.

The movement of a crane to any part of the Underground system imposes severe limitations upon design if it is to negotiate tube tunnels successfully. The limitation was overcome in 1955 when two Taylor Hubbard cranes, each weighing 36 tons, were put into service. Previously, over 100 miles of Underground open track could be reached only by long detours or not at all. Although required to operate within tube gauge, the cranes had to be capable of slewing a complete revolution and to have a tail radius which would effectively clear cable posts and platforms with the minimum of obstruction to traffic on parallel tracks when working; axle loading was not allowed to exceed 12 tons. This required some design ingenuity, particularly in the articulation of the foot of the jib, which is necessary to negotiate curves in tube tunnels. The articulation is automatic when the jib is lowered on to the jib carrying wagon, and the re-engagement of the foot of the jib when raised for use is also fully automatic.

A five-car tunnel cleaning train was built at Acton in the 1970s, and acts as a giant vacuum cleaner in

tube tunnels during non-traffic hours.

A fleet of tamping and lining machines from the Austrian firm of Plasser and Theurer carries out by machine tasks that a few years ago were left to careful observation and measurement followed by hard physical work. To find out where this work is most needed, a new Track Recording Train entered service in 1987. It consists of an instrumented 1973 stock trailer, specially modified by British Rail at Derby, between two 1960 stock pilot cars. Other pilot cars for ballast trains and moving trains or parts of trains around the system other than under their own power are formed from old passenger driving motor cars.

Traction for engineers' trains was provided by the fleet of retained steam locomotives after passenger train haulage passed to the L&NER in 1937. These locomotives eventually wore out, and it was ironic that just as the British Railways publicity machine was being cranked into action to extol the advantages of modern types of traction, Britain's most completely electrified system should issue a confession of faith in steam, albeit for very specialised purposes only. In 1957, the Underground acquired Western Region Pannier Tanks Nos 7711 and 5752, renumbered them L90 and L91, painted them in lined maroon livery and set them to work on miscellaneous duties. According to London Transport, the minimal use to which the locomotives were put meant that retention of steam was a viable proposition. Battery locomotives were considered, but their cost and the practice of working them in tandem told against them. So, replacement with WR surplus steam was proceeded with until a maximum of 11 Pannier Tanks was in service. They were finally withdrawn in

1971, being replaced by three Sentinel diesels (themselves now defunct) and more battery locomotives…

Most haulage around the system is now provided by the battery locomotive fleet, usually placed one at each end of their trains to speed reversal. All are of 'tube' loading gauge to enable them to pass anywhere without restraint, and have variable height drawgear to suit both 'tube' and 'surface' stock coupling heights. Wherever possible they operate on current obtained from the conductor rail, during which time the batteries (on the more modern locomotives) are recharged in readiness for use where no live supply exists. Charging time is about 1hr for each hour of discharge. A fleet of 32 such locomotives is seen as about right; built by various manufacturers over the last 50 years, they cost about £2.5 million each.

In some years, winter weather precautions are hardly needed. Sleet locomotives were used to help in solving the current collection problems during

Below:
The battery locomotive fleet has been built in small numbers over many years. They have driving positions at both ends and may use traction current from the live rail when this is available. This is No L44, the first of 11 machines built by BREL Doncaster in 1974 and pictured there before delivery.
British Railways Board

winter weather by the use of antifreeze solution, liquid sprayers and wire brushes on the conductor rails. Electrically-operated pneumatic control actuated the valves controlling the de-icing fluid, and the cylinders which lowered the brushes and ice-cutting rollers to the rails. These locomotives were built out of redundant CLR motor cars of 1903 vintage, but have now been replaced by equipment on a number of passenger cars. Night-time heating of conductor rails was tried as a frost precaution; the method used was to short circuit the negative and positive rails so that their resistance to the 600V dc traction current being passed through them raised the rail temperature and melted any snow or ice. This method could only be used out of traffic hours, but once trains started to run, their passage was usually enough to keep the current rails clear. In 1963, 17 miles of track on rising gradients on the Metropolitan, Piccadilly and Central Lines were being thus treated.

The autumn has always brought the problem of falling leaves, and various methods of removing them before they are ground to a slithery paste on the rail have been tried. This included water cannon, but in 1983 a Unimog tractor and trailer which could run on road or rail was acquired to vacuum up the leaves as they fell. The tractor unit had a cabinet containing a centrifugal fan, and a flexible hose with suction nozzle to draw up the leaves from the track into the cabinet. They then passed into the trailer van where they were

collected for disposal. This unit was kept at Chalfont & Latimer station high in the Chilterns, where many of the worst problems are to be found, and made night time sorties. However, it was found that Unimogs could not be relied upon to operate track circuits at all times; the two which remain are now restricted to depot shunting purposes only.

No precautions were possible for the night of 15–16 October 1987, when hurricane-force winds swept southern Britain, after which over 600 trees had to be cleared from the tracks. The more serious damage was to signal cables, cut by falling debris, while the stability of some embankments previously bound by tree roots had to be attended to in the longer term. Even the Epping–Ongar line, which had 60 fallen trees to itself, was back in business three days later.

The early tube railways began the tradition of self-sufficiency in power generation, and the City & South London Railway built its own power station at Stockwell when it opened in 1890; the Central London Railway's establishment was at Wood Lane. The electrification of the Metropolitan and the Metropolitan District Railways spawned coal-fired power stations at Neasden and at Lots Road, Chelsea respectively in 1905. By this time, the District and three of the tube railways were under the unified control of Yerkes, and Lots Road which was them claimed to be the biggest power station in the world, provided power for them all. Later, the power station at Greenwich was added, after being

Left:
A four-wheeled hopper ballast wagon, No
HW235; this 1936-built vehicle was fitted with
both central and side ballast chutes controlled
by wheels on the near end. Both surface height
shackle couplers and tube height ward couplers
were fitted.
Modern Transport/Ian Allan Library

Below:
The pair of brake vans converted from 10-ton
flat wagons in 1950 provided little
accommodation for the guard! In the midst of
the Metropolitan's Amersham electrification,
during which they were used on long-welded
rail trains, work progresses at Northwood.
J. A. Rosser

released from its former role of supplying power to
the LCC tramways and, later, trolleybuses. Supply is
now standardised at 630V dc on all lines, using the
fourth rail system.

Lots Road was built on the banks of the Thames.
It burned about 6,000 tons of small grained 'pea'
coal a week coming in by barge. Conveyors
transported the coal by bucket conveyor to bunkers
over the 32 boilers in the basement. These were fed
mechanically, and the draught for the fire raised by
the four 275ft chimneys and assisted by fans. An
agreeable description referred to 'the old warm,
gently roaring power house with its glowing, slowly
moving chain grates; its glistening rows of humming
generators; and its parquet-floored control room, all
knobbly with polished dials and instruments with,
above, thin plumes of smoke drifting from its tall
chimneys'.

Each boiler produced about 50,000lb of steam
each hour, used to turn the nine turbo-generators

arranged in two rows above the boiler basement.
Their output was electricity at 11,000V, three phase
at $33\frac{1}{3}$Hz. Jutting out into the river bed were the
two water intake pipes of 9ft and 7ft 6in diameter
respectively, supplying cooling water at up to nine
million gallons each hour. After passing through
screens to remove debris, the water was passed over
the condensers to cool them, and returned to warm
up Chelsea Creek. The condensed steam in the
boilers was then recycled, and any losses were made
good after purification by supplies from artesian
wells.

All this was swept away in a modernisation
programme in 1968, with natural gas or oil taking
the place of coal as the primary energy source.
Neasden was closed at the same time, and provision
made in the investment programme for supplying
power to meet the needs of the expanding
Underground system. Lots Road was re-equipped,
with six vertical oil-fired boilers serving new turbo-

alternators. The voltage generated is now 22,000V at
50Hz, and the total capacity of the plant increased
by 7% to 180,000kW. Shortly afterwards, in 1972,
Greenwich was also re-equipped, but with gas
turbine alternators.

Although outer sections of the Underground have
been fed by the National Grid for half a century, the
principle of generating the base requirement of
electricity was not challenged until recent years.
However, a number of failures of power supplies for
technical reasons served to bring trains to an abrupt
stop all over the system. In October 1979, an
explosion in one of the boilers blew out the other
two which were in use at the time. As this happened
at 14.30 when Greenwich was not operating, this
caused a complete power loss in the central area.
Although Greenwich came on load within a couple
of minutes, this was not sufficient to prevent a
shutdown.

Supply was restored in 20min, but it took more
than an hour to get most of the trains running
again, with disruption lasting for the rest of the day.
Industry sources were highly critical of the
Underground's generating policy. 'London
Transport has two choices — find an alternative

Above:
The Tunnel Cleaning Train is made up of former 1938 cars and intermediate purpose-built trailers. Two filter cars unload dust collected by the nozzle car. *John Glover*

Left:
A new layout was installed at Minories Junction, Aldgate, in 1922. This picture shows the complications of fourth rail electrification and the precautions needed to ensure that collector shoes are not damaged when passing over pointwork. *Real Photos/Ian Allan Library*

source of economic electricity to operate in parallel with Lots Road, or go on taking the risk of spasmodic shutdowns' said the Electrical Times. 'Its problem is that one of its power stations is specifically designed for base-load operation and the other for peak demand. It could overcome some of its difficulties if it improved the efficiency of one or two of its gas turbine sets at Greenwich and ran them continuously in parallel with Lots Road.' However, it turned out that internal power supplies were not necessarily any more secure than the Grid could offer nor, as it happened, any cheaper.

Further incidents in 1993, which crippled the Central Line and up to five others for extended periods, were traced to three separate faults. These were in an earthing cable at Lots Road, a cable failure between Mile End and Greenwich, and a transformer failure at Newbury Park. They demonstrated both the vulnerability of the Underground to power supply problems (with a bill estimated at £2 million for repairs, lost revenue and passenger compensation), and the importance of adequate investment in the largely unseen infrastructure.

A review of long term requirements and the cost of running power stations and installing new generation plant every 30 years or so has come to the view that Lots Road should be closed. Normal supplies would be taken from the National Grid, with bulk supply points at Lots Road and Aldgate, together with an existing point at Neasden. Back-up battery systems installed at stations will be capable of powering emergency lighting, PA systems and train radio.

Above:
London Underground's Track Recording Train consists of an ex-1973 stock trailer car No TRC666 marshalled between two 1960 Cravens motor cars Nos L132/2. The whole is turned out in a fetching red, grey and black livery and works around the system on a regular basis. The ensemble is seen here at Wimbledon on 28 October 1988.
Chris Wilson

Greenwich would be retained but restricted to providing emergency cover. Four gas turbines at Greenwich would insure against a total power failure in southeast England, and could be brought into use within a quarter of an hour to take over from the batteries and to provide power for tunnel and station lighting, ventilation, pumps, lifts and escalators. This would enable passengers to be evacuated from tunnels; however, there would be insufficient power to provide for traction purposes.

Traction supplies for the Underground are fed from Lots Road and other supply sources to switch houses located at Cromwell Curve, Coburg Street and Stockwell, where they are transformed down to 11,000V.

The function of substation equipment is to receive high tension current, step it down to the traction voltage, and rectify the supply from alternating current as generated to direct current at 630V as required by the traction motors. The current then flows through track feeders to the conductor rail, each length of which is bonded or welded to its neighbour to minimise voltage drop.

Over the whole system there are approximately 100 substations owned by London Underground or, in some cases, by Railtrack. The substations are unmanned, and use mercury arc or silicon rectifiers. Current can be cut by the operation of relays in the substation which trip the track breakers; all stations have the facility to do this in emergency, as have train drivers when underground by pinching together the tunnel wires.

Each section of track is fed by the substation at each end (double end feed), apart from terminal sections (single end feed). Electrified sections are

Left:
An unidentified sleet locomotive at Neasden, 6 February 1963. Each was converted in 1939/40 from a pair of 1903 Central London Railway Driving Motors, welded together to form one vehicle. The de-icing equipment was carried on two central unpowered bogies with the tank for the fluid above them. The outer bogies retained the traction equipment. *J. A. Rosser*

Above:
Two rail grinding cars were introduced in 1956, rebuilt from pre-1938 tube stock. The cars carry grinding equipment and operate between a pair of pilot cars. On 16 July 1981 car No RG803 visited the Kingston–Shepperton line on trial between motor cars L13^1/$_2$; the objective was to see if grinding could help solve the wheelslip problems on the BR Class 508 EMUs.
Colin J. Marsden

Left:
The maintenance of the Underground takes many forms. In this 1989 picture of Euston, Northern Line Charing Cross branch, a vacuum cleaner is being used to clean station track areas.

discrete, and separated from each other by gaps in
the conductor rails; in the event of a failure a
section can be neutralised without affecting nearby
parts of the line. If a section in advance of an
approaching train is dead, a triangle of three red
warning lights alerts the driver to an approaching
train. The driver should attempt to stop short or, if
this is not possible, to ensure his train is completely
on the dead section. Otherwise, he will bridge the
section gap and render the section in advance live,
which could endanger persons on the track or
otherwise exacerbate the incident which caused the
current to be discharged in the first place.

Substations also provide current for ventilating
fans, lifts, escalators, lighting and pumps.

The City & South London Railway used a third-
rail system from its opening in 1890. The current
rail carrying a potential of 500V dc was laid between
the rails, offset to one side to keep the pick-up
shoes clear of the couplings. The return current
used the train wheels and the running rails. The
Central London Railway adopted a true centre third
10 years later. This arrangement was not popular;
another principal British exponent (who used the
sleepers and ballast as well for the return) was
Meccano Ltd, makers of Hornby Dublo electric
trains!

In 1898, the Metropolitan Railway decided at last
that it would electrify its lines, after 35 years of
steam operation underground. The means by which
the choice of system was made has been related in
Chapter 3; here it is necessary only to record that
the preference for fourth rather than third rail
electrification stemmed from fears of corroding
pipes and cables. The arrangement placed the
positive rail outside the running rails, usually on the
far side from the platform face in stations. The
return rail is located centrally between the running
rails. All underground lines were built or later
converted to this standard, although on the CLR
(today's Central Line), the changes in curvature in
the tunnels still require a limited repositioning of

the positive rail to maintain clearances.

North of Queen's Park on the Bakerloo Line and
on the Richmond and Wimbledon branches of the
District, Underground trains run over lines
electrified on the third-rail principle. The fourth rail
here is effectively a dummy, provided to
accommodate the shoes of Underground trains. It is
bonded to the running rails, through which the
current is returned via the wheels and axles of third
rail BR trains.

A disadvantage of using relatively low voltage dc
traction current is the need for frequent substations
by the lineside. The heavy currents involved and the
cost of equipment were among the reasons that
British Railways eventually adopted ac overhead
traction supplies in the 1950s, but clearances in any
case would have been insufficient in the
Underground tunnels. One wonders how Messrs
Ganz would have fared if given the chance! In the
event, the fourth-rail dc system has worked
superbly; its only real operational vices for urban
applications are the susceptibility to frost and snow,
and the potential safety hazard.

Chapter 10

Victoria Line to the Greater London Council

Above:
One of the most visible signs of work on the Victoria Line was the Oxford Circus 'umbrella' bridge, erected over August Bank Holiday 1963. Its purpose was to allow the construction of the new station booking hall below the road junction, which took nearly five years to achieve. The umbrella was removed in April 1968.
London Transport Museum 440/102A/A5

In August 1962, the Government finally approved construction of the Victoria Line northwards from Victoria to Walthamstow. Not surprisingly, London Transport was well prepared. General principles aimed at in building the new line were:

- avoidance of curves sharper than 20 chains radius;
- stations built on a hump or saw-tooth profile (giving a falling gradient to accelerate a train leaving a station and a rising gradient approaching it);
- tunnel diameter sufficient to minimise air resistance; and

- the line to be as straight as possible (not following street patterns above) between any two points.

These ideals had to be modified as necessary to fit the line into the pattern of existing stations, tunnels and sewers.

Approval came just before a pleasant interlude to mark the Underground's centenary in 1963. A gathering of invited transport officials from various parts of the world was shown the modern system at work and, in contrast, part of its history in review. The description provides an interesting snapshot of the Underground of over 30 years ago. A plaque commemorating the centenary was placed outside

Baker Street station.

Essentially, this was a Metropolitan Railway occasion, which was reflected in the exhibits. The parade of 15 trains took place at Neasden Depot, on

Above:
**Concrete segments to line 20 miles or so of
running tunnels plus station tunnels and
escalator shafts are trainload-type traffic. A BTH
Class 15 delivers segments to Oakleigh Park for
Victoria Line construction on 13 April 1964.
This site is now occupied by a housing estate.**
British Railways

23 May. The first was Metropolitan Railway Class A
locomotive No 23 and two contractors' wagons.
No 23 was built in 1866 and survived in traffic until
1948, when it was withdrawn after 82 years of
service. The locomotive was subsequently restored
externally to its 1903 condition and resided in the
(then) British Transport Museum at Clapham. The
two contractors' wagons had been doctored to
resemble the vehicles used by Smith and Knight,
builders of the Paddington–Euston Square section
of the original Metropolitan Railway, to convey a
party of VIPs along the still unfinished line on
24 May 1862. Twenty-four members of the LT
Musical and Dramatic Society, attired in period
costume, recreated the scene. Cheating slightly, the
entourage was propelled by battery locomotive
No L76.

The train was followed by Metropolitan Railway
Class E 0-4-4T No L44 with milk van No 3 and four
bogie coaches. No L44 was the first of the Class E
locomotives to be built at Neasden works in 1896
for the extension of the Metropolitan's services into
the Chilterns. The milk van was built at the same
time by the Birmingham Railway Carriage & Wagon

Co, and was used in passenger trains on the outer
sections of the Metropolitan until 1936, when it was
transferred to the engineers' department for use as
a tool van in the breakdown train. The four
passenger coaches were built between 1898 and
1900, and were withdrawn and sold to the Bluebell
Railway when the Chesham branch was electrified.

Third in the procession was electric locomotive
No 1 *John Lyon* with a six-coach train of
'Dreadnought' stock. Locomotive No 1 was the first
of a batch of 20 which replaced the original 1905
locomotives in 1922/23. They were employed
primarily on through London–Aylesbury trains as
far as Rickmansworth until 1961. At this time, four
were still in use for shunting.

First in the line of multiple-units was a three-car
train of compartment T stock. The Metropolitan
preferred compartment stock for its longer distance
trains, due to its greater seating capacity compared
with saloons. It was followed by a four-car train of
District F stock, by then confined to East London
Line services.

Next came a three-car train of P stock with
Metadyne control, which had replaced early
Metropolitan electric trains on the Uxbridge line
just prior to the 1939–45 war. This stock was still in
the process of being converted to normal resistance
control with PCM equipment. To bring the surface
stock story right up to date, the P stock was
followed by a single unit of silver A stock, built by
Cravens of Sheffield in 1961.

The inclusion of some tube stock in the parade

was justified by the projection of Piccadilly Line
trains to Uxbridge and the Bakerloo extension to
Stanmore, a former Metropolitan appendage. Pre-
1938 stock was used initially on both these
extensions although it was by then fast
disappearing; it was compared with the 1938 tube
stock with its increased carrying capacity due to the
PCM control equipment being placed beneath the
floor. A few of these trains were then in service on
the Piccadilly, but they monopolised the Bakerloo,
albeit with one trailer of pre-1938 stock in each
train.

An example of the 1959 aluminium successors for
the Piccadilly Line was then shown, which was
eventually to oust all the pre-1938 rolling stock and,
with the similar 1962 stock, most of the 1938 stock
as well.

Attention next turned to Metropolitan 'F' class
0-6-2T No L52 with an engineers' train. No L52 was
one of four engines which were built in 1901 for
use on freight trains on the Aylesbury and Uxbridge
lines. In 1937 they were transferred to engineers'
duties, with No L52 being the last survivor and
about to be superseded by a further arrival of
0-6-0PT locomotives from BR's Western Region.
Pannier No L98 was shown on a cable-laying train,
with special wagons carrying drums of new power
or signalling cable; one end of the cable was fixed to
a convenient point by the track and the wagon
pulled slowly along, paying out the cable which was
supported on brackets at the side of the track.

Battery locomotive No L57 used battery power

Left:
The Victoria Line was a triumph of the 1960s. Entirely underground except for the depot, great use was made of its connectional potential with other lines. Only Pimlico has no interchange facilities. At Finsbury Park, rearrangement of the station tunnels took place to give a cross-platform facility to the Piccadilly Line. Using one of the tracks originally used by the Northern City Line, a 1967 stock train for Brixton was photographed on 18 March 1982. *John Glover*

Below:
At the beginning of the afternoon peak period, a 1967 stock train makes its way from Northumberland Park depot to the ramp which will take it down into the tunnels and Seven Sisters station, a mile away. *John Glover*

while the current in the conductor rails was switched off and the crew of the long welded rail train which it was hauling gave a demonstration using 400ft rails. When being transported from the depot to the working site the rails — up to 18 may be loaded at a time — are secured only to the middle wagon; with the ends free to move, the rails bend with the train as it goes round curves. Further lateral movement is prevented by the stanchions located along the sides of the wagon. The whole then resembles a gigantic leaf spring. The assembled guests were then shown the ease with which these rails, weighing over $4\frac{1}{2}$ tons each, are handled. To load a rail length, the end is winched up and placed in a roller mounted in a hinged frame on the rear wagon. The whole train is then propelled under the rail, until the last 20ft overhangs the roller. This is hauled on by the

Above:
A station which owes its appearance almost entirely to its former Great Eastern Railway parentage is Chigwell, seen here with both the Woodford-Hainault shuttles. The trains are composed of single units of 1967 Victoria line tube stock. The Automatic Train Operation equipment was still in use at the time that this 3 October 1980 picture was taken.
John Glover

winch. Both loading and unloading operations were carried out by the eight-man crew, the entire manoeuvre taking 10min.

Also on view was the Chief Mechanical Engineer's Instruction Train. This consisted of five yellow painted ex-Bakerloo Line 1920 Cammell Laird trailers of 1920 vintage, which had been fitted out as a mobile school. These were the first production tube cars to have air doors from new. Using adapted pre-1938 motor cars as power, the train was taken from depot to depot to give instruction courses on new train equipment and refresher courses to staff responsible for maintenance work on Underground trains.

The 1960s were the age of the big holes in London, when the scars left from the bombing of WW2 were finally healed. The Barbican was one of the largest construction projects, and at the behest of the City of London, London Transport diverted

the Metropolitan Line to a straighter and more southerly route between Aldersgate (now Barbican) and Moorgate. This work first entailed the moving of the Widened Lines. The 500yd of new railway were constructed by the 'cut and cover' method, reinforced concrete being used both to enclose the line and support the Barbican development above. This work was completed in 1965.

Meanwhile, progress with Victoria Line construction by September 1966 saw the work of the shields, in cutting the running and station tunnels, complete. The earlier experimental work with a 'drum digger' shield and a groutless method of installing the tunnel lining had proved useful and had been adopted for the main construction. During 35 months, this had involved 44 different tunnel drives starting from 21 shafts sunk for that purpose, the last drive breaking through an already completed tunnel section near King's Cross. There remained only a few short sections of running tunnel to be excavated without the use of a shield. The whole of the line is underground apart from the depot, located at Northumberland Park.

At Victoria, the ticket hall for both the Victoria and District Lines was sited under the existing forecourt of the main line station. The Victoria Line's platforms lie 59ft below; beyond, to the south, there were four sidings, two of which subsequently formed the start of the Brixton extension.

The Railtrack station was largely built over a filled in canal basin. It was necessary to stabilise part of

the thick stratum of water-bearing sand and gravel to permit deep mining beneath it, by injecting chemicals through a large number of narrow pipes driven 35ft into the gravel over the affected area to harden it.

A large part of the land south of Victoria down to the Thames was ancient low drainage ground, referred to as early as the year 951 as Bullinga Fen, into which the River Tyburn is thought to have drained. This once open river is now either non-existent or reduced to a subterranean trickle, but it is roughly beneath and along its alignment that the Victoria Line now runs. This is northward to cross deep under The Mall opposite the Queen Victoria Memorial, then beneath Green Park to the station of that name.

The Victoria Line platforms lie just to the west and above the Piccadilly Line station, connected to the latter by a subway, and to the new ticket hall by a bank of three escalators. From Green Park the line, having crossed the Piccadilly Line roughly at right angles, runs north again beneath Mayfair to Oxford Circus for interchange with the Bakerloo and Central Lines. It has climbed steadily to follow the land contour rising from the Thames, but is still 70ft below the surface.

Tunnelling here was a major job, as the tubes swing out to flank the Bakerloo on both sides, thus providing the ideal cross-platform interchange. Building this composite station below ground took longer than any other along the line, and the only visible surface evidence of the day and night activity

going on below was the 6,600-ton steel 'umbrella' bridging the whole of Oxford Circus itself. This carried all the street traffic 3ft 6in above its former level. Below the Circus is a large circular ticket hall and below that are five escalator shafts, separate Victoria Line station tunnels, subways, passages and concourses linking it all together, including the Central Line at right angles.

At Oxford Circus, the engineers were faced with an unusually intricate task in underpinning part of a large store and transferring the load from its foundations to the southbound Victoria Line station tunnel. Below the third basement, the building's columns were underpinned with massive prestressed concrete, the bottom layer cast in weaker concrete. Later, the tunnel shield drove beneath a saddle shape cut in the base of the concrete, and finally the station tunnel segments were expanded by jacks to produce the necessary stresses in the ground.

The line continues north from Oxford Circus station, cutting diagonally across a grid pattern of streets above to Warren Street. Along the route the northbound tunnel was made to roll over the southbound and continues thus to the station 90ft below ground level. New escalators connected the Victoria Line platforms with the existing escalators to the Northern Line at an intermediate landing; there is no low level connection between the two.

Beyond Warren Street the tunnels swing northeast to Euston, another deep level underground complex which provides

interconnection between the Railtrack terminal station above, and both the City (via Bank) and West End branches of the Northern Line. The reversed tunnels emerge into a combined, one level, double-island Euston station, with the northbound tunnel on the right and the southbound tunnel on the left. Across their respective platforms are the northbound City branch trains to Camden Town and the southbound City trains to King's Cross. These platforms are unusual in that trains run in opposite directions on each side of them. One mildly odd result is that to travel from Euston to King's Cross one can catch either a northbound Victoria Line train or a southbound Northern Line via Bank service. Pedestrian subways give access to Northern Line via Charing Cross trains.

The line rises gradually to King's Cross, a congested maze of tunnels between which the new line and its platforms had to be threaded. A complicating factor was the brick arch of the Midland curve, now used by Thameslink services. This had to be removed and replaced by a new structure of reinforced concrete so as to provide room for a subway. Lower down, part of the Victoria Line's station tunnel crown is positioned a few feet below the foundations of the Midland curve and the Circle Line tunnels. As these are in brick with either no inverts or inverts of varying depth, an extra robust tunnel shield was employed here to exert great pressure in the ground at its working face during excavation. Finally, extra heavy steel tunnel lining was expanded against the

Above:
Former GWR 0-6-0PT No 7760, now L90, passes Northwick Park with the 'Croxley Tip' train from Neasden in March 1969. Steam had already departed from main line BR by this date; on the Underground it was to continue until 1971.
Victor C. K. Allen

ground by powerful jacks and steel wedges, so as to maintain at all times equilibrium of ground stresses and prevent settlement of the brick tunnel foundations.

Presently, King's Cross is the only 'four-tier' station on the Underground system. The work here included the excavation of two horizontal tunnels, one 12ft and one 15ft in diameter, both of them for draught relief and each about 75ft long. They connect the Piccadilly and Victoria Line stations to a new vertical air shaft. The Victoria Line is above the other tube lines but below the Metropolitan. At ticket hall level, the Fleet River sewer had to be diverted and recontained in a new concrete ring and box construction, which at one point nearly obtrudes into the ticket hall. All this work had to thread between existing tunnels and shafts in deep earth, without any visual means of pinpointing obstructions as would be the case above ground.

Beyond King's Cross the tunnels curve and ascend to follow the rising ground to Highbury & Islington, providing interchange there with what was then the Northern City Line and later became part of the Great Northern Electrics.

About half-way along this 1½-mile stretch, the running tunnels resume their normal positions by the southbound crossing over the northbound. The old Highbury station was rebuilt extensively both above and below ground, and a joint station building constructed to serve also BR's North London Line. The northbound Northern Line platform became the Victoria Line southbound; the other pair of lines use new tunnels and platforms. The result was a very positive improvement to interchange facilities.

The running tunnels continue a further mile to Finsbury Park, where the old Great Northern & City Line and the Piccadilly Line stations, opened in 1904 and 1906 respectively, were utterly transformed. The below ground works here involved building step-plate junctions around tunnels through which trains continued to run, building underground crossovers, and ultimately switching trains from old lines to new. This resulted in southbound Piccadilly and Victoria Line trains using the old GN&C former terminal platforms, while the northbound trains of both lines used the former Piccadilly station. Again, the result was cross-platform interchange between a pair of lines in both directions of travel, with further BR services available 'upstairs'.

Descending steadily now to Seven Sisters, the 1.96 miles of this stretch became the longest distance underground on the system between adjacent stations. This is the interchange with BR electric services to Enfield Town and Broxbourne. The station has three platforms, the centre one leaving the eastbound line just west of the station and subsequently offering access to Northumberland Park depot. The outer ones are the north and southbound tracks, the latter receiving the exit road from the depot a little to the east of Seven Sisters. The pair of depot tracks swing northward in tunnel for about ½ mile, coming to the surface alongside the Railtrack Lea Valley line. The extensive site was built to cater for the complete fleet of 1967 stock trains.

The tube running tunnels continue northeast, descending to Tottenham Hale where Lea Valley rail connections are made for passengers. The line then rises again and swings eastward to continue a mile to Blackhorse Road (interchange of a sort with the Tottenham and Hampstead Railtrack line), and to its terminus below the Railtrack Chingford branch station of Walthamstow Central.

Beyond Finsbury Park, the Victoria Line broke virgin territory for the Underground; from Tottenham it followed beneath the old road over the River Lea and then through misty marsh and reservoir country on the route to Epping Forest. The Great Eastern Railway colonised Walthamstow and other parts of northeast London with steam trains from the 1870s on, but the Victoria Line had no such development aspirations. Instead, it aimed to attract traffic from this builtup area and beyond through interchange with the surface railways.

All this northern end of the line's running tunnels were driven through blue clay, as was part of the southern end, and excavated by shield and rotary cutters. For the larger diameter station tunnels and for a crossover at Walthamstow the tunnel lining is in cast iron segment form, and the running tunnels in concrete segments. Much of the southern end was lined with cast-iron segments, some of the new design similar to those used in the experimental tunnel, but for water-bearing and other difficult ground, conventional bolted cast-iron

segments were used.

Furnishing of the line was according to the practice of the time, and used wood sleepers concreted into the road bed to support bullhead rail, long welded into 300ft lengths at Northumberland Park and fed into the tunnels from there. A narrow concrete shelf was affixed to the tunnel walls at platform height to contain the noise of steel wheel on steel rail. The station decor was plain to today's eyes with grey tiling everywhere (except where it has since fallen off), relieved only by a motif illustrative of each station. While the maze at Warren Street and the cameo of Queen Victoria were apt and well chosen, the association of seven trees with Seven Sisters was tenuous, while the use of the Doric Arch, then so recently demolished, to denote Euston seemed almost vindictive.

The opportunity to construct a brand-new line was unique for London Transport, and the decision was made to go for full automation of operation as represented by Automatic Train Operation (ATO). As applied, it reflected the technology of the time, and

is described here in some detail.

Under non-automatic conditions, the train driver applies power to the traction motors, cuts it off or applies the brakes as dictated by the track and signalling conditions. With ATO, the human element is almost completely removed, and the train is under a dual system of control. The most important system safeguards the train by employing an inductive pick-up to receive continuous coded signals from the track, with equipment on board the train to interpret and act upon these signals. No code means no movement. This is the safety signalling system. The other, the 'driver command' system, receives impulses at predetermined spots along the track. These cause power to be applied, or cut off for coasting and the brakes to be applied; a series of commands controls the stopping of trains in the station platforms.

In more detail, the safety signalling codes are formed by current from the mains supply. In a relay

Below:
Victoria Line Automatic Train Operation.

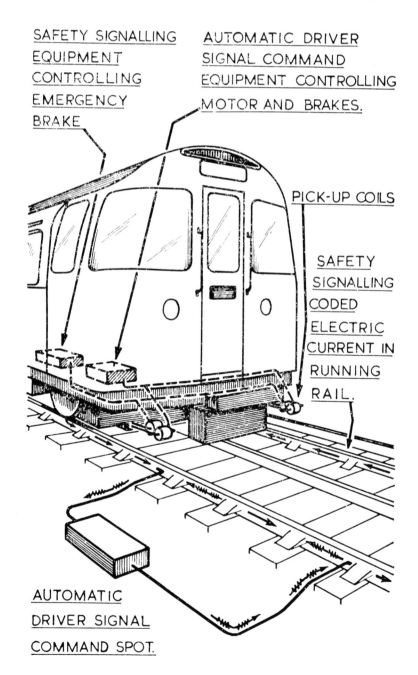

SAFETY SIGNALLING EQUIPMENT CONTROLLING EMERGENCY BRAKE

AUTOMATIC DRIVER SIGNAL COMMAND EQUIPMENT CONTROLLING MOTOR AND BRAKES.

PICK-UP COILS

SAFETY SIGNALLING CODED ELECTRIC CURRENT IN RUNNING RAIL.

AUTOMATIC DRIVER SIGNAL COMMAND SPOT.

issues a command to
cut the motors.
For example, in
operation a train
may have left one
station, but some
distance ahead
another train is
standing in the next
station. Between the
trains would be a
'420' signal coded
section (speed unrestricted), followed by the
restrictive '270' and then '180' coded sections.
Ahead of that a 'no code' section protects the train
in advance. When the advance train clears the
station to leave an unimpeded run to the following
train, the latter would be able to proceed under
'420' code to a 15,000Hz command spot, cutting
the flow of current to the motors and causing the
train to coast to the first of the command spots at
the approach to the station. Here it would pass
successively command spots at 3,000, 2,500, 2,000,
1,500 and 1,000Hz, each producing a 5mph speed
reduction through to a final halt. This would be at a
predetermined platform stop, which the train
would approach and stop at in a gradual braking
curve, regardless of its load at the time.

All that is left for the driver, or rather 'train
operator' to do is to initiate starting the train by
depressing simultaneously a pair of buttons on the
control desk, and operating the passenger doors.
(Manual driving can be performed in the case of
ATO failure.) For this he was deemed to need a
clear view back along the length of his train,
supplemented by closed circuit television cameras
to view from the rear. This meant straight, or nearly
straight, platforms, a condition which could not be
provided on the existing system. The Victoria Line
was the first application of One Person Operation
on the Underground, which was a welcome gain in
productivity. But overall, not using the driver as a

room this current is interrupted into codes
electronically or by the action of pendulums
operating electronic switches. One pendulum,
swinging 180 times a minute, produces a '180'
impulse code. A faster swinging pendulum
produces a '270' impulse code. This coded signal
current is fed into the running rails (which are
sectionalised by insulated joints), passing along one
rail, through the wheels and axles at the front of the
train, and then back by the other rail. Coils
mounted on the front of the train are affected by
the code in the rails, and a signal is passed to the
train equipment, amplified, and recognised by the
electrical circuits responding only to an appropriate
code frequency. A '180' code indicates that the train
is safe to proceed at up to 25mph provided current
is not being fed to the traction motors. It is made to
conform to this speed by a mechanical governor,
actuated by the train wheels, that ensures that this
speed is not exceeded for as long as the '180' code
is being transmitted. A '270' code allows the train to
run under power at up to 25mph; a '420' code
indicates that a train may proceed at full speed.
While one of these safety signal codes is being
received by the train, current from the train battery
holds an emergency brake valve in the closed
position. If the code should cease to be picked up
by the train, the current would be cut off from the
brake valve and an emergency application of the
brakes would result.

The other part of ATO is described as 'automatic
driver signal command'. These commands are also
derived from current fed into the track, but in this
case only in short 10ft sections of running rail. An
electronic generator produces current of a special
frequency which is obeyed by equipment on the
trains. Current at 100Hz equals 1mph permitted to
the trains; at 1,000Hz it equals 10mph, at 3,000Hz
30mph, and so on. One of the main purposes of the
driver command equipment is to apply the brakes
to stop the train accurately in the station, and
careful calculations are made to enable command
spots to be positioned along the track at the right
places. This, incidentally, is one of the major
difficulties in applying ATO to lines in the open,
since rail conditions and hence braking
requirements vary according to the weather.

The command signal frequency, picked up by an
inductive coil on the train, is counted by an
electronic counter and the frequency compared
with the frequency produced by a speedometer
generator on the train. Electrical circuits regulate
the train's progress to the correct predetermined
speed required, by causing brake application or
release. This occurs at station approaches, but there
are also command spots along the line where the
train has reached sufficient speed to allow it to
coast to the next station. The frequency at these
spots, 15,000Hz, is outside the speed range of the
train, and is recognised by a special circuit which

skilled man seemed to represent rather a waste of talent.

The Victoria Line is now alone in being ATO operated, the Woodford–Hainault 'guinea pig' service having reverted to normal One Person Operation. The only other installations were experiments on the District Line in the early 1960s.

Work on extending the Victoria Line south to Brixton began in 1967, shortly before the main section to the north was opened in sections in 1968 and 1969. Twin tunnels driven south led to Pimlico (built at the behest of the local authority and the only station without interchange to another railway), and on under the Thames. Crossing at its lowest point 24ft below the river bed, the line reaches Vauxhall, with interchange for British Rail. The familiar cross-platform arrangements were provided once again at Stockwell with the Northern Line. Brixton station is the terminus, serving a particularly densely populated area. The finished product, largely completed in July 1971 but with the opening of Pimlico delayed until September 1972 brought Brixton and Walthamstow, 14 miles apart, within 32 minutes of each other. It was indeed a tour de force, and in its time was hailed as the world's most highly automated underground railway.

The 1960s had not been good years for London Transport, which found itself sinking slowly into deficit despite the demands of the 1962 Act for the undertaking to pay its way. This was compounded by growing staff shortages and industrial relations problems. The Greater London Council had been created in 1963, and was complaining that if it was to be the strategic planning authority for London, it should also have control of London Transport. In their 1968 'Transport in London' White Paper, the Labour Government agreed, and was determined to hand the undertaking over to the GLC. The hope was expressed that this would offer a comprehensive approach to the efficient planning, provision, operation and financing of transport in London. There would be the 'closest possible harmony' with the wider aspects of land use and development. A new London Transport Executive was set up in 1970 under the control of the GLC (Transport London Act, 1969), 'for the purposes of implementing the policies which it is the duty of the Council to develop'. The GLC therefore became responsible for appointing the members of the Executive, establishing their general policies and approving their budgets and fares policies. The government heaved a sigh of relief; it was very much

'over to you'.

While the Victoria Line was being built, the question was inevitably 'what next?' Office space in central London was being expanded, and it was thought that further travel demands would arise. By the end of 1965, Parliamentary powers to extend the (then) Aldwych branch to Waterloo had been obtained, while proposals for a new 'Fleet Line' saw the light of day. In both cases, what actually happened proved to be somewhat different!

Both in the inter-war period and the 1950s it had seemed as if the growth in demand for travel by the Underground network would go on expanding for ever. Yet the growth was faltering. The Location of Offices Bureau did its best to encourage firms to move out of London, and by the time that the London Rail Study reported in 1974, the extensive plans and optimistic proposals for capacity increases had to be judged against a background of static traffic levels. The growth that there was began to be taken up in the outer suburbs, with centres such as Croydon, Watford and Uxbridge bearing the brunt. And, in these, there was little or no traffic for the Underground.

One development represented a loss to the Underground network. What had become a detached part of the Northern Line north of Moorgate in the frustrated expansion of the 1930s finally had its fate determined. From autumn 1975, Underground trains were withdrawn from the Moorgate to Finsbury Park (latterly Drayton Park) section, and the line was handed over to British Rail's Great Northern Electrics. It had always been a difficult part of the Underground to work; for instance, to transfer trains to Acton Works, it was latterly necessary to drag them via a spur up to British Rail at Finsbury Park, haul them down to King's Cross and the Widened Lines, and back on to the Underground. Transfer was then via the Circle Line, Earl's Court and Hammersmith.

British Rail's suburban electric services started late in 1976, connecting Moorgate with Welwyn Garden City and Hertford North. The Class 313 trains were dual voltage, using 25kV ac south to Drayton Park where they entered the tunnel section. While standing in the platform, the pantograph was lowered and the current pick-up was made from the 750V dc third rail instead. A dead overhead wire section is installed in the tunnel as far as Highbury in case the pantograph does not lock down!

Great Northern services on the Widened Lines were withdrawn. These tracks were later transferred to British Rail for the use first of 25kV ac Midland

Suburban Electrics to Moorgate, and subsequently the Thameslink service through the Snow Hill tunnel via Farringdon, City Thameslink and Blackfriars. This brought the third rail through to Farringdon in 1988, where a similar pantograph ceremony takes place.

The Bakerloo Line south from Baker Street had long been the most overcrowded of the Underground lines in Central London, and relief was planned to enhance its capacity by eliminating the junction of the Queen's Park and Stanmore lines at Baker Street. The Stanmore branch would henceforth be connected to a new 'Fleet' Line, running via Bond Street and Green Park to Charing Cross (Stage I), on to Aldwych, Ludgate Circus, Cannon Street and Fenchurch Street (Stage II), and finally to Surrey Docks (now Surrey Quays), New Cross and Lewisham, with a branch from Surrey Docks to New Cross Gate (Stage III). Or such was the plan, amended many times since, especially in the vexed question as to the direction the line should take east of the City of London.

For the main problem was that traffic on the Underground system was falling, quite fast. The go-ahead for Stage I was obtained in 1971, with work starting the following year. When Stage I was opened well behind time in 1979 and two years after the Queen's Silver Jubilee, to honour which the line's name was changed, the need for the line to exist at all was being questioned, as were most certainly the extensions. Consequently, the cost of further construction which would largely parallel the District Line was not favoured, while a new concept (named the River Line) arose for the further eastern projection. The 1974 London Rail Study had pronounced in favour of an underground link binding together the north and south banks of the Thames, to be tagged on to the Fleet Line by a junction at Fenchurch Street. The line would cross beneath the Thames no less than four times, with a terminus at Thamesmead. However, without Stage II, discussion of Stage III alternatives foundered; they came to be resurrected in totally different circumstances several years later.

Separating the Bakerloo Line branches at Baker Street, deep underground, so that each branch would have its own two platforms but all four interconnecting in the same station, presented problems. Two new step plate junctions were built, one just to the south of Baker Street and one 1,000ft to the north about 50ft below Marylebone main line station. Additionally, a new station tunnel and a new running tunnel were driven on the north

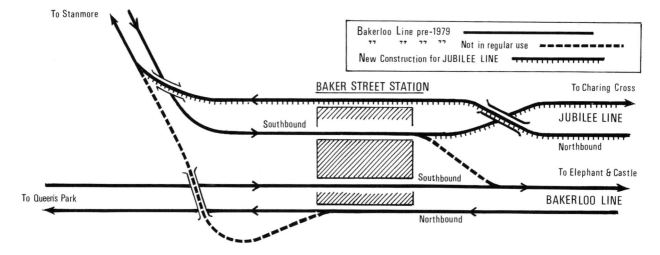

side of the existing Stanmore platform. The end result is that this latter now became the southbound Jubilee Line platform, and the new station tunnel and platform became the northbound Jubilee tunnel and platform. To achieve this the northbound Jubilee running tunnel had to be made to roll over the southbound tunnel both north and south of the station, which resulted in the new line's running in the station being the reverse of that of the Bakerloo Line. Readers are invited to examine the diagram and work this out for themselves, and also perhaps to ponder on how a simple design concept in terms of passenger convenience can be met through an ingenious and complex, but thoroughly elegant, solution.

At depths of between 70ft and 140ft, the twin tunnels run south and east for 2½ miles. At Bond Street, only 7ft separates the station tunnel from the Post Office Railway's driverless trains above, an indication of how existing services and building foundations can constrain the future provision of new lines and facilities under the capital. Bond Street ticket hall was much enlarged, and as at Oxford Circus some years previously an umbrella raft was erected over the roadway to allow work to proceed more or less unhindered. The line then veers southeast to Green Park, where it passes beneath both the Piccadilly and Victoria Lines to reach the new station platforms, east of and below the latter's station. There is interconnection between all three lines, aided by new passages and escalators, but geography here as elsewhere on the Jubilee Line has imposed limitations on how convenient these interchanges can be made.

Reconstructing the Northern Line station at Strand and the Bakerloo Line station at Trafalgar Square resulted in the disappearance of both those names and the appellation Charing Cross being applied to them as well as the new Jubilee Line terminus. (The then Charing Cross station was renamed Embankment.) During the building work, Strand had to be closed, as a shaft for a bank of three new escalators was to be driven diagonally through the former lift shafts. Here too an umbrella was constructed in the Railtrack station forecourt, after carefully underpinning the 300-ton Queen Eleanor memorial.

Tunnelling followed established practice, but a laser beam was used to assist in setting out the tunnels and keeping the tunnelling machines on course. A beam from a point in the rear of the workings is directed on to a mark at the face, where it appears as a spot of light and thus acts as a guide for the shield operator. The line continues with over-run tunnels for another 0.3 miles, ending just north of Waterloo Bridge.

The new part of the line was constructed with Automatic Train Operation in mind, but it was Driver Only Operation which was adopted eventually without the complications of ATO. From its opening by HRH the Prince of Wales on 30 April 1979, the line was operated by the 1972 Mk II stock, although subsequent reshuffles led to its being equipped with the purpose-built 1983 stock. A consequence of the divorce from the Bakerloo was the depriving of that line of its maintenance depot, and a new facility was built at Stonebridge Park. The connection between the lines at Baker Street remains, though not in normal passenger use.

The further development of the Jubilee Line Extension project is discussed in Chapter 13.

In 1929, grass runways for test flying were established at a site in west London. During World War 2 the aerodrome was chosen as a base for RAF long-range transport flights, and by 1945 military aircraft were taking off from its sole runway. Civilian airlines arrived in 1946, and LHR or London Heathrow was officially opened in May of that year. At that time, with an annual passenger usage of under two million, it was said that an Underground link would probably be built within six years. However, false prophets in a 1956 study concluded that the expected passenger use would not justify the cost, and that the proposed M4 motorway would suffice.

After a skirmish between British Rail and London Transport interests had finally been resolved in favour of the latter, and with air passenger traffic predicted to reach 20 million a year in 1973 (now over 50 million), the go-ahead for the Piccadilly Line extension was received in 1971. Few pretended that the Underground was the perfect solution for Heathrow; the Piccadilly is an integral part of the Underground, carrying commuters to and from Central London and used for a variety of journey purposes within London. It is thus an ordinary urban railway and accordingly passengers have to handle their own luggage up and down escalators and in and out of trains. Extra floor space for luggage was provided in the 1973 tube stock with which the Piccadilly Line was re-equipped, but with limited success when it came to impeding other passengers.

However, there were also advantages. One was that the scheduled service needed to be very frequent to cater for the combined needs of airport users and others; another gain was the multiplicity of destinations available directly or with a single change of train. King's Cross proved to be the single most popular destination.

The Piccadilly Line runs in the open between Barons Court and Hounslow West, from which point it was extended mainly in 'cut and cover' tunnel 1.81 miles to Hatton Cross (save only to emerge into the open for a short distance to cross the River Crane), and then in deep-level tube tunnels under the runways for the further 1.37 miles to Terminals 1, 2, 3. That station is built in a reinforced box nearly 400ft long and 75ft wide, right in the centre of the airport. Escalators join the platforms 44ft below ground to a subsurface concourse, from which there is direct access via subways built by the British Airports Authority (BAA) to the three terminals. A further exit is to the bus station immediately above. Her Majesty the Queen formally opened the Heathrow extension on 16 December 1977.

A modernisation scheme for the East London Line, which sorely needed it, was started in 1979. In the pre-Docklands boom days, traffic levels were low and declining, but the condition of the stations was deplorable. Refurbishment was later to become a major programme on the principal Underground stations; that on the East London was confined mostly to installation of fluorescent lighting, platform resurfacing, repainting and minor works, together with the plastic faced panels to cover up the grimy platform walls. At Wapping, the panels tell the story of the Thames Tunnel. However, Shadwell was provided with lifts to replace stairs, and a new surface building. Wapping got new lifts,

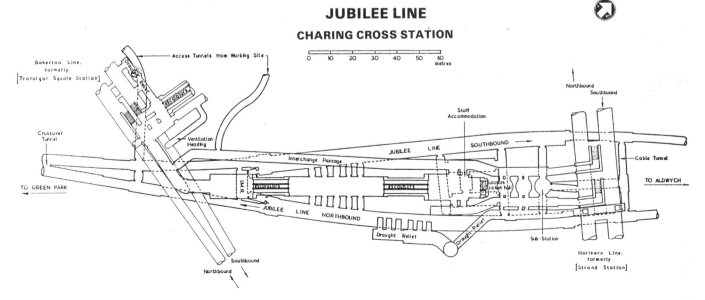

JUBILEE LINE
CHARING CROSS STATION

fares charged, but the financial consequences were not perhaps appreciated. This was peripheral territory, of marginal profitability at the best of times, with both the Watford and Ongar branches having been less than successful ventures financially. 'The Counties shall pay for these services if they want them', said the GLC. It turned out that the Counties did want them, but politely declined to contribute, arguing quite reasonably that it was a mere historical quirk that such services were operated as part of the Underground rather than

Rotherhithe's rebuilding featured a pair of escalators, and Surrey Docks received a complete new surface station. At Whitechapel, the ticket hall was renewed.

The London Transport Museum was opened in the former Covent Garden flower market building in 1980, replacing the display at Syon Park and at Clapham before that. Major as well as minor exhibits, many of which are mentioned in this book,

are displayed here permanently.

Travelling beyond Northwood on the Metropolitan or the far side of Woodford on the Central, a curious change took place. For this was territory outside Greater London and hence beyond the writ of the GLC.

It cannot be said that the 1969 Act ignored this spread of the Underground beyond the GLC boundaries, since that authority had to approve the

British Rail. Faced with this, London Transport was instructed to raise fares to a quite ridiculous extent (Ongar to Debden, under 10 miles, £1.55 single at 1980 prices).

In an effort to save costs, the Epping–Ongar line was staked out as a closure proposal; the usage of this rural branch which had already been reduced to operation by one train, was less than 1,000 passenger journeys a day. The Minister refused

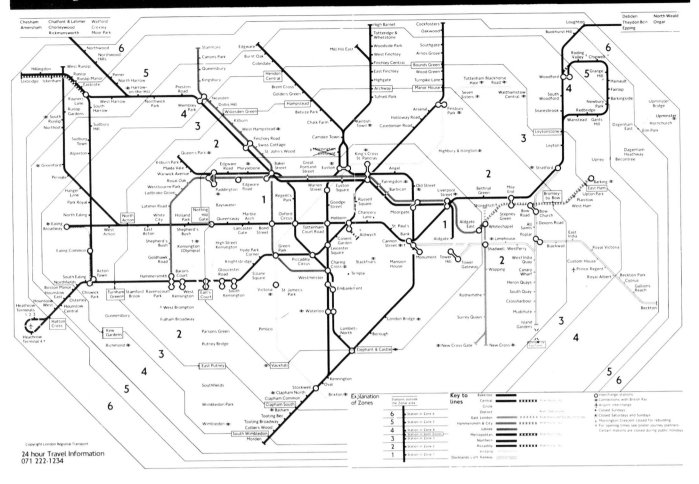

outright closure, but Blake Hall station in its remote glory was having difficulty in generating even double figures of passengers on a good day and was closed in 1981. It was then claimed to have the lowest patronage of any underground line station in the world. The rest of the service was reduced to run in rush hours only, which were generously interpreted in the 1982 timetable revisions. Unexpectedly, a local management decision, albeit short-lived, was to restore the all-day service in 1989.

Although the GLC years produced some tangible results in terms of new trains and some line extensions, the whole period was characterised by the warring which took place with central government, to which the Council was often politically opposed. The Jubilee Line was a case in point; denied a capital grant from the (Labour) Government to continue east from Charing Cross, the (Conservative) leader of the GLC said that 'the line would be built whether the Government agrees and helps or not... if we cannot borrow the money we will raise it from the rates and damn the government'. The extensions were not built. GLC influence was far from consistent over the years, as administrations oscillated from one party to the other. Policy shifts are all very well, but when capital investment can last for a century or more for infrastructure and 30–40 years for rolling stock, a degree of continuity and freedom from political meddling is called for.

Fares provided the graphic example of shifting priorities. At first, London Transport was expected to break even after depreciation expenses, to provide for any surplus which the GLC might determine, and to set aside a general reserve. The incoming GLC administration of 1973 decided to implement a fares standstill until 1975, when spiralling inflation led to a policy reversal. The original wholly unrealistic remit was thus turned into a fares relief grant, first made in 1974. The cost escalated alarmingly, and fares were doubled in 18 months during 1975–76 to restore the position. After that, fare levels continued to climb slowly in real terms, reaching a historically high level in 1981. 'Fares Fair' then intervened. This was a GLC attempt to put fares back to their 1969 levels in real terms. But such had been the growth of inefficiency in London Transport with staff levels up, traffic levels down, a falling London population and a miserable operating performance, that the cost was too much for some to swallow. Prime critic was the London Borough of Bromley, whose High Court action succeeded in having the policy declared unlawful on appeal. Consequently, fares were increased by 96% in March 1982, with the result that patronage, which had been rising, took a nosedive again. Services were reduced to match the new traffic levels in December of that year.

In many ways, this was the Underground's darkest hour; from such a position, matters could only improve. Fewer than 500 million passenger journeys were recorded in 1982, the lowest since 1943 when the network was much smaller and circumstances wholly different. Yet in the turmoil of the Greater London Council's fares policies for London Transport had been the introduction of zonal pricing on the Underground — a necessary precondition for what was to follow in the bestselling product of the Travelcard.

The essentials of today's London Travelcard scheme, which is a season ticket offering travel to the holder within a specified geographical area, are:

■ definition of six concentric zones around central London, Zone 1 encompassing the Circle Line and a little more, Zone 6 coinciding more or less with the Greater London boundary;
■ tickets available and priced for the number of zones required;
■ valid for unlimited travel on London Underground, London bus services, Docklands Light Railway and British Rail services within the zone(s) selected; and
■ issued for one week or for any period between one month and one year.

A further one day ticket gives similar benefits, but is not available before 0930 on Mondays to Fridays. Underground single journey fares were also converted to a zonal basis.

The original Travelcard scheme was launched in

121

Above:
Wapping is one of the lesser known Underground stations. In 1982, the access and street level ticket office were rebuilt, new lifts provided and the station generally smartened up. The station was photographed on 13 March 1995.
John Glover

Below:
The GLC sanctioned the re-equipment of all District main line services with the 'D' stock which, after ventilation problems had been sorted out, might fairly be described as the most comfortable vehicles in the Underground fleet. An westbound service arrives at Whitechapel on 13 March 1995.
John Glover

Right:
Work on the Terminal 4 loop for the Piccadilly Line includes the laying of drainage pipes in the step plate junction at the end of the over-run tunnels from Heathrow T1,T2,T3 station, seen here on 5 April 1984. The T4 loop was opened in 1986.
Ian Allan Library

May 1983. This date marked the introduction of the GLC's 'Balanced Plan' for transport, whereby a strategy for transport as a whole in the capital was unveiled. For London Transport this meant an overall fares reduction of 25%, the legality having first been verified by a 'friendly' High Court action between LT and the Council. The result was a restoration of the real fares level to a position midway between that before and after 'Fares Fair'. By the end of that year there were 600,000 holders of Travelcards, and passenger miles travelled on the Underground rose by no less than a fifth. The number of passenger journeys made over the early 1980s reflected the fares structures; for the years 1981, 1982, 1983 and 1984/5 these were, in millions, 541, 498, 563, and 659 respectively.

It was, however, too late to save the GLC, and the Government abruptly wrenched London Transport away from the Council's control with its London Regional Transport Act on 29 June 1984.

Before leaving the GLC period, it is perhaps timely to consider the major project of the Terminal 4 loop at the western end of the Piccadilly Line, completed under LRT auspices. Underground traffic

at Heathrow had built up very satisfactorily but, unfortunately, the planners had anticipated that if a fourth terminal was built, this would be on the Perry Oaks site further west. The station, originally Heathrow Central, was thus aligned on a northwest — southeast axis, which posed something of a problem when the decision was reached to construct Terminal 4 a mile or so away on the southern perimeter! After desultory talk of a travelator link to Hatton Cross, the decision was reached to build instead a terminal loop for the Underground starting at Hatton Cross. Trains would proceed in a clockwise direction only around this loop calling successively at Terminal 4, Terminals 1, 2, 3 and Hatton Cross again. This meant the effective abandonment of one of the two existing running tracks west of Hatton Cross constructed only a decade previously.

The building of the loop led to some novel problems. Excavation just west of Hatton Cross station had to take place almost directly under the flight path of aircraft. No component part such as

lifting gear and stacked material could be allowed to rise above a level which would have created radar interference and thus affected aircraft in flight. So the large working area had first to be turned into a kind of shallow pit, and in a deep trench below that a new rail junction plus a 1/4-mile section of tunnel had to be built and then covered in.

The new junction was built within a concrete subsurface formation, necessitating careful demolition of the original box. Then followed an ascending section of tunnel with cast-iron lining, built in trench and backfilled. Tunnelling shields were used from all three working sites to drive the running tunnels through the London clay, thrust forward by hydraulic rams. Face cutting was by boom cutters, and the spoil was removed rearwards by conveyors. Eventually this reached the surface up inclined drift tunnels. Most of the running tunnel was lined with pre-cast concrete rings.

Where the new single track tunnel divided to link with the two original over-run tunnels, a step plate

junction was constructed. Flat-bottom welded rail on prestressed concrete sleepers made its first appearance on the tube system here. In an effort to reduce noise, sleepers on part of the new track rest on rubber fittings. Finally, two ventilation shafts were constructed. It was a shame that delays in deciding how the new terminal should be served resulted in the station at T4 not being ideally sited, and rather a long walk from the vast terminal proper. The station and loop were opened in April 1986.

The proposed Terminal 5 is considered in Chapter 13.

Chapter 11

Light Rail in London

Above:
Above:
A pair of the original DLR P86 cars meet at Canary Wharf in 1989. The original station here, on the left-hand side of the picture, was constructed but then demolished without being opened. Its replacement has three tracks and six platform faces. *John Glover*

If the Jubilee Line was too costly to extend into Docklands, were buses the only alternative? Could a cheaper means of providing a railed solution be found? What ought to be done about the intermediate level of flow requirements which is above what buses can handle comfortably, but below the really heavy traffics which are needed to support a full scale Underground system or similar?

The London Docklands Development Corporation was created in 1981. Its purpose was to provide a lasting regeneration in the eight square miles of London's derelict docklands in the ensuing 10–15 years. The intention was that this would be achieved by awarding speedy and unrestrictive planning permission to would-be entrepreneurs; an essential part of the package was the provision of transport infrastructure.

At an early stage, it became clear that the LDDC wanted a railway, and preferably one using the latest technology. If industry was really to be attracted and new life injected into the area, a high-quality public transport system was seen as essential — and that meant rail, however much the Department of Transport might have hankered after buses. Evaluation suggested that a rail system might attract 9,000 extra jobs, being the key element which would entice businesses to move to the area and people to live and work there. It was always admitted that justification in transport terms alone was low, at least for the first few years, but that was to miss the point. The Docklands Light Railway was to be a catalyst and justified on what it would achieve for the community and the area, not as the result of a commercial decision by a transport operator.

In the event, public funding covered the whole of the cost of the initial section. London Transport were able to build the railway on the cheap; not so much from skimping the specification, although that was pared right down wherever possible, but from

the extensive use of existing railway rights of way and infrastructure, which accounted for two-thirds of the original system.

What were these lines? The London & Blackwall Railway of 1840 was a remarkable creation. Carried for most of its length on a 4,020yd viaduct, trains on this double track line were cable-hauled using a drum-to-drum system and seven miles of hemp rope for each track. Winding engines were built at each end of the line. Track gauge was a non-standard 5ft 0½in and carriages, each with their own brakesman, started every 15min from each terminus. Thus from Minories to Blackwall a group of carriages started out together and as each station was approached, the rope gripper was released and the carriage braked to a halt, while the rest of the train continued on its way. From Blackwall to Minories the rope direction was reversed, and a cumulative train, as it were, returned to the City. To ensure efficient and regular operation, the railway relied on the electric telegraph, one of its first commercial uses.

It will be apparent from this description that a major shortcoming was the impossibility of

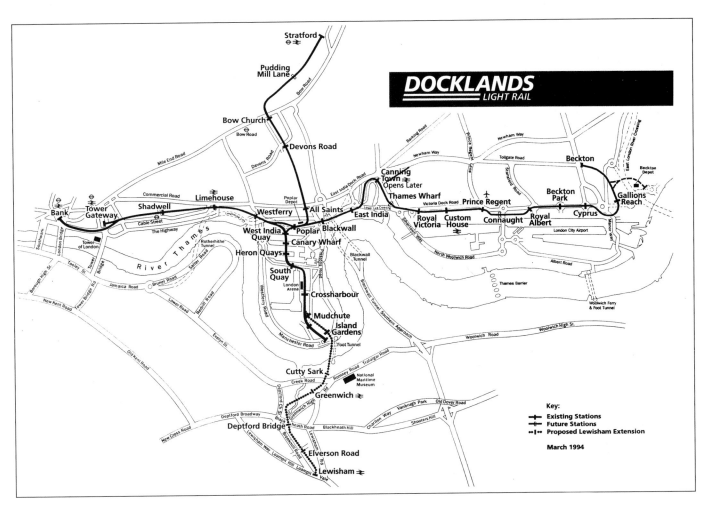

Above:
Docklands Light Railway.

travelling between any pair of intermediate stations, while on the technical side the cables had a tendency to twist or snap. By 1849, it had been rebuilt as a conventional railway to standard gauge. The Millwall Extension Railway forms the southern part of the line, built as part of the Millwall Docks complex to exploit the southern part of the Isle of Dogs. It was connected to the London & Blackwall at Millwall Junction, the whole coming under the Great Eastern Railway. The third railway was the grandly titled East & West India Docks & Birmingham Junction Railway, later known by the more homely (and more accurate) name of the North London Railway. The company created their own docks at Poplar, while their former workshops at Bow much later became the first depot on British Railways to be turned over exclusively to diesel traction. The combined effects of motor bus competition and the war saw all passenger traffic cease by 1944, while the fortunes of the freight traffic declined with those of the docks. All conventional rail traffic had ceased by 1980.

By the time the Docklands Light Railway was being planned, there was thus much ready-made railway. The NLR portion even had some track remaining. The brick-built viaducts had been disused for years, but their availability did ease the land acquisition and construction costs. After ideas of street running to Mile End had been discarded as unnecessarily complicating an otherwise completely segregated railway, plans were quickly finalised.

The 'London' end was built at Minories, squeezed alongside the Fenchurch Street station throat next to a multi-storey car park. It was a far from ideal site, several minutes' walk away from Tower Hill Underground station, but at that stage of the game the costs of going any further would have

prevented the project from proceeding at all. Tower Gateway, as it was named, is in standard Docklands style of unstaffed station built from a kit of modular parts. Platforms, originally built for 28m-long articulated pairs of cars, were extended subsequently to permit two-unit operation. They feature canopies with distinctive curved roofs. Self-service ticket machines, 'Next Train' indicators and closed circuit TV monitoring complete the picture. Normally, access to the stations is by stairs with a lift for the disabled, but Tower Gateway features a pair of escalators plus a stairway in a shaft, rising up from a glass rotunda at pavement level.

From here, the DLR lines took over the two southernmost BR tracks on the Fenchurch Street lines viaduct, leaving all the 23 trains/hr of the Southend line's peak service to be accommodated on the two which remained. Shadwell station construction involved building out from the existing viaduct to accommodate an island platform. Interchange of a sort is available to the East London Line, but unfortunately the new station entrance for the Underground which was constructed only in 1982/83 was further from the DLR station than the original! At Limehouse the DLR takes the course of the former London & Blackwall Railway along a route disused since 1962. A fine view of Regent's Canal Dock is afforded from the viaduct. From West Ferry, the railway embarks on the 'ski-jump', which forms the 1 in 23 approach to the elevated triangular junction at the centre of the system. It also features curves at the 40m minimum radius which, although allowing a truly compact (and economical to build) set of junctions, stretches the technology to its limit and must induce severe wear on the wheel tyres and rails.

In the passage of this junction the trains turned

due south, as for the time being the northern side was not used by trains in passenger service. Immediately beyond the triangle is the exposed and recently rebuilt West India Quay station, where inter-changing passengers descend to a lower level to cross between the two island platforms. This section is all new construction, as the line jumps the three stretches of dock on a series of brand-new bridges. The next station is Canary Wharf, now a six-platform, three-track station to serve the financial centre.

Immediately following, at only about 100yd beyond, is Heron Quays station. More bends (corners?) follow through the South Quay area and across Millwall Cut before the old North Greenwich branch embankment is reached and the line descends to Crossharbour and then reaches Mudchute. Use of the former viaduct here complicates matters, since it was built for single track only; the splayed pattern of the twin tracks at the Island Gardens terminus denotes another unusually laid out station. From here, passengers have the option of walking through the pedestrian tunnel under the Thames to Greenwich.

The Stratford branch diverges at West India Quay and descends to Poplar station. Poplar has now been rebuilt and extended to provide for the Beckton branch. It is also the point where trains enter and leave the system from the adjacent operations and maintenance depot. The Stratford line, which turns north and now follows the former BR Poplar Dock branch, is in a shallow cutting or at ground level. Stations are at All Saints, Devons Road

and Bow Church; between the latter there is even a short tunnel where flats bridge the line. One of the Docklands speciality sharp curves on a steep gradient, and single track at that, heralds the BR Great Eastern main line, which is joined via the connection from Fenchurch Street. The single track continues, albeit via a passing loop soon to be a station at Pudding Mill Lane, to a formerly disused bay platform at Stratford, where there are extensive interchange facilities.

The Docklands line is self-contained, with no physical connection to Railtrack. Although this left the way open for truly innovative technology, the familiar standard gauge steel wheel on steel rail was used. For economy, little purpose is usually served by reinventing the wheel where well-tried solutions exist. In this case, extensive existing trackbed was also available. Current collection at 750V dc uses third rail, but with a difference: the aluminium rail is shrouded with a plastic cover, and is of bottom contact type. Hopefully, this will minimise failures in conditions of ice and snow, but so far this has remained largely untested.

Initially, Docklands trains ran every 10min as a minimum frequency. They are automatically driven, the starting command being given by the Train Captain on board. However, he has the commercial duties of ticket checking to perform, as well as looking after the passengers generally, and does not drive the train in normal operation. This task is performed by the ATO system on the train. Using data received from a transmitter at the platform, the system 'knows' when to accelerate, coast or brake. The Automatic Train Protection (ATP) system is a limiting arrangement which ensures that the train is driven correctly either by the ATO or the Train Captain. By means of loops laid in the track which are detected by the train, codes are received which ensure that the maximum speed permitted is not exceeded, and that there is a safe distance maintained behind the train in the section ahead. Automatic Train Supervision (ATS) regulates the train service by adjusting departure times to maintain even intervals after disruption, or to instruct the ATO system to forsake economy by the use of coasting, and to go flat out to recover from delays. There is also the option for the supervisor to key in additional instructions.

The three systems together control the whole of the operation; this includes the door operation, the setting and the locking of the points, and the driving of the train indicators.

The whole, though, has been replaced by the Alcatel SELTRAC moving block (or transmission-based) signalling system. Some upgrading was essential for the vastly more complex railway that the DLR has now become. It was installed initially on the Beckton branch, which was opened in 1994 before SELTRAC was extended to the whole of the DLR. One consequence was the enforced physical separation of operations on the Poplar to Beckton line from the rest of the DLR until that work was completed.

In the 'moving block' signalling concept, each train 'knows' the position of all the trains ahead and can regulate its own position. There are four elements:

- On Train. The on-board computer 'talks' to the central computers via trackside equipment. Messages between the two are exchanged every second. It controls the

operation of the train along the tracks, stops the train in the next station and opens the doors. It also tells the central computer of the train's location.

- Trackside. The trackside equipment provides the communication link and operates the points as instructed by the central computers. It also features axle counters, which log the movement of trains along the track as a computer back-up.
- Central Computers. These are the heart of the system and run the trains to predefined rules. They control the operation of the trains in accordance with the safety criteria of the signalling system. They also manage train movements according to the timetable and make adjustments for any delays.
- Control Room. This is the staffed operations room where the system is monitored. It is also the source of public address announcements.

For the DLR, headways of 60sec or even slightly less are considered achievable with the £30 million SELTRAC system.

The 11 original P86 stock trains each comprised a twin articulated unit of welded steel construction, seating 84 but with the ability to take 200+ including standing. They are 91ft 10in long, weigh 39 tonnes, and are of typical continental design and appearance. Two-axled motor bogies are located at each end of the unit, with a central non-motored two-axle bogie under the articulated joint. Trains have 'gate turn off' thyristor or 'chopper' traction control equipment, which is a modern electronic alternative to older systems which made extensive use of mechanical switching. Both rheostatic and disc friction braking equipment are fitted. The braking system automatically compensates for the passenger load, and a load compensating air suspension system is also fitted.

As trains are driven by an automatic system, they have no driving cabs, although driving controls are provided at each end of the trains to allow manual operation in sidings or in the case of system failure. Maximum service speed is 50mph. While the initial 11 cars were built by Linke Hofmann Busch in Germany, the subsequent batch of 10 P89 cars were assembled by BREL (1988) Ltd at York. Seating is mostly in bays of four, but there are longitudinal seats in the centre of the car, where provision is also made for the carriage of wheelchairs.

The system is fully accessible to the disabled, with hydraulically-powered lifts giving access to street level — much used by mothers with push chairs. All platforms are straight, to minimise the car-to-platform gap. The system is monitored from the control centre by CCTV with recording facilities; a passenger alarm system at the stations enables contact with the controller in emergency, and its use automatically activates the cameras. Public address is installed at all stops, and a 'next train in x minutes' is displayed. The Train Captains keep an eye on what is happening at the stations.

The initial system as described with its 15 stations and 7½ miles of track was designed to link the Isle of Dogs with both Central London and Stratford, and this was reflected in the 33,000 or so journeys made daily in 1988/89. The average service speed of 15–20mph is between that of buses and Underground, and so is the average journey length of just under three miles. Besides work journeys, the DLR caters extensively for shopping and leisure journeys made by residents of the area, as well as

for visitors and tourists. The system was opened formally on 30 July 1987 by Her Majesty the Queen, who travelled from Island Gardens to Poplar, visiting the Operations and Maintenance Centre, and then to Tower Gateway. Public opening was postponed until 31 August, to allow further time for reliability testing. Operation was originally in the hands of Docklands Light Railway Ltd, a wholly-owned subsidiary of London Regional Transport. It was never, therefore, part of London Underground.

With so much new in a short period of time, it would have been remarkable if all had proceeded entirely smoothly. True to form, it was the train doors and the ticketing system which offered the most trouble.

The doors were of the inward opening variety. This resulted in their taking up space inside the car as they opened, which was proving to be increasingly difficult when the cars were full. The alternatives were bleak: folding doors as on buses carried with them the risk of pinching fingers, while outside plug doors would foul the platform edges which had deliberately minimised the gap so as to ease wheelchair access. Nevertheless, a way was found of fitting internal sliding doors to the P89 trains.

Ticketing is by machine purchase at stations, but tickets once purchased needed to be validated. This was done by inserting the ticket in a separate machine, which code-marked it with date, time and station to prevent it from being reused. Coding was in magnetic as well as visible form. Stations are 'open' in that there are no barriers, and a 'paid area' is denoted by crossing a red line, within which all passengers must have a ticket. Sadly, the ticket machines did not work at all well, and the validation arrangement was not well understood. Ticket issue arrangements were altered during 1989, with ticket machines automatically validating tickets as they issued them. This was one of the aspects of the DLR which had been most criticised by the public, another being information systems when services were disrupted.

The success of the Isle of Dogs was undoubtedly encouraged by the existence of the DLR, but was that enough? Built at the bottom end of the capacity scale, major developments threatened to swamp it. Olympia & York, the developers of Canary Wharf, were quite certain that they wanted direct access to the City of London, and hence were instrumental in putting forward a private capital grant for the extension to Bank. This deep-level section leaves the DLR near Royal Mint Street and just short of the Tower Gateway terminus, and drops down a 1 in 16 ramp to run underground for the 0.94 miles. Because the P86/P89 car designs did not anticipate underground operation, no end exits were provided on the cars. Thus the twin tunnels are of 5m diameter with a continuous walkway on one side, more like that of a tube station tunnel than that of a bored tube. However, safety changes in the wake of the King's Cross fire mean that none of the 11 original cars were allowed to work underground; they have been sold to the Essen operator in Germany. Opened in 1991, the DLR platforms at Bank are at very deep level below the Northern Line; a shunting neck beyond the pair of platforms allows terminating trains to run forward after discharging their passengers and then reverse into the other platform.

The Bank extension though was only part of the story. With Canary Wharf employment growing rapidly, it was expected that there would be 100,000

employed there in the mid-1990s. Trains needed to be lengthened and frequencies increased — to the extent of producing 10 times more railway. This has being achieved by doubling train lengths from one to two units, which required platform extensions, and increasing the peak frequencies to every 8min on all sections of the line.

A further order for trains was clearly required since, quite apart from service expansion on the existing system, the Beckton extension was now going ahead. This five-mile projection eastwards from Poplar, with 10 stations initially, was intended to open up both the Royal Docks and the housing area beyond. To be paid for out of land development values (the land already being in the hands of the LDDC), major works were needed, including the construction of a flying junction to supersede the original arrangements at Delta Junction outside West India Quay.

Much of the extension is on newly-constructed viaduct sections, although it is of some surprise to find the line descending to the two stations at Beckton Park and Cyprus. Both of these are located under roundabouts in road intersections! The extension also required the building of a large rolling stock depot and workshops at Beckton. A new control centre has been constructed at Poplar to meet the needs of a growing railway.

For all these enhanced services, 70 B stock trains were built by Bombardier BN in Bruges, Belgium. There are two variants: 22 (B90 cars) had the original ATO/ATP signalling equipment; the remaining 47 (B92 cars) are fitted with SELTRAC equipment. All the B90 cars will be converted to the B92 standard.

The B cars are distinguishable from their predecessors by having outside sliding doors, achieved by a slight narrowing of the overall body width. They also have emergency doors in the outer ends of the vehicles, while seating capacity is reduced from the 84 of the P stock to 70. This allows a corresponding expansion in standing room.

For the DLR, presently carrying 50,000 passengers per day, further expansion is likely. Parliamentary powers have now been obtained to extend south of the Thames from Mudchute (new station) to Island Gardens (underground), Greenwich, Deptford Creek, Elverson Road and Lewisham. A station at Cutty Sark may also be provided. The private consortium which constructs the £140 million project will also be responsible for maintenance, but the operation will remain in DLR hands.

The Government took the Docklands Light Railway away from one public sector organisation, London Regional Transport, and gave it to another, London Docklands Development Corporation in 1992. They announced in 1994 that it was their intention to franchise DLR operations to the private sector from 1996, initially for a seven-year period. Subsequently, the railway would be transferred as a whole to the private sector.

The DLR was not the first time that light rail had been considered for London. Croydon to New Addington was an old favourite, while consideration was given to Finsbury Park and Muswell Hill along what was once to be part of the Northern Line. Cost was the main reason for abandonment, but light rail was a serious contender for the Terminal 4 link at Heathrow before the Piccadilly Line loop was decided upon. Docklands thus provided the first

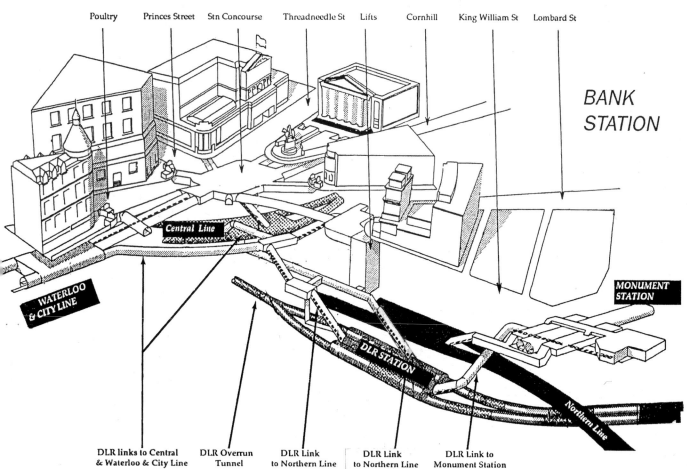

Poultry   Princes Street   Stn Concourse   Threadneedle St   Lifts   Cornhill   King William St   Lombard St

BANK STATION

MONUMENT STATION

Central Line

WATERLOO & CITY LINE

DLR STATION

Northern Line

DLR links to Central   DLR Overrun   DLR Link   DLR Link   DLR Link to
& Waterloo & City Line   Tunnel   to Northern Line   to Northern Line   Monument Station

Above:
Bank station, and how the platforms of the various lines relate to each other.

actual installation and, if nothing else, the experience has demonstrated how flexible light rail schemes can be. Fears expressed that technical excellence in Docklands might not be matched with sufficient traffic potential do not seem to be a problem. However, the new-found belief in the efficacy of light rail to solve urban transport problems and indeed regenerate run-down urban areas is fragile, and there is no scope for an engineering, operational or financial fiasco. Too often light rail is equated with trams, and the words of the Chambers Committee in 1955 still find an echo in some quarters:

'We have no hesitation in saying that, having considered the evidence, we are satisfied that the decision (to cease tram operation) was right, but that whatever the merits of railed electric traction in some Continental cities with wide streets, such a system is clearly obsolete and impracticable for London. There can be no doubt that the removal of the trams has done more than anything else to improve road traffic conditions...'

What is light rail? The following is a generalised definition, representing more the concept rather than a specific technology:

- driver only, manual operation;
- standard gauge, steel wheel on steel rail vehicles;
- wholly or partially segregated rights of way, or completely unsegregated from road traffic;

- simple, low cost, closely spaced stops;
- minimum signalling;
- lighter vehicles built to less onerous end loading and other design criteria, which are capable of negotiating sharper bends and curves and steeper gradients than conventional rail vehicles.

All the above are, in a sense, negotiable, and trade-offs exist. If the proposed system merely replaces an existing railway using the same structures, there is no need to use vehicles capable of negotiating 20m radius curves. On the other hand, if high accessibility is the goal through providing frequent stops, then good acceleration and braking characteristics are required. Wholly segregated systems (as in Docklands or Tyne and Wear) can consider automatic operation, but drivers are essential elsewhere. Light rail is the intermediate transport mode: ideally flows will range between 5,000 and 15,000 passengers an hour, with route lengths a maximum of 15 miles. Outside these rough orders of magnitude it will be bus for lower levels of traffic and conventional heavy rail (or metro) above.

What is in it for London? With the requirements for Docklands now looking as if the Jubilee Line Extension ought to have been the prime project after all, where might one look next?

For central London the conventional heavy rail or Underground system will continue to be the unchallenged answer, but there are a number of intriguing possibilities for light rail in outer London. Although simple conversion of existing railways to light rail standards is not thought worthwhile, there are a number of sections of line which might benefit from light rail development, particularly outer branch lines and some local orbital routes in the

inner suburbs. Of those schemes which have survived initial evaluation, that for the Croydon area is of most interest.

Croydon is an important regional centre and a focus for bus and rail services; it also suffers badly from traffic congestion. However, neither East nor West Croydon stations are particularly well sited; there is a need to penetrate the office and shopping areas. Light rail offers the potential for greatly increasing the accessibility, while not causing the environmental disasters associated with road building.

Another objective is to segregate the rail system from road traffic to avoid importing traffic delays. Tramlink has achieved either total segregation or shares roads with buses only, apart from a 120m section leaving Croydon on the Wimbledon route. The alternatives, of going underground or elevated, have not been necessary. In fact, the only flyovers required are those to keep Tramlink clear of Railtrack lines at Mitcham Junction and in crossing the West Croydon to Sutton line. The other major engineering requirement when going 'on street' is to divert the pipes and cables of statutory undertakers such as gas and electricity, while still enabling Croydon to function properly.

The 18-mile scheme, which has now received Parliamentary powers, includes:

- conversion of the Wimbledon to West Croydon Railtrack line to light rail, and its extension on street to West Croydon and East Croydon stations;
- conversion of the Elmers End to Woodside Railtrack line to light rail, and its extension to East Croydon station in one direction and to Beckenham Junction in the other;

129

Above:
Royal Albert is typical of the Beckton line stations, with the station name displayed for the benefit of passengers on approaching trains. *John Glover*

Below:
This view of West India Quay station from Canary Wharf shows an approaching service with P89 car No 21 from Stratford, while on the right a Canary Wharf–Stratford service proceeds towards Poplar. The tight geometry achievable with light rail is evident in the track layout. *John Glover*

■ establishment of a new light rail route on street from East Croydon station to New Addington. (This latter is the largest urban area in the southeast without rail transport. It has a population of 25,000 and is economically entirely dependent on Croydon.)

Of the total route, about 11 miles will be on presently used or abandoned railway, two miles along existing highways and five miles on new rights

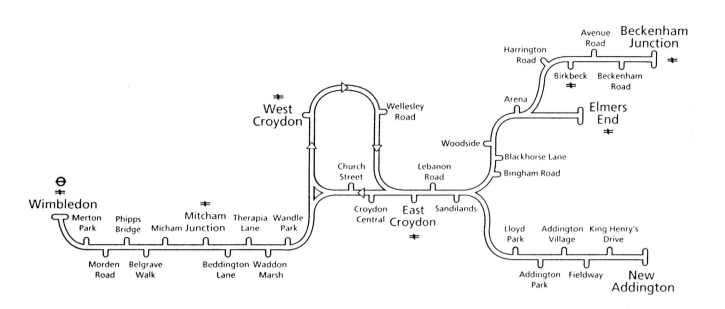

Harrington Road · Avenue Road · Beckenham Junction
Birkbeck · Beckenham Road
Arena · Elmers End
West Croydon · Wellesley Road · Woodside · Blackhorse Lane · Bingham Road
Church Street · Lebanon Road · Sandilands
Wimbledon · Merton Park · Phipps Bridge · Mitcham · Micham Junction · Therapia Lane · Wandle Park · Croydon Central · East Croydon · Lloyd Park · Addington Village · King Henry's Drive
Morden Road · Belgrave Walk · Beddington Lane · Waddon Marsh · Addington Park · Fieldway · New Addington

Above:
Croydon area proposed Tramlink system.

Below:
Cyprus is one of the two stations located underneath a road intersection — officially a 'bowl' station. B92 car No 53 leads the Poplar-bound train. *John Glover*

of way. These latter are mostly alongside existing roads. The economics of light rail will enable service frequency to be at least every 10min on all routes, compared with a 30min BR norm at present. This would require a fleet of 23–27 cars. One possible service pattern is to run Wimbledon to Elmers End and also Beckenham Junction to New Addington.

In all cases, new intermediate stations are to be constructed, and there will probably be around 32 stops in total. Tramlink will be totally segregated from other rail operations. There is thus no possibility of through running to or from Railtrack destinations, notably London termini, but this is offset by achieving far better penetration of the centre of Croydon on all routes. It is not possible to have both.

The high platforms at Railtrack stations are likely to be demolished and replaced with platforms, whether on street or elsewhere, set at 350mm above rail level and of simple construction. Platform lengths need be no more than 45m. Where it is

intended to use one side of a Railtrack island platform, as at Wimbledon, Tramlink track levels can be raised. Electrification will be at 750V dc, with overhead pick-up.

Automatic operation as on the Docklands Light Railway is not practicable, given the intermixing with other traffic; trains would be manually driven with traffic signals controlling rail/road intersections.

The £150 million scheme is presently being

Below:
This interior view of B92 rolling stock shows the spacious interior and how this is continued across the central articulation. Sadly, few passengers are apparent, though there are two members of staff.
John Glover

evaluated by private sector consortia with a view to bidding for a fund, design, build and operate scheme; a 99-year concession is to be offered to the successful bidder. Up to one third of the cost is likely to have to come from central government grant.

The study which came up with the Croydon proposal looked at the whole of the British Rail and London Underground network in the London area, and about 40 sections of line were involved. The most important of the study findings was that a simple conversion of existing railways to light rail standards is unlikely to be worthwhile; the main scope is in applications where the special attributes of light rail can be exploited. These include the ability to use low cost stops (a more appropriate term than stations), street running, and the ability to

negotiate track geometry more akin to the big dipper than a conventional railway. It was concluded that the best chances of success were in situations where there was scope for:

- cost savings on an existing lightly used line;
- improving access by constructing additional stops;
- joining existing lines by new links built to light rail standards;
- extending existing lines which stop short of traffic objectives;
- a small network rather than one route only.

Besides the Croydon area, three other schemes were dubbed worthy of detailed study. These were the conversion of the East London Line to light rail standards and its extension to Shoreditch High Street or Liverpool Street; linking Rickmansworth via the Watford branch of the Metropolitan and a short link to the Croxley Green branch of British Rail, and thence to Watford Junction; and conversion of the relatively underused ends of the Central Line (beyond Greenford in the west and north of Woodford and Hainault in the east) to light rail operation. Subsequent traffic growth stilled such talk, and light rail work is now concentrated on new or lightly used Railtrack alignments. Two of the lines just mentioned we shall meet again, but in a different context.

Top right:
A pair of B92 cars approach Prince Regent from Beckton on 13 March 1995. The building above the tracks is merely the station entrance, reached by either a staircase or a lift.
John Glover

Bottom right:
Steep gradients are of little difficulty to light rail, subject perhaps to autumn leaf problems (not very likely here) or snow. A pair of B92 sets climbs on to the viaduct section taking them eastwards from Prince Regent towards Beckton on 13 March 1995.
John Glover

Chapter 12

London Underground Ltd

The creation of London Regional Transport in June 1984 and the subsequent formation of London Underground Ltd as a wholly-owned subsidiary in 1985 represented a complete change of direction. Originally, LRT had three main tasks:

- an overall responsibility for the planning of public transport services in London;
- securing the provision of those services, and
- the effective running of a series of businesses related to bus and Underground operation.

LRT was created as the strategic planning and management body, while London Underground Ltd, London Buses Ltd and Docklands Light Railway were its three transport operations. They were separate subsidiary companies operating independently, but co-ordinated by LRT. Just to confuse matters, 'London Transport' is the collective name now used for London Regional Transport itself. London Transport also includes the bus services which are provided by outside contractors as an integral part of the network, and the common activities such as ticketing, marketing and service information. The collective name was also applied to the activities of London Transport Advertising, London Transport International (the consultancy), London Transport Lost Property and London Transport Museum.

Times, however, change. The (already noted) loss

of the Docklands Light Railway to the LDDC, the privatisation of the London Buses subsidiaries during 1994 and the sale of other businesses has left London Underground as LRT's only directly controlled transport operation.

In discharging its principal job of determining what services should be provided or secured for Greater London, LRT has to have regard for London's transport needs, and to satisfy the financial objectives laid down by the Secretary of State for Transport. This means that it must break even after grants. Early in the life of the new undertaking, these objectives were set:

- real fares to be held broadly stable beyond January 1985;
- no programme of major route closures on the Underground;
- improved interchanges and travelling environment;
- improved co-ordination with British Rail
- the needs of disabled people to be given special attention;
- advice of the Passengers' Committee to be carefully considered;
- unit costs to be reduced by at least $2\frac{1}{2}\%$ each year;
- revenue support to be reduced to £95 million in 1987/88.

In response, the annual business plan for 1985/86 set out the action it was intended to take.

Above:
Passengers at Earl's Court eastbound platforms await their next service which is for Upminster. London Underground is heavily dependent on peak traffic revenues, despite the physical and financial problems that catering for the peak brings. Will the numbers travelling rise or fall in the next decade? *John Glover*

Overall Underground mileage would increase slightly, with the aim of maintaining service quality as measured by the average waiting times for passengers. Investment in station modernisation was to press on apace, with one quarter of the capital budget being thus committed; the intention was that by the end of 1990 more than 80% of stations would have received some attention since the programme began in 1981. Work on interchanges would continue as would a number of measures to enhance security for passengers and staff. On stations, the extension of centralised public address would become virtually universal, and the dot matrix train indicators would appear at more locations.

The initial emphasis of London Regional Transport was on cost reduction and consolidation after the turbulent years of the previous decade. But other forces were also at work, and one of the main factors causing the strategy to be rethought was the upsurge in passenger usage, fuelled by a growing economy and the runaway success of the Travelcard.

134

Top:
Angel station had one of the less satisfactory layouts, with entry to and exit from the narrow island platform being restricted to a single stairway at one end. This view, on 10 March 1983, shows a High Barnet train of 1959 stock arriving. This is a peak hour scene, with the Underground fulfilling its major role. *John Glover*

Above:
By 1995, the scene has changed entirely. This view is from the opposite end of that same platform, looking north; a Morden-bound train approaches. It is difficult to realise that the northbound track, now diverted to the west in a new tunnel, would once have been on the left of this picture. *John Glover*

The first moves away from the traditional charging methods based on distance travelled were made in 1981 with 'Fares Fair', which established a system of zonal charging on buses throughout Greater London and on the Underground in the central area. It was not until the May 1983 fares revision though that zoning was fully established. Beyond the central zone, an inner zone equivalent to its bus counterpart was formed, to be followed by three concentric ring zones roughly three miles apart, covering broadly the same area as the bus outer zone. The most significant change, however, was the replacement of Underground season tickets and bus passes with Travelcards. These gave their holders freedom to interchange without penalty, and to make additional journeys at no additional cost. Indeed, the greater the use made of the Travelcard, the better value the user obtained from buying it — irrespective of whether the fare level was low or high. Usage shot upwards. This was, of course, still under the GLC regime. Progressive improvements subsequently added in British Rail services in 1985, initially at a premium, and one day tickets available outside the morning peak. In 1991/92, Travelcard sales accounted for 62% of all London Underground revenue.

There were two basic thrusts to the fares policy. Simplification asked whether the complexity of graduated fares was really necessary, and found that it was not. Integration was a more positive and creative approach, which attempted to develop new and attractive ticketing products for passengers. It was hoped that this would in turn result in a fundamental shift in the market for travel, thus enlarging the core of intensive users whose patronage is critical in sustaining the system, and abating the drift towards the use of the private car. After all, Travelcard and the car have similar

Above:
Reconstruction has also taken place at Hammersmith (District and Piccadilly) station. This view of the new structure on 14 March 1994 shows the eastbound platforms and a 1973 stock train departing.
John Glover

economics for their users. Following the initial outlay, the marginal cost of use of Travelcard is zero; what is more, its user doesn't have to park the vehicle!

The fares policies were certainly successful. Starting from such a low base, the system at first had ample capacity to absorb traffic growth. But traffic grew and kept on growing, and in time coping with the effects became a major preoccupation. Overcrowding and congestion thus once again became part of the vocabulary of public transport operators in London, matters which had been of limited importance, other than in respect of road traffic generally, for a long time. Demand was racing ahead, stimulated also by economic growth. Such was the turnaround that the 498 million passenger journeys of 1982 — the low point — reached 815 million in 1988/89, an increase of over 60%.

The studies of and possibilities for new rail services are discussed later. Meanwhile, how was the Underground being managed? In the real world, productivity measures were being pursued, as exemplified by the Underground Ticketing System and Driver Only Operation of trains, as already described; in the five years from 1983, unit costs were cut by 15%. Infrastructure investment has been more than doubled, both to secure reductions in future running costs and to modernise and improve the amenity value of the system. After years of underfunding, much of the Underground was still undeniably squalid, and perceptions of the quality of service offered were correspondingly low. 'Tubular Hell' was one newspaper's way of

describing it, while an (often exaggerated) view of crime in the Underground caught the public attention. Neither public nor staff confidence had been improved by the major fire at King's Cross in November 1987 in which 31 persons died, and the sad tale of shortcomings unravelled by the public inquiry was followed by the deafening sound of stable doors being very expensively bolted. The railway was not being run professionally, and it ran out of luck. The most lasting result to come out of this incident was a realisation that safety has to be managed positively: hazards must be identified and rated according to their potential impact and likelihood of happening — and of the cost of remedial measures. This includes not only standards, materials, communications and emergency arrangements, but also the need for crowd control plans at major stations and thus the means of providing for the growing problem of congestion relief.

Another result was a complete change of top management.

If poor quality in a world of rising expectations was one problem, the other conundrum was growth. The level and pattern of demand for Underground travel is a resultant of multiple factors, many of which are way outside the control of any transport undertaking. Population, employment, personal incomes, car ownership, road conditions and tourism are among those factors. As with personal investment warnings, 'passenger volumes may go down as well as up'. And down by 10% they have gone since the heady days of 1988/89 when 815 million journeys on London Underground were recorded, to reach a low of 728 million journeys in 1992/93. But, by 1994/95, volumes had recovered to 764 million. What next?

To start with, sustained growth when it comes may not be uniform. If, for example, future

employment is associated with major developments in Docklands, the City, King's Cross and Heathrow, the loads imposed on the Underground network will be very uneven. It all boiled down to a conclusion that without action being taken, probably irrespective of any fares levels which might be considered reasonable, system capacity would become totally inadequate.

There were five strategic issues facing London Underground Ltd:

- The network capacity was constrained at the peak.
- There were service quality, as well as safety, problems as a result.
- The anticipated growth of demand would be a further 20% at peak and 30% at off-peak by 1997/98.
- Major additions to capacity needed large investments and long lead times.
- LUL had neither the cash nor the borrowing powers to fund extensive new investment in either the short or medium term.

What, then, would be the likely effects of taking various broad courses of action? Four scenarios were painted:

- Commercial network. This would make money, and be cash rich within a decade through high fares and the lopping off of the extremities, such as everything north and west of Harrow-on-the-Hill. Lines such as the Bakerloo which are paralleled (in this case mostly by the Jubilee Line or BR North London Railways) would close completely. Overall, the network would shrink to about half its present size.
- Quality network. The quality of provision would be brought up to predetermined levels, but essentially the system would

Above:
**A 1992 stock train for the Central Line arriving
at Epping on 29 September 1994; on its return
journey it will proceed to Ealing Broadway.**
John Glover

remain within the limits of the existing
infrastructure.

- Expanded network. As quality network, but
  providing additional works to relieve
  congestion and serving new areas of
  London as could be justified.
- London showpiece network. This would be
  an attempt to make London resemble Paris,
  but at a capital cost of £10 billion which
  could come only from outside sources.

What would the pursuit of a commercial network
mean for London? High fares would certainly
reduce passenger congestion on the Underground,
and enable service quality to be improved
significantly; the revenues could be used to fund
investment. However, higher fares would also
reduce demand and encourage relocation away
from London. Was that what London Underground
(and its LRT parent body) were there to do? A
reading of the 1984 London Regional Transport Act
confirms that LRT is there 'to have due regard to the
transport needs for the time being of Greater
London'.

If, however, unchecked demand-led growth were
to resume, perpetuation of the present financial
regime would result in service volume, quality and
safety all suffering. The problems of inadequate
capacity have to be addressed; unfortunately, the
levels of investment needed are not related to the

volume of business, nor to the fares levels charged,
nor even the latent demand for services. It is simply
not tenable to allow more and more passengers to
crowd into the system unless it is expanded to
cope: the safety of passengers in overcrowded
conditions is at risk, and the congestion factor as on
the roads would result in the overall throughput
diminishing as trains were forced to spend longer at
station platforms. This raises the spectacle of certain
central London stations having to be closed for the
duration of the peak. This situation was nearer than
it might have seemed, with for example Chancery
Lane being available for exit only during the
morning rush hour, while King's Cross adopted an
elaborate one way system to keep the two flows of
passengers apart.

Financial performance of the business cannot be
separated from the above, and it is just not possible
to have everything. An equation has to be found
which balances financial performance against
adequate quality, volume of service provision and
safety. What the customers of London Underground
merited was a policy which allowed government
funding for major investment in expanding service
provision, offset against internal efficiency
improvements and restructuring of the business to
improve its management, and the results showing
within a five-year time scale. There needs to be a
co-ordinated framework.

During this period, the standards of customer
service and company performance must improve
steadily, the gains must be consolidated with past
standards restored, and the strength of the
improved position used as a justification for further
expansion. While the first stages were a matter for

Underground management, the latter could only be
accelerated or even achieved at all with the financial
help of the government and/or the private sector.
Realistically, the returns for private investment in
rapid transit are just not there, with the result that
public cash is needed in the vast majority of cases.
With LUL at present, a substantial proportion of
investment comes from operating profits, and the
rest from external sources.

If that is the strategy, how could it be made to
happen? The management organisation now
consists of a small executive Board of Chairman,
Managing Director, Engineering and Finance
Directors; there are also four non-executive
positions. Each Underground line has been made a
profit centre and been given its own General
Manager, responsible for the volume, quality and
safety of the service operated. These Managers are
also responsible for costs and revenues, the
performance of the physical assets over which they
have charge, and of that all-important asset —
people. Everything else is dealt with as a support
function. As part of that shake-up, all staff are
responsible to one named manager, who controls
directly a maximum of 100 individuals. This
number was selected to enable all of them to be
known personally to the manager, and replaces a
system where an individual member of staff might
be responsible, in turn, to a succession of shift
supervisors.

What was the then state of London
Underground? Sadly, the situation was not
encouraging. Customer perception was decidedly
poor, rating the Underground's value for money as
inadequate. Both the capacity of the system and the

Above:
The 'C' stock trains have now been refurbished, a task which included the substitution of four longitudinal seats for the facing/back bays of four previously installed. This maintained total seating capacity on these trains with four sets of double doors per side, albeit with a reduced width available for each seat. Also added were the windows in the car ends, to enable passengers to see into the adjoining vehicle.
John Glover

conditions in which people had to travel were found wanting. Staff were perceived as unhelpful, restrictive practices abounded, and their efficiency was poor. This was partly due to uncompetitive pay levels not attracting the staff quality needed. Many assets were near life-expired and thus more costly to maintain than they should have been. Where investment had taken place, much of it had been fragmented and incomplete. There had been many improvement measures, but overall they had not been focused sufficiently; frustratingly, in spite of all the efforts made, the results did not show and were neither recognised nor appreciated. Finally, management's ability to measure and control performance had been severely limited.

It was not just the politicians who had been at fault, as the Underground's 1988 'Plan for Action' frankly admitted:

'Though this thoroughly unsatisfactory situation derived in large part from the political and national economic context of the business, there were also major weaknesses in the organisational structure and performance of management in the Underground.'

From such a base line, the only way to go is up. In 'PLEASE', the Company set out a 'mission statement' of its aims:

Partner (in London's prosperity and development)
Leader (among world rapid transit systems)
Enjoyable (for both passengers and staff)
Affordable (fares for both Londoners and visitors)
Safe (and seen to be so)
Efficient (and perceived to be so by all concerned)

The long term objective was that the total service will be of the same standard which is implied by new trains, updated control systems and signalling, well maintained track and modernised stations. The financial performance must be maximised within the constraints of volume and the extension of quality and safety of service. Market potential must be optimised, and it was essential that long term total costs were brought down to the lowest possible level.

The immediate response provided for a number of major upgrading proposals, of which the Central Line was by far the most extensive and exciting project. This offered its complete re-equipment. The 85 new trains of 1992 stock and their derivation

from the 1986 stock have already been discussed. The Central Line refurbishment included the installation of new fixed block signalling and centralised control. The power supply system was also to be replaced and uprated, to allow trains to run faster and thus reduce journey times by 12%. There were also minor track realignments to raise speed limits. The new signalling aimed to increase the previous 30 trains per hour (tph) throughput to 33/34tph; the restrictions such as speeds over the tortuous curves at Bank and the time taken to discharge passengers at Liverpool Street and other busy stations were as much limits as was the signalling, when it came to increasing service frequency further. Speed control signalling, a feature of inter-war installations, had been removed in the declining traffic years of the 1960s and the 1970s. The new signalling offers the opportunity to get back to frequencies achieved in the past. While a transmission-based signalling system based on a moving block section and offering a potential 38 or even 39tph is now available, it was not judged as yet being sufficiently developed or cost effective for Central Line use.

The whole project, which increases the total line carrying capacity by about 16%, is due for completion in 1996.

The Northern Line is the second busiest, with around 700,000 passengers a day. Large scale investment to catch up on 35 years of backlog was needed, and one of the major schemes was Angel station. New office building at Angel had seen traffic rise by 123% in six years, with more to come as the area is ripe for redevelopment. The station was

Northern Improvements.

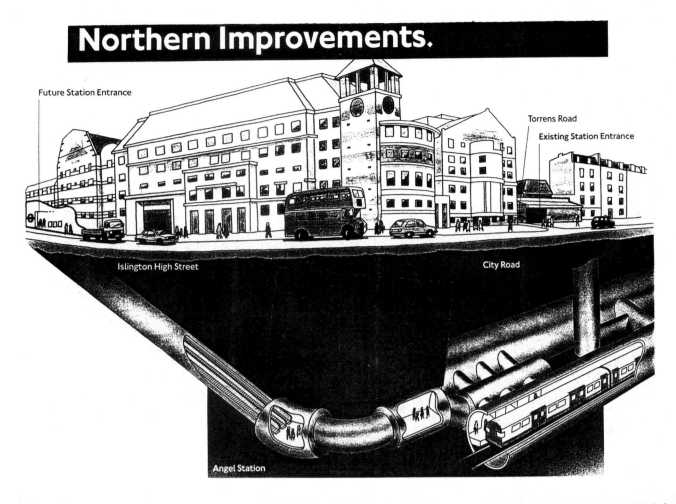

Future Station Entrance

Torrens Road

Existing Station Entrance

Islington High Street

City Road

Angel Station

Above:
Angel station reconstruction.

provided only with lifts, but under a £70 million scheme, a new entrance and ticket hall were built to lead to the longest escalator shafts on the Underground. From there, a second short escalator flight descends to a circulating area to the west of the previous island platform. The northbound track of this was filled in as was done at Euston (old Northern City Line southbound platform) when the Victoria Line was built, and a direct passageway made to the new circulating area. A totally new northbound platform was constructed in a new station tunnel, and the line diverted into it. Work was completed in 1992.

Although the Northern Line is next in the queue for wholesale updating after the Central, a number of shorter term improvements have been undertaken. Transfer of additional trains from the Bakerloo as part of the repercussions of the delivery of the 1983 tube stock boosted the number in service. Highgate depot was reopened and modernised, while 11 stations at the southern end of the line are being extensively refurbished — with special attention paid to anti-graffiti measures. The dot matrix information displays are being upgraded at all 49 stations on the line, and a further extension of passenger security measures is anticipated at the southern end, which has seen some growth of late evening traffic in response. Dot matrix indicators are being provided in some ticket halls so that passengers need to descend to platform level only when their train's arrival is

imminent. Aerials are now being installed in the ceilings of underground passages so that staff can remain in contact by personal radio.

The Northern is operated by a mixture of 1959-62 and 1972 Mk 1 stock trains. Refurbishment work concentrated on the 1972 stock as the remainder were too old to justify much expenditure. The new décor is designed to offer a brash exterior and a homely interior. Lighting was softened to reduce glare, while providing the much liked end bulkhead lights to brighten up the gloomy corners. Repositioned grab rails are intended to encourage standing passengers to move away from the door area. Ceiling panels and other fittings which have been assessed as potential fire hazards have been replaced, and public address fitted. Comparable work has been carried out on the very similar Victoria Line (1967) and Bakerloo Line (1972 Mk II) stock.

Replacement of the Northern Line rolling stock will not result in carbon copies of the Central Line stock. The Northern has long continuous tunnel gradients to the north, and a much higher proportion of the line is in tunnel. Station platforms are also relatively restricted in length, and operationally it would be desirable to get away from an inflexible seven car formation. It was announced late in 1994 that a new fleet of 106 trains will be built by Metro-Cammell (now part of GEC-Alsthom) in Birmingham in an entirely new form of contract.

GEC-Alsthom will be responsible for maintaining the trains and supplying sufficient for LUL to operate in service on a daily rental basis. The contract is for a 20-year agreement and is performance related. The reliability target includes a failure rate of 1 in 19,000 miles; this compares

with 1 in 2,500 miles for the present elderly fleet. There will also be a 'small payment' related to the number of passengers carried on the Northern Line. The first trains are expected to be delivered in 1996/97 and by the time the last train is delivered in 1998/99 the annual usage payments, excluding maintenance, will be in the order of £33 million escalating thereafter at 3% per annum.

The maintenance staff at Golders Green and Morden depots will transfer to GEC-Alsthom. The strengthening of power supplies and the renewal of signalling now take on an added priority. In prospect are a reduction of journey times, for which the permanent way will also need to be brought up to scratch, coupled with increased service frequencies. Flat-bottomed long-welded rail will become standard equipment.

Among the capital works intended are the making of East Finchley into a useful four-tracked station with a loop in each direction, and the provision of more stabling sidings at some points to reflect a changed balance of service patterns between the various destinations.

The Northern Line capacity had been reduced in the years of passenger losses by signalling simplification schemes, which are now much regretted. The practical maximum on each of the Charing Cross and City branches is presently 25tph although theory says that more ought to be possible. Transmission-based signalling is now the favoured means to overcome the problem; through the use of this, the train service might be increased to 32tph. Journey times via the City are 4min longer than via Charing Cross. This tends to lead to movements at junctions which conflict with each other at either Camden Town or Kennington.

The 106-train fleet would signal its position and its speed via the track to a central computer, which then analyses the information every 0.5sec and 'instructs' the train accordingly. Such measures are now favoured over earlier ideas such as splitting the line into High Barnet/Mill Hill East to Morden via the City, and Edgware to Kennington via Charing Cross. Difficulties with this option include the vast numbers of passengers who would have to change (especially at Camden Town) and the implication for station dwell times, and the likely imbalances of peak and off-peak traffic requirements on the two routes. A further complication would be the imbalance of depot engineering facilities. Spending £75 million or so to rebuild Camden Town seems a lot merely to inconvenience passengers.

Throughout the system, station modernisation has absorbed large chunks of funds. The work is difficult as it has to be carried out around times when trains are still running and the station is in use. Consequently, much of the retiling and platform resurfacing can only be done at night or during periods of extended line closure. There were also unforeseen hazards; it was a materials store being used by a contractor during station modernisation at Oxford Circus in 1984 which caught fire and wrecked the northbound Victoria Line platform. A wide variety of schemes has been tried; one of the most successful was that at Baker Street on the original 1863 Metropolitan and Circle platforms. The original station was lit by gas at night, but by day natural daylight came from the shafts above the platforms which had been installed to allow the escape of smoke from the locomotives. Later, accumulated grime, advertising hoardings and fluorescent lighting made it a dismal place indeed. The refurbishment involved stone cleaning, the introduction of artificial daylight through sodium lights in the old shafts, and new seats and fittings.

Other notable past refurbishments have been David Gentleman's mural on melamine panels of the mediaeval craftsmen building the original Eleanor Cross above at Charing Cross (Northern Line), and a complementary portrayal of some of the treasures of the National Gallery and the National Portrait Gallery on the Bakerloo Line platforms. Eduardo Paolozzi's unique hi-fi inspired mosaics at Tottenham Court Road, the British Museum theme at Holborn, and the Brunel tunnelling shields at Paddington are others which catch the eye. Throughout, fittings such as cable ducts and seats are in the Line colour, and standard roundel-style station names are used. Various experiments have taken place with signing, and illuminated 'Way Out' indicators, for instance, are all now in yellow.

The relief of station congestion has produced a list which included Monument (District Line) and Bank (Northern Line), both as a result of the DLR extension, and Goodge Street as a result of UTS. The problems varied between locations; lift or escalator capacity (eg Russell Square), the ticket barrier or ticket hall capacity (eg Bayswater, High Street Kensington), platform capacity (eg Liverpool Street, Central Line and Victoria, Victoria Line). At Euston Square, consideration was being given to 'double-ending' the station by providing a ticket hall at each end of the platforms; here that would have the additional advantage of improving the access to Euston Railtrack station. At Tottenham Court Road, better street access was needed, and a new escalator shaft. A total of 24 or 25 stations have a measurable present problem, while an eye to future expansion as a result of new lines is also important. Thus a rebuilt Tottenham Court Road would include embryonic provision for both CrossRail and the Chelsea–Hackney lines.

The difficulties at Victoria were complex. The Victoria Line ticket hall needed enlargement, with augmentation to the escalators and the lower concourse. Restricted platform widths increased station stop times, which had serious implications for the train service which could be operated. If trains are halted by up to a minute to allow passengers to alight and board (preferably in that order!), this constrained the number of trains per hour which could be run on the whole line. The possible solutions, all of which were exceedingly costly, included widened station platforms, additional platforms, and 'double-ending' the station. In such cases, and Liverpool Street Central Line was as bad, the aim must be to control stop times, and if this needed new track layouts, rolling stock modifications, staff training or signalling changes, these had to be built into the plans.

The capacity of lines is governed primarily by train lengths and frequencies. More trains and longer trains were one of the options being pursued by British Rail, but on the existing Underground with traditional signalling, it is considered that something like 30 trains per hour is the realistic maximum, despite schedules in the past on the Bakerloo and District Lines offering a (perhaps theoretical) 34 or 36tph. Train capacities vary, but using the Underground's formal loading standards, an 8xA stock formation will carry 680, while both 6xC stock and most tube stock trains will carry 550. More passengers can of course squeeze themselves on. The new six-car trains being built for the Jubilee Line Extension are billed as seating 250 with a capacity for a further 1115 standing. This equates to 229 passenger per car, or more than four standing for every seated passenger!

In the spring of 1989, London Regional Transport were set new objectives for their rail services by the government. These were:

- to carry through the recommendations arising from the King's Cross fire;
- to provide for the continuing increase in traffic on the Underground, and for growing needs in Docklands and
- to improve the quality of services and security for the traveller.

With the scene having changed significantly, formal targets have been set for service quality. Among these is the performance of lifts and escalators. Only 75% were in working order in

1989, which was freely admitted to be unacceptable. Those on the Victoria Line, which were only 20 years old, were failing. Underground escalators may now be the cleanest in the world in the aftermath of King's Cross, but the incapacity of the industry and the high loads being carried for hours at a time have played havoc with performance. New escalators are being installed at 12 a year for the foreseeable future.

In escalators, as in so much else, the largely unsung role of the engineer is crucial. Here too there are changes. Technology offers the ability to squeeze more out of existing infrastructure, to increase construction benefits and to reduce operating costs. But new technology is also demanding: new skills are needed, control over specifications is essential (including the interfaces between disciplines), while exploitation needs to encompass learning from outside. It is much more cost effective to learn from the mistakes of others!

Power electronics for rolling stock offer tremendous potential. The positive effects include energy saving, regenerative braking, jerk-free operation, wheelslip control, elimination of fire hazards through doing away with dc starting resistances, response to supply variations, and no contactor maintenance. Conversely, they add weight, interact with signalling and power supply, and need a greater engineering input.

Similarly, there are huge gains to be made in the interrelated fields of signalling, traffic control, communications and passenger information. What could be more antiquated in concept than traditional block signalling when track capacity is the most precious asset? Computer-aided

engineering enables calculations on matters such as safety and immunisation to be made more accurately. This therefore reduces the likelihood of wasteful over-engineering. Simulation for site specific designs can be carried out, and the testing of trade-offs. The need to build prototypes for engineering reasons has now largely passed. Another fast developing field includes management information systems; the instant calculating ability of computer systems vastly enhances the capability of flexible systems scheduling. The concomitant need is for wholly satisfactory agreements to be reached with the staff.

The conclusion is that the sheer scale of potential technology impacts must be managed, with London Underground determining where it is going and organising itself accordingly. Engineering activities are a service which is focused to meet the needs of business managers. Engineers determine standards. Equipment procurers (not all of them engineers) draw up specifications. Contractual obligations on outside purchases ensure (one hopes) reliability. However, while procurement by performance specification encourages the supplier to innovate (compared with technical specification), it has to be seen also in the context of managerial responsibilities. What is the best value for the business?

The Underground needs more revenue. By the end of the 1980s, it was noticeable that official noises were beginning to be made about fares levels; a slow increase in real fares since LRT took over in 1984 was approaching a cumulative 20% five years later. The harder line asserted that fares had not grown faster than earnings, and that fares

Above:
The Class 482 cars for the Waterloo & City Line were all but indistinguishable from their Central Line counterparts. New unit No 482501 is seen inside Waterloo depot on 13 May 1993 for artisan training. Brian Morrison

still offered good value for money. Indeed, the average fare per passenger journey in 1993/94 was 87p, compared with the then minimum fare of 90p applicable in the Central Zone 1. The users of the system are predominantly under 35 years old, while 70% are in the ABC1 social groups and relatively well off. With a government view that passengers must pay for the benefits they receive, further real fares increases with alterations to the Travelcard zonal system in order to finance investment, at least for renewals, seemed inevitable. However, pricing limitations by the Rail Regulator on BR fares will also affect London Underground pricing.

Such, at any rate, was the view of the Monopolies and Mergers Commission, which reported on London Underground in 1991. With economic recession biting into traffic levels, and following some financial misjudgements, the Company has had to make economies in all areas. The MMC were critical of the physically decayed state of much of the infrastructure. 'The public's perception of an erratic, overcrowded and poorly maintained service in many areas is broadly correct,' they said, albeit acknowledging that the overall picture was more

favourable. They too concluded that higher fares would be needed in order to finance investment and renewals, endorsing as they did the need to inject £³/₄ million a year for the foreseeable future.

Meanwhile, the public were invited to see how perceptions matched up with reality through the Customer Charter.

There is a key need to catch up on the investment and renewals expenditure which was denied in the mid-1980s. Otherwise, insufficient investment leads to higher asset age and failure rate, to higher maintenance costs and the costs of inspections and repairs. This results in a reduction of funds available for investment and thus to even higher asset age and failure rates… and so on.

Yet, it was not to be, for in their autumn 1992 statement the Government cut the promised 1993/94 investment programme by a third, with similar reductions in subsequent years. The result was a drastic slowing down or cancellation of projects, with station refurbishment being the worst hit area. Station modernisations, like those carried out successfully at Edgware Road (Bakerloo), Gloucester Road, Hammersmith (District and Piccadilly), and Hillingdon were among the schemes most easily dispensed with. Track reconditioning plus attention to tunnels, earthworks, bridges, power supplies, pumps, drainage and ventilation, lifts and escalators, and lighting are, perhaps regrettably but certainly realistically, far more important.

London Underground returned to the fray in 1993, when the 'Decently Modern Metro' was launched. Its aim is to provide up-to-date infrastructure supporting a railway which is safe, quick, reliable, clean, comfortable and efficient, and which gives good value for money. As Denis Tunnicliffe, LUL Managing Director, suggested to the Chartered Institute of Transport: 'This is not too much for Londoners to expect of their Underground system'.

With a total spend of about £7.5 billion over a decade, the main components of the 'Decently Modern Metro' are:

- Trains, including signalling, power supplies and depots £1.2 billion
- Stations £1.1 billion
- Infrastructure £2.0 billion
- Line developments (eg Central and Northern Lines) £1.6 billion
- Other expenditure (eg new line development) £1.6 billion

Total **£7.5 billion**

Of this, London Underground themselves might fund a quarter out of revenue gains and cost reduction; the remainder has to come from government, at a rather higher rate than they were intending to spend! Nevertheless, London Underground was setting itself a goal to become financially self-sufficient by the year 2004/05, once the investment backlog was cleared.

Customer Charter: Refund Form

Claims must be submitted within 14 days of the delay.
Please complete this form in capital letters.
USE EITHER BLUE OR BLACK INK.

Customer Services Centre
London Underground Limited
55 Broadway
London SW1H 0BD
Telephone 071-918

215214

1 Personal details

Surname

Date   30 April 1994

Claim   179488

Customer Charter refund Valid for 13 months

Value of single journey

£1.70   (One pound, seventy pence)

For terms and conditions see reverse

London Underground's 1994 Customer Charter

'...the best possible service...'

However, London Underground also warned that a 'Decently Modern Metro' could not be achieved for over 20 years if the level of investment implied in the autumn 1992 statement was the best which could be managed.

One indirect consequence of the Railways Act 1993 was the transfer of three parts of the railway system in the London area to the Underground. This took place on 1 April 1994, when London Underground became the owner and operator of the Waterloo & City Line, the Wimbledon branch of the District Line beyond Putney Bridge station, albeit excluding Wimbledon station itself, and the Kensington (Olympia) stub end.

The Underground-owned network increased in length by about five miles as a result. Acquisition included the liabilities as well as the benefits; thus Fulham Bridge (the railway bridge over the Thames at Putney) needs £7 million worth of repairs after being struck by a barge in 1991. Power supplies and signalling are, for the time being, bought in from Railtrack. Also new to the Underground was the inheritance of the two Travelators installed at Bank W&C station.

Although there are many possibilities for system expansion, times change, and there are also those parts which have perhaps outlived their usefulness. An Underground line closure is a rare event, yet on

Above:
There is much more to a railway than rolling stock. The complexity of the trackwork and associated signalling is evident in this view of the north end of Golders Green station looking towards the tunnel mouths, with a 1959 stock train approaching. All the infrastructure will need attention if the Northern Line is to make the most of the new trains to be provided under the Private Finance Initiative. *John Glover*

Below:
Kensington (Olympia) sees a 'D' stock train on the shuttle operation from High Street Kensington on 2 May 1983. The line is now wholly in LUL ownership, though this station remains in Railtrack ownership. *John Glover*

Above:
The last week on the Aldwych branch sees the three-car train of 1973 stock at Aldwych on 28 September 1994. *John Glover*

Below:
On 29 September 1994, a 1960 stock train, also of three cars, arrives at Epping from Ongar. *John Glover*

30 September 1994 both the Aldwych branch and the Epping–Ongar line saw their last trains. At Aldwych, the *coup de grâce* was the need for replacement of the 1906 lifts; usage by 450 passengers/day was judged inadequate to justify around £3 million in engineering capital expense.

For Ongar and the one remaining intermediate branch station of North Weald, a residual traffic of 80 people/day over a six-mile single line with deteriorating track was clearly insufficient. This third attempt at line closure succeeded, the last having been over a decade earlier.

Railways thrive on volume; urban systems are in their element when moving perhaps 20,000 passengers per hour, per direction. If, however, there are no more passengers than a few buses can carry, it is difficult to defend the incurring of operating costs, let alone spending on maintenance and renewals for a specialised right of way with no alternative uses.

For an outside view, it is perhaps instructive to quote Alan F. Kiepper, President of New York City Transit

Above:
The Underground has 'exported' two sets of rolling stock to the Isle of Wight. Class 485 No 485001 in blue and grey livery arrives at Ryde St John's Road from Shanklin. These pre-1938 cars monopolised Island rail services from 1967 until their own replacement by 1938 stock. *John Glover*

Below:
The Underground at sea. Class 483 No 004 approaches Ryde Pier Head station, with Ryde Esplanade station in the background, in June 1992. The 1938 stock displaced the Class 485 units in 1989/90. *John Glover*

Authority, in his London Transport lecture, 1994.

'We clearly have not found a satisfactory way to properly manage and maintain public transportation services and facilities over the long haul.'

'We have vacillated between private ownership with government regulation and total public ownership and operation. Neither has proved satisfactory and, more importantly, we cannot live with the consequences of either. Moreover, the transition between the two can be terribly destructive and unsettling.'

'The fact is that few, if any, societies are prepared to either let privatisation and the laws of supply and demand set the level of service and fares or, alternatively, to pay the continuing public price to provide extensive service at low cost. We move from one to the other and, in so doing, keep public transport in a constantly unsettled state. London and New York are cases in point.'

Chapter 13

A New Railway Age?

What do we mean by a metropolitan or Underground railway? This definition was coined by Michael Robbins in 1981 for the International Union of Public Transport (UITP):

'A metropolitan railway is one designed to provide a system for the carriage of large numbers of passengers within a city area by means of railed vehicles under external control, within space which is wholly or partly in tunnel and is completely devoted to their use.'

To which was later added:

'A transport system using its own reserved infrastructure to handle traffic in excess of 10,000 per hour, based largely on the railway technology currently available or in course of development.'

Underground railways offer high capacity, but only at a high cost. They are ideal for serving high density corridor movements, which they also encourage. In this lies their fundamental challenge. Their conception, planning, financing and construction are so complex and involve so many different interests that it is a major challenge to bring them into existence. In addition, when those hurdles have been overcome, the operating railway can be a major determinant of land use patterns and development (Ridley, 1989).

What is the market for rail services in London? According to London Underground's 1991 Company Plan, there are around 130 million trips per week by all modes in Greater London, of which about 12% are made by Underground (out of the 38% which use public transport). However, the Underground is particularly strong in journeys to work and school, which account for just over half of the total.

This in turn means that the system's market share is unevenly distributed by the day of the week, with only 6% of Saturday trips by Underground and 4% of Sundays. The share is much larger on Mondays to Fridays.

It is in journeys to, from and within central London where public transport is really dominant; in the morning peak commuting market, the Underground is used by 52% or just over half a million passengers daily. This includes those who also travel by BR for part of their journey. Hence, economic trends in general and employment trends in particular are highly important to the undertaking.

The embarrassment of custom for the Underground in the late 1980s was to offer an unparalleled opportunity for network development. The Central London Rail Study (CLRS) of 1989 was a joint approach by the Department of Transport,

Above:
CrossRail services to Aylesbury will curtail the Metropolitan Line interests north of Moor Park, but will continue to serve Watford. This is Watford South Junction when it was being rearranged as part of the Amersham electrification. The date is 8 June 1962.
J. A. Rosser

which brought together British Rail, London Regional Transport and London Underground Ltd to address the wider issues. The terms of reference of the CLRS were as follows:

- To develop a strategy for improving services for rail passengers.
- To provide for forecast demand.
- To have regard to the need to maximise the use of existing resources.
- To put forward packages of measures whose costs were justified in terms of revenue and external benefits.
- To present the strategic choices.

Such a remit forces a position to be taken on a number of critical issues. Would the traffic growth of the last few years persist — and what proportion could be attracted to rail? Alternatively, if the system remained static, would that have the effect of throttling the growth, which would then take

147

place outside the London area altogether (and, if so, did that actually matter?). What were the various options for dealing with that growth, and what could be the basis for a justification of the expenditure needed for a really major increase in capacity?

Compared with 1987, the year 2001 was then expected to see a further rise of between 20% and 30% in peak traffic, with the off-peak growing between 30% and 45%. Employment was undoubtedly the key; around one million people were employed in the Central Area in 1987, a number which it was anticipated would grow by 100,000 (10%) or even by 150,000 (15%) by the end of the century. In Docklands the growth rates were much higher, given the relatively insignificant base levels, leading to employment there of between 120,000 and 150,000 in 2001.

It is the peak period where the capacity problem becomes acute. The system had, more or less, coped with the growth until then, albeit with severe discomfort in some areas. Identified sections of lines which were now overloaded in the peak included:

Above:
This is a Metro-Cammell interior, as provided in their Type C train of 1986 rolling stock. It will be interesting to see what changes are wrought for the Jubilee and Northern Line trains.
Metro-Cammell

Left:
The Jubilee Line Extension underground stations will be provided with platform doors, which will open only when there is a train present and the doors are lined up with those on the train. *LUL*

Opposite top:
The JLE will have a depot at Stratford Market to supplement the Neasden facility. This is an artist's impression. *LUL*

Opposite bottom:
The East London Line has ample dimensions to take BR rolling stock, as this 'A' stock train disappearing into the tunnel north of Surrey Quays demonstrated on 3 May 1990. *John Glover*

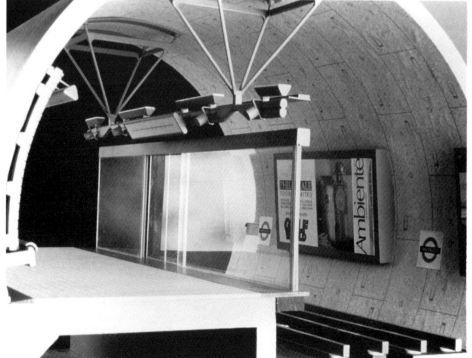

- Oxford Circus and Euston
- Oxford Circus and Swiss Cottage
- Bank and Elephant & Castle
- Arsenal and Holborn
- St James's Park and Sloane Square

- Archway and Warren Street
- Leyton and Holborn
- Fulham Broadway and South Kensington, and
- Green Park and Victoria.

Given the forecast additional peak traffic on the system by 2001, overloading would take in all the eastern part of the Central Line, large chunks of the Northern and Victoria Lines, the District and Piccadilly Line corridors to west London, and the

WATFORD HIGH STREET

Metropolitan and Jubilee Line corridors to north west London.

So far, then, the potential bill for the base network looked something like this:

Relief of station congestion	£420 million
Improving operating performance	£60 million
Service enhancements (LUL)	£200 million
Service enhancements (BR)	£550 million
Major changes to service structure	£100 million
Total	**up to £1,500 million**

Beyond that, the answer had to lie in network extensions. The most exciting schemes were those for the new lines across Central London. There were two CLRS schemes with a high claim to priority for implementation. West of London, the CrossRail scheme would run from Aylesbury through Amersham and Harrow-on-the-Hill to a tunnel mouth near Royal Oak, and from Reading via Slough to the same tunnel mouth. Stations in central London are to be Paddington, Bond Street, Tottenham Court Road, Farringdon and Liverpool Street. East of London, CrossRail is to run from a tunnel mouth near Bethnal Green to Stratford, Romford and Shenfield.

With CrossRail, there would be no Metropolitan Line services at all north of Watford South Junction to Rickmansworth and Amersham/Chesham; the Chiltern Line services from Marylebone via Amersham would also disappear. CrossRail trains would follow the existing Great Central line to Neasden and thence use a mixture of freight lines and new construction to reach the GW main line near Old Oak Common. The scheme aims both to reduce overcrowding on the radial routes and to ease passenger distribution within central London.

The existing British Rail suburban services out to Reading would be superseded, while a few CrossRail trains would also be able to proceed to and from Heathrow by the Heathrow Express Railway.

Paddington-Liverpool Street on the brand-new underground alignment, with gradients in places as steep as 1 in 30, would be a 10min journey. Initially 24 trains/hr would use the link, but with provision made both for longer trains and more frequent services. A journey such as Amersham to Tottenham Court Road could be completed within a running time of 28min due, in part, to the restoration of 70mph running north of Harrow. The CrossRail system would offer limited stop, high quality services, designed to match rising social expectations.

It is intended that new Class 341 25kV ac electric multiple-units would provide all services; although considered, dual-voltage units are not favoured. As a result, part of the present Metropolitan would be converted to ac overhead. Of all the schemes tested in the CLRS report, CrossRail was the one which came closest to eliminating overcrowding on the most heavily laden section of the Underground between Chancery Lane and Liverpool Street. It was also the only one to reduce loads to below the planning standard on the Metropolitan and Circle Lines east of Baker Street. Furthermore, it even had some effect on the District and Piccadilly Lines around Earl's Court, by attracting people in the Ealing area away from the Underground.

Even so, the CrossRail Bill failed to pass into law, and a new application is being made under the Transport and Works Act procedures.

The north–south link has long been expected to be provided by a new Chelsea–Hackney

Above:
Will the Underground return to Watford High Street and Watford Junction? Bakerloo services were withdrawn north of Stonebridge Park in 1982 and then restored in 1984 — but only as far as Harrow & Wealdstone. Restoration now depends on the Croxley link. A 1938 stock train arrives at Watford High Street in April 1977 on a southbound working. John Glover

Right:
Maybe there is scope for more intermixing of Underground and BR operations, as happens as a matter of course north of Queen's Park, between the Bakerloo Line and North London Railways. As dusk gathers on 14 March 1995, a 1972 Mk II train arrives at Kensal Green with a Stonebridge Park service. John Glover

Underground line, taking over the present Wimbledon branch of the District Line as far as Parsons Green where it would enter tunnel. It might then proceed via King's Road, Chelsea, Sloane Square, Victoria, Piccadilly Circus, Tottenham Court Road, King's Cross, Angel, Essex Road, entering new areas for the Underground at Dalston, Hackney Central and Homerton. The line would surface near Leytonstone and then take over the Epping branch of the Central Line.

However, changes of plan are continuing. Chelsea–Hackney is presently seen as a tube loading-gauge line, though construction to surface stock standards has certainly been considered. An alternative being canvassed in 1995 was the southwest to northeast Metro.

Still starting from Wimbledon, one possibility is for the Metro to run eastwards from East Putney alongside the Railtrack line to Wandsworth Town and Clapham Junction, thence in tunnel to a station in the Battersea power station area. The line would then have stations at Victoria, Tottenham Court Road and King's Cross. Surfacing beyond the last named, the Metro could run on Railtrack's North London Line to Highbury & Islington, Dalston and Hackney Central. From there, further choices include access to Leytonstone by tunnel and hence to Epping, or continuing to Stratford and beyond to North Woolwich or, possibly, with the addition of a new tunnel under the Thames to Woolwich and up to the surface by Abbey Wood. The alternatives in southwest London include the previous Chelsea–Hackney route or one via Clapham Junction and Chelsea Harbour before reaching King's Road, Chelsea.

In contrast with Chelsea–Hackney, the southwest to northeast Metro would be of not less than Underground surface stock and probably BR stock loading gauge. The tunnelled portion would be reduced from 11.7 miles to around 6.5 miles, depending on which sub-option was taken forward.

Together with the omission of a station at Piccadilly Circus, this has a perhaps decisive advantage of much reduced tunnelling costs. The result is that the capital costs of the Metro ideas are put at something around one half of the £2.5 billion Chelsea–Hackney proposal.

With the possibilities of through running to and from Railtrack lines, this would be a remarkably flexible piece of railway. Consultation is proceeding on the various alternatives offered.

To the surprise of many, though, it was the Jubilee Line extension (JLE) to Stratford for which a Parliamentary Bill was deposited in 1989, following pledges of financial support from private sector developers in Docklands. However, it transpired subsequently that private contributions would match no more than 15% or so of the costs. The Jubilee, on its chosen alignment, did not even appear on the list of the Central London Rail Study options, but was the subject of the later East London Rail Study.

The £1.9 billion scheme was authorised in October 1993, after interminable financial wranglings over construction funding. It is now

being built, a task which is expected to take nearly five years. All the new running tunnels are to be bored to an enhanced 4.35m diameter, to allow for the installation of a side walkway. This aids maintenance and eases the detraining of passengers, should this be necessary for any reason.

The route of the JLE diverges from the existing line at the south end of Green Park station. From here, new tunnels pass beneath part of the St James's area, Pall Mall, under St James's Park and close to the Palace of Westminster. At Westminster, new platforms are being built below the present station. From here, the JLE passes under the river for the first time and below the old County Hall before reaching Waterloo. Here it will be the lowest of the four Underground lines, at a depth of about 100ft. Upstairs, there are many domestic rail services and also Eurostars to Paris and Brussels.

At Southwark, the next station, there is to be interchange with the southern end of the nearby platforms of Waterloo East Railtrack station; at London Bridge the line will be below the Railtrack concourse, with an escalator link to the Northern Line. Bermondsey is a new station, but at Canada Water the JLE passes beneath the East London Line. The latter was closed completely in 1995 for an extended period to enable the Canada Water interchange station to be constructed and the whole of the East London Line to be resignalled. The JLE then crosses again beneath the Thames to reach Canary Wharf.

On the Isle of Dogs, the 'cut and cover' station is being built in the bed of the dock, between Canary Wharf and the Docklands Light Railway's Heron Quays. This is expected to be one of the busiest on the line, and will be double-ended with a bank of escalators at each end of the platforms. Access will be through three glass domes rising out of a newly created park. Back under the river for a third time, the objective this time is the presently derelict wasteland site of North Greenwich. Here a three platform station with turnback facilities is being constructed.

By now, the JLE is heading north. It crosses under the river for the fourth and last time and rises to the surface just short of Canning Town. This will be a three way interchange station, the other lines being the North London Richmond–North Woolwich service and the DLR's Beckton branch.

From here the JLE uses the western side of the former four-track railway formation, alongside the present North London Line. At West Ham there is also an interchange with the District Line; perhaps this will also one day boast interchange facilities with the London, Tilbury & Southend line. At the Stratford terminus, of course, available options include the Central Line, BR services and the DLR; in the future one might be able to add in CrossRail and a Channel Tunnel Rail Link International and Domestic station.

The Jubilee Line extension is 10 miles in length, three-quarters of which is underground. A total of 59 new six-car trains are being built by GEC-Alsthom to re-equip the whole line right through to Stanmore. The design of the pairs of three-car units will allow the subsequent insertion of an additional seventh car if required. A rolling stock depot is being built at Stratford Market. Fourteen works locomotives are also being supplied, as well as wagons. The existing 31 train fleet of 1983 stock, for which a new use has yet to be determined, becomes surplus to requirements.

There will be a line control centre at Neasden,

Speed around a Winter Wonderland

UNDERGROUND

You can't beat the Tube

Above:
The extension of existing lines may have unwelcome hazards. A 1992 stock train arrives at Tottenham Court Road. It is approaching the section of station tunnel which was enlarged in the late 1930s, as part of the Central Line extension work, to enable longer trains to be run. However, although the new tunnel diameter increased conductor rail clearances as may be seen, this had no effect on the original sections. The Central Line's outside conductor rail thus remains above the standard height used elsewhere on the Underground.
John Glover

Left:
A poster displayed on the Underground during the winter 1994/95 period.
John Glover

and the initial service is intended to be 27 trains/hr. However, the transmission-based signalling will allow up to 35 trains/hr to be provided. Journey times may be calculated at around 2min between each pair of stations. This puts Canary Wharf a mere 10min away from Waterloo, 8min from Stratford, or 6min from London Bridge. The presently available alternatives, one might add, are rather slower.

The stations represent a considerable upgrade on previous practice. A typical station layout underground will include a ventilation shaft at each end, emergency stairs and a lift for disabled passengers. This could also be used by those accompanied by children or luggage. On the edges of platforms, automatic platform doors will be installed for the first time anywhere in Britain. Escalators will be in banks of three or four, with either one or two banks needed to cover the vertical distances. Thus, a remarkable total of 115 escalators will be provided, representing very nearly half as many again as existed previously on the whole of London Underground. This is all for a mere 11 stations, three of which are above ground!

Tunnelling access is being made from six of the 36 construction sites overall. Geological conditions for tunnelling are superior at the western end, where London Clay is a much more favourable medium than the Woolwich and Reading Beds and Thanet Sands east of London Bridge. Much use is being made of the New Austrian Tunnelling Method,

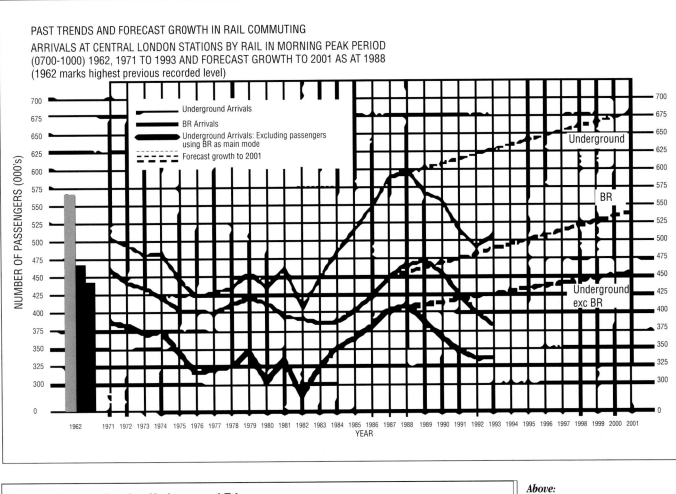

PAST TRENDS AND FORECAST GROWTH IN RAIL COMMUTING
ARRIVALS AT CENTRAL LONDON STATIONS BY RAIL IN MORNING PEAK PERIOD
(0700-1000) 1962, 1971 TO 1993 AND FORECAST GROWTH TO 2001 AS AT 1988
(1962 marks highest previous recorded level)

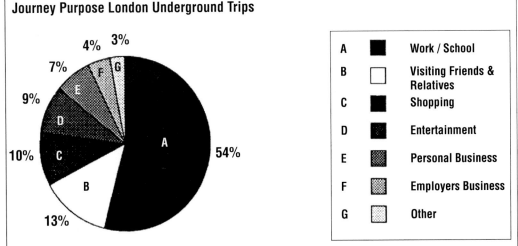

Journey Purpose London Underground Trips

A	■	Work / School
B	□	Visiting Friends & Relatives
C	■	Shopping
D	▨	Entertainment
E	▨	Personal Business
F	▨	Employers Business
G	▨	Other

Above:
Past trends and future changes in rail commuting: Central London Rail Study, 1989.

Left:
Journey purpose, London Underground trips.

present Shoreditch. The platforms could be incorporated in a major property development on the Bishopsgate Goods Yard site. The ELL route then joins the southern end of the disused Broad Street rail viaduct and proceeds north along it with new stations at Hoxton and Haggerston. It would terminate, initially anyway, at a station on the site of the former BR Dalston Junction.

Phase 1 of this project would also see the construction of a new servicing facility at Silwood, south of Surrey Quays. The inquiry Inspector's report is awaited for this £100 million scheme. Meanwhile, proposals for Phase 2 would see a southern extension to East Dulwich, mostly over Railtrack infrastructure, while Phase 3 offers a possible continuation from Dalston Junction to Highbury & Islington. This latter, however, needs to be related to the southwest and northeast Metro proposals. The whole project has the remarkable attribute of being achievable almost entirely over past or present railway infrastructure. It would also provide a useful new north–south link and forge

by which sprayed concrete reinforced with steel mesh and lattice girders takes the place of bolted segments. However, the collapse of the Heathrow Express station tunnels being built using NATM at the airport in October 1994 has cast some doubts upon the suitability of this method.

Where possible, JLE spoil is being removed by river barge. This is fine, provided that the barge does not turn turtle and spill its contents into the river, as happened early in 1995.

Opening of the Jubilee Line throughout is anticipated for 1998; it will not be opened progressively, section by section. The fate of the present Charing Cross terminus is unclear. It would seem to serve little useful purpose in future, other than as a bolt hole for trains from Stanmore if there

is a train failure or another problem on the Extension section.

Another and separate scheme which is making progress is that for the East London Line, which runs presently between Shoreditch and New Cross/New Cross Gate. The East London has a long and chequered history; the opportunity now exists to make it a more useful part of London's rail network by extensions both to the north and to the south.

An application under the Transport and Works Act 1992, the first for London Underground, has been made for a northern extension from Whitechapel. The line is to have a new station at Bishopsgate, to the west of, and replacing, the

153

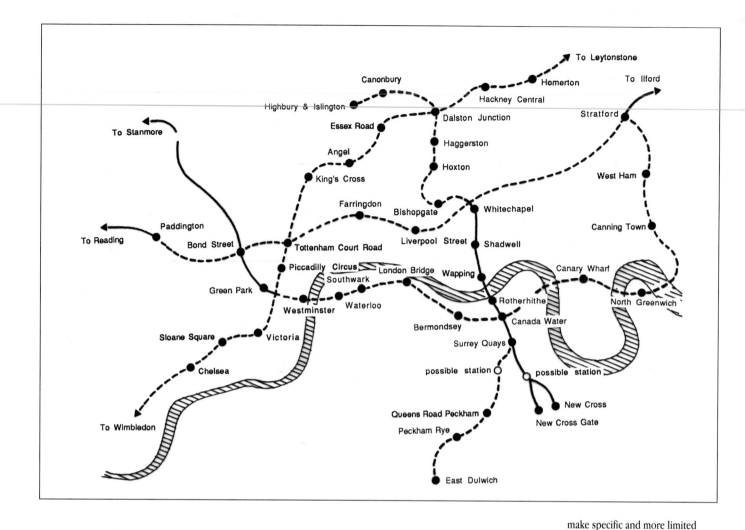

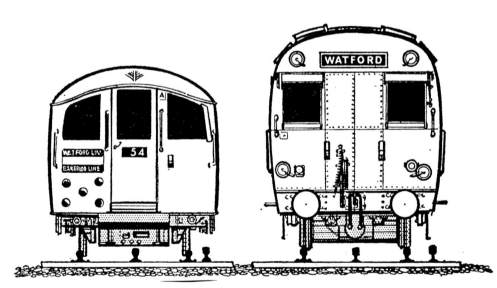

Top:
The Jubilee Line Extension, CrossRail, Chelsea–Hackney, and East London Line proposals.

Above:
The differential dimensions of tube and BR rolling stock.

many new interchanges.

The Transport and Works Act procedures replace those of the private Parliamentary Bills, under which railways have been constructed since Victorian times. Under the previous procedures, a Bill was introduced into either House of Parliament with a period allowed for petitioners to object. Such petitioners could then expect to be referred to the Select Committee of Members of Parliament appointed to consider the Bill.

The Committee listened first to the promoter making his case and then the objectors; the latter could either be against the project as a whole, or

make specific and more limited objections. The Select Committee had wide powers to reject the Bill, or impose changes in it or restrictions before it became an Act.

This procedure has now gone. Today, an application for an order is made to the Secretary of State for Transport by the promoters, and published. If objections are received, then a public inquiry will normally be held. An Inspector is appointed, who then submits a report to the Secretary of State for his decision. The Secretary of State may approve or reject the order, with or without modifications. The only exception is for projects judged to be of national importance, for which the hybrid Bill procedure has been retained. This is currently the case for the Channel Tunnel Rail Link Bill.

One of the dafter results of past railway construction was the L&NER/Metropolitan Watford branch of 1925. This never managed to reach Watford proper, via Cassiobury Park as intended. To the south and about 200yd away at its nearest, the London & North Western Railway's branch from their Watford High Street station ended at its own less than satisfactory terminus of Croxley Green.

A scheme to link the two and which would involve the closure of the present LUL Watford station and diversion of its trains to Watford Junction over the refurbished and doubled Railtrack branch is now being pursued by London

Underground. This modest scheme is costed at £25 million. The earliest possible date for the link to open would be 1998.

Another Central London Rail Scheme proposal included a western package. This requires the construction of two new underground links, which are rather more direct than the Journey Planner would lead one to believe. The links would be as follows:

- from Shepherd's Bush, Central Line, to Turnham Green, District Line; and
- from Queen's Park, Bakerloo Line, to North Acton, Central Line.

The first would allow the Central Line Ealing Broadway branch services to be diverted to and take over from the District Line branch to Richmond. This would relieve the District Line of one of its western branches and allow an enhanced service to be provided to Wimbledon and Ealing Broadway. The second scheme would permit the extension of Bakerloo Line services on to the Central Line, thus replacing the discontinued Central Line services to Ealing Broadway.

In each case a little over two miles of new tunnelling would be required, at a total cost estimated at £150 million (at 1989 prices). This scheme helps east and west of central area traffics of the Central, and relieves the Piccadilly Line corridor west through Hammersmith and Earl's Court.

Heathrow Airport continues to be less than adequately served by rail; the proposed Terminal 5, if constructed, will add to the daily passenger and staff movement requirements. As part of the overall scheme, London Underground propose to extend the Piccadilly Line from a new junction to the west of Terminals 1, 2, 3, in a double track formation to T5. The new Terminal is to be located just over a mile away to the west of the Central Terminal Area. One possible service pattern would be for all trains to run to Terminals 1, 2, 3. From there, most would continue to T5, with some proceeding in an anticlockwise direction to Terminal 4 and terminate. All trains would then return via Terminals 1, 2, 3 on their way back to Central London. (This would result in the effective abandonment of the Hatton Cross–Terminal 4 link.)

There is, of course, no need to terminate at T5; a further projection of the Piccadilly Line to an interchange station on the GW main line could well be feasible.

It might be observed that one of the difficulties associated with the Piccadilly Line generally is the need to interrupt the Heathrow service pattern to offer trains from central London to the Rayners Lane branch. An alternative way of providing for the branch has to be found if an enhanced service is needed for Heathrow.

Not all schemes involve London Underground as an operator. Albeit that the new construction is below ground level and in tunnel, the Heathrow Express Railway has no operational interface with London Underground. It may well, of course, affect Piccadilly Line traffic levels. Likewise, the Channel Tunnel Rail Link (CTRL) will incorporate long lengths of tunnelling in north London as it makes its way from the Dagenham area to its St Pancras terminal. Given its planned domestic as well as international use, there are substantial implications in the numbers who may wish to access St Pancras by Underground. Yet, again, Thameslink 2000 might help, or will construction of the Chelsea–Hackney Line or the Metro proposal take priority?

Other schemes outside the central London area include the CTRL-related Union Metro from Ebbsfleet (Kent) to Woolwich and under the Thames to Stratford on the North London Line, an orbital 'Outer Circle' scheme to link up various Railtrack lines, and the general sorting out of heavy rail activities south of the river. Ideas for the extension of the Charing Cross branch of the Northern Line southwards from Kennington, or the Bakerloo from Elephant & Castle, both have long pedigrees.

Throughout, the loosening of the informal lines of demarcation between heavy rail and Underground is noticeable. Yes, there are real problems of mixing the two on the same infrastructure, whether they be operational, engineering or technical snags. Any solution must meet the requirements of Her Majesty's Railway Inspectorate, but overcoming them where there is a real advantage to be gained is perhaps a challenge the industry faces.

There is much scope to relieve existing lines, make better use of what exists and to reach new markets. Perhaps it should be stressed that London Underground needs to look primarily for financial returns and revenue benefits, not social benefits. But, if London is to grow as people appear to want, massive investment is unavoidable, with the only rail alternative being demand management through fares. With major road building rightly ruled out as a practicable alternative, rail must be the mode to be exploited further. After all, the formal function of London Transport is to best meet the transport needs of Greater London.

It is system expansion which seems to cause the most difficulty. Who benefits? Who will pay for it? How much can users be expected to contribute? What can be expected from the private sector — and from government by means of grant?

Transport projects are typified by having initial spare capacity, which is filled only over time. This means long pay-back periods. Then, while revenues are stable and predictable once the asset is operational, there is considerable uncertainty at the feasibility and development stages. Also, once built in a location, infrastructure cannot be moved if better opportunities subsequently appear to lie elsewhere. Finally, transport projects are always up against competition with those from other industry sectors, which may have better cash flows and less risk attached to them.

The result is that public cash is needed in the vast majority of cases, justified by the benefits which are received by the non-users and by London as a whole.

How reliable are the forecasts of employment and activity generally? Over the years, there have been three classic and interlocking mistakes:

- underestimating the future rate of growth,
- providing insufficient investment to meet demand, and
- a lack of foresight on the best way forward.

Somehow, the same errors must not be made again. When it comes to new Underground railways, the costs are enormous and the time-scale for building is extended, but once complete they are there for ever. The premium which is to be placed on stable policies is incalculable. Underground railways quickly become the unseen but essential parts of the cities which they serve. But their conception, planning, financing and construction are so complex and involve so many different interests, that it is a major challenge to bring them into existence. New railways, or extensions to an existing system, can only be long term solutions to long term problems.

And so the development of London's rail transport services continues. Let us not lose sight of the purpose of the system: people congregate in cities because of the greater opportunities which they offer in terms of employment, education and social life. These opportunities can only be grasped if efficient transport is available at a reasonable cost; otherwise the whole purpose of the city is lost. Roads alone can never have the capacity to be the sole solution.

It will take time and effort. The following extract is from a book published in 1862, discussing the Metropolitan Railway a year before the first section opened:

'These works… will give employment to many, and be a nuisance to others, as long as they are being constructed. But when the mess is cleared up and the new channels (of railway) are thrown open, a sense of comfort and relief will be felt throughout the vast general traffic of London.'

In modern speak, the author was presumably predicting a highly positive cost/benefit ratio.

The years to come promise great things; let us hope that a combination of political will, managerial excellence and the garnering of political and public support will enable them to be achieved. As a nation, we cannot afford to take London's transport system for granted.

Appendices

1 Chronology of Principal Events on London's Underground Railways

Opening dates of sections of line until 30 June 1933

Metropolitan Railway

10 January 1863	Farringdon-Paddington
1 October 1863	Connection to Great Northern Railway at King's Cross
13 June 1864	Paddington-Hammersmith
23 December 1865	Farringdon-Moorgate
13 April 1868	Baker Street-Swiss Cottage
1 October 1868	Paddington-Gloucester Road
24 December 1868	Gloucester Road-South Kensington
1 February 1875	Moorgate-Liverpool Street, connecting to the Great Eastern Railway
12 July 1875	Moorgate-Liverpool Street (Metropolitan)
18 November 1876	Liverpool Street-Aldgate
30 June 1879	Swiss Cottage-West Hampstead
24 November 1879	West Hampstead-Willesden Green
2 August 1880	Willesden Green-Harrow-on-the-Hill
25 September 1882	Aldgate-Tower Hill
6 October 1884	Liverpool Street-Whitechapel
25 May 1885	Harrow-on-the-Hill-Pinner
1 September 1887	Pinner-Rickmansworth
8 July 1889	Rickmansworth-Chesham
1 September 1892	Chalfont & Latimer-Aylesbury (old)
1 January 1894	Stoke Mandeville-Aylesbury
1 April 1894	Aylesbury-Verney Junction (absorbed)
1 December 1899	Quainton Road-Brill (absorbed)
4 July 1904	Harrow-on-the-Hill-Uxbridge
1 January 1905	Electrification, Baker Street-Uxbridge
1 July 1905	First stage of Inner Circle electrification inaugurated
2 November 1925	Moor Park and Rickmansworth-Watford
10 December 1932	Wembley Park-Stanmore

Metropolitan District Railway

1 October 1868	High Street Kensington-Gloucester Road
24 December 1868	Gloucester Road-Westminster
12 April 1869	Gloucester Road-West Brompton
30 May 1870	Westminster-Blackfriars
3 July 1871	Blackfriars-Mansion House and High Street Kensington-Earl's Court
9 September 1874	Earl's Court-Hammersmith
1 June 1877	Hammersmith-Richmond
1 July 1879	Turnham Green-Ealing Broadway
1 March 1880	West Brompton-Putney Bridge
1 May 1883	Acton Town-Hounslow Town
21 July 1884	Osterley-Hounslow West
6 October 1884	Mansion House-Whitechapel. Inner Circle completed and junction made with East London Railway at Whitechapel
3 June 1889	Putney Bridge-Wimbledon
2 June 1902	Whitechapel-Upminster
23 June 1903	Ealing Common-Park Royal
28 June 1903	Park Royal-South Harrow
1 March 1910	South Harrow-Uxbridge
2 June 1932	Through working Barking-Upminster begun

East London Railway

1 October 1884	Underground services operated Whitechapel-New Cross and New Cross Gate until 3 December 1906
31 March 1913	Shoreditch-New Cross and New Cross Gate, using electric traction

Great Northern & City Railway

14 February 1904	Finsbury Park-Moorgate

City & South London Railway

18 December 1890	King William Street-Stockwell
25 February 1900	Borough-Moorgate; closure of King William Street previous day
3 June 1900	Stockwell-Clapham Common
17 November 1901	Moorgate-Angel
12 May 1907	Angel-Euston
20 April 1924	Moorgate-Euston reopened after reconstruction. Through running to Hampstead line via Camden Town
1 December 1924	Moorgate-Clapham Common reopened
13 December 1926	Clapham Common-Morden. Through running via Kennington and Embankment to Hampstead line

Waterloo & City Railway

8 August 1898	Waterloo & City, worked by London & South Western Railway

Central London Railway

30 July 1900	Shepherd's Bush-Bank
14 May 1908	Shepherd's Bush-Wood Lane
28 July 1912	Bank-Liverpool Street
3 August 1920	Wood Lane-Ealing Broadway

Baker Street & Waterloo Railway

10 March 1906	Baker Street-Lambeth North
5 August 1906	Lambeth North-Elephant & Castle
27 March 1907	Baker Street-Marylebone
15 June 1907	Marylebone-Edgware Road
1 December 1913	Edgware Road-Paddington
31 January 1915	Paddington-Kilburn Park
11 February 1915	Kilburn Park-Queen's Park
10 May 1915	Queen's Park-Willesden Junction
16 April 1917	Willesden Junction-Watford Junction

Great Northern, Piccadilly & Brompton Railway

15 December 1906	Hammersmith-Finsbury Park
30 November 1907	Holborn-Aldwych
4 July 1932	Hammersmith-South Harrow
19 September 1932	Finsbury Park-Arnos Grove
9 January 1933	Acton Town-Northfields
13 March 1933	Northfields-Hounslow West and Arnos Grove-Oakwood

Charing Cross, Euston & Hampstead Railway

22 June 1907	Charing Cross-Golders Green and Archway
6 April 1914	Charing Cross-Embankment
19 November 1923	Golders Green-Hendon Central
18 August 1924	Hendon Central-Edgware

Major events from 1 July 1933

1 July 1933	Formation of London Passenger Transport Board under Act of 1933
31 July 1933	Opening, Oakwood-Cockfosters, Piccadilly Line
18 September 1933	Monument-Bank escalator link opened
25 September 1933	Opening of reconstructed Holborn station; closure of British Museum previous day
23 October 1933	Opening, South Harrow-Uxbridge, Piccadilly Line
5 June 1935	New Works Programme 1935–40 announced
30 November 1935	Quainton Road-Brill closed

4 July 1936	Aylesbury-Verney Junction closed
1 November 1937	All steam locomotives and goods rolling stock transferred to London & North Eastern Railway (except service stock)
30 June 1938	1938 tube stock enters revenue earning service
31 October 1938	Opening of new Aldgate East station
4 December 1938	Opening of new Uxbridge station
3 July 1939	Opening, Archway-East Finchley, Northern Line
1 September 1939	Control of undertaking passed to government through the Railway Executive Committee
20 November 1939	Opening, Baker Street-Stanmore, Bakerloo Line
14 April 1940	Opening, East Finchley-High Barnet, Northern Line
19 October 1940	Latimer Road-Kensington (Olympia) closed
19 January 1941	Opening of Highgate station, Northern Line
14 March 1941	Opening, Finchley Central-Mill Hill East, Northern Line
4 December 1946	Opening, Liverpool Street-Stratford, Central Line
5 May 1947	Opening, Stratford-Leytonstone, Central Line
30 June 1947	Opening, North Acton-Greenford, Central Line
23 November 1947	Opening of new White City station; closure of Wood Lane previous day
14 December 1947	Opening, Leytonstone-Woodford and Newbury Park, Central Line
1 January 1948	Formation of London Transport Executive as a Nationalised body under the British Transport Commission, following Transport Act 1947. End of wartime controls
31 May 1948	Opening, Newbury Park-Hainault, Central Line
21 November 1948	Opening, Woodford-Hainault and Loughton, also Greenford-West Ruislip, Central Line
25 September 1949	Opening, Loughton-Epping, Central Line
18 November 1957	Opening, Epping-Ongar, Central Line
26 January 1958	First installation of programme machines for automatic junction signalling at Kennington
1 March 1959	Opening of interchange between Central and District/Circle Lines at Notting Hill Gate
28 February 1959	Acton Town-South Acton closed
12 September 1960	Opening of electrification, Rickmansworth-Amersham and Chesham, Metropolitan Line
10 September 1961	Metropolitan Line services north of Amersham withdrawn; end of steam passenger working of Underground services
18 June 1962	Completion of four tracks, Harrow North Junction-Watford South Junction, Metropolitan Line
1 January 1963	Formation of London Transport Board, following Transport Act 1962
10 January 1963	Centenary of first Underground railway
5 January 1964	First automatic ticket barrier installed at Stamford Brook
5 April 1964	Full scale trials of Automatic Train Operation commenced between Woodford and Hainault
3 October 1964	Finsbury Park-Drayton Park closed
9 October 1964	District Line services withdrawn between Acton Town and Hounslow West
5 February 1967	Opening of new Tower Hill station, District and Circle Lines
1 September 1968	Opening, Walthamstow-Highbury & Islington, Victoria Line
1 December 1968	Opening, Highbury & Islington-Warren Street, Victoria Line
7 March 1969	Opening, Warren Street-Victoria, Victoria Line
1 January 1970	Formation of London Transport Executive under the control of the Greater London Council, following Transport (London) Act 1969
6 June 1971	Steam working of engineers' trains ceases
23 July 1971	Opening, Victoria-Brixton, Victoria Line
14 September 1972	Opening of Pimlico station, Victoria Line
28 September 1975	42 killed and 74 injured in tunnel wall end collision at Moorgate, Northern City Line
19 July 1975	Opening, Hounslow West-Hatton Cross, Piccadilly Line
6 September 1975	Moorgate-Old Street closed
3 October 1975	Old Street-Drayton Park closed
16 August 1976	British Rail commences services Old Street to Drayton Park
8 November 1976	British Rail commences services Old Street-Moorgate and Drayton Park-Finsbury Park BR station
16 October 1977	Opening, Hatton Cross-Heathrow Central (later renamed Heathrow Terminals 1, 2, 3), Piccadilly Line
1 May 1979	Opening, Baker Street-Charing Cross, and transfer of Baker Street-Stanmore line to new Jubilee Line. Opening of interchange at new Charing Cross station
28 March 1980	Opening of London Transport Museum at Covent Garden
4 October 1981	'Fares Fair' introduced by Greater London Council, reducing fares by 32%
17 December 1981	Law Lords rule 'Fares Fair' unlawful
21 March 1982	Fares increased by 96%
24 September 1982	Bakerloo Line services withdrawn north of Stonebridge Park
22 May 1983	GLC reduces fares by 25%. Travelcards introduced
1 July 1983	Golden Jubilee of London Transport
26 March 1984	Introduction of One Person Operation, surface lines
4 June 1984	Bakerloo Line services restored between Stonebridge Park and Harrow & Wealdstone
29 June 1984	Formation of London Regional Transport under control of the Secretary of State for Transport following London Regional Transport Act, 1984
1 April 1985	Formation of London Underground Ltd as a subsidiary of London Regional Transport
12 April 1986	Opening, Terminal 4 station, Piccadilly Line
31 August 1987	Opening, Tower Gateway and Stratford-Island Gardens, Docklands Light Railway
31 August 1987	Introduction of One Person Operation, conventionally driven trains, on tube lines
18 November 1987	31 killed in fire at King's Cross, Piccadilly Line escalators
29 July 1991	Opening, Shadwell-Bank, Docklands Light Railway (single line only)
29 November 1991	Full opening, Shadwell-Bank, Docklands Light Railway
1 April 1992	Docklands Light Railway transferred from London Regional Transport to the London Docklands Development Corporation
28 March 1994	Opening, Poplar-Beckton, Docklands Light Railway
1 April 1994	Waterloo & City Line, Kensington (Olympia) line, and Putney Bridge-Wimbledon transferred to London Underground Ltd
30 September 1994	Holborn-Aldwych and Epping-Ongar closed 1998 Opening, Green Park-Stratford, Jubilee Line
10 July 1995	Docklands Light Railway fully converted to SELTRAC signalling system.

Notes

Dates shown as 'Openings' refer to the first day of public service. Thus although the Jubilee Line was officially opened by HRH Prince Charles on 30 April 1979, public services south of Baker Street did not commence until the following day. Sometimes opening dates refer to the first Underground involvement. 14 April 1940 was the first day of electric traction from East Finchley to High Barnet, the Underground having supplanted the previous L&NER steam service. Withdrawals refer to the last day on which services ran; thus the last steam passenger services ran on 10 September 1961, and British Railways took over all services north of Amersham on 11 September. Throughout, present day names of stations have been used to avoid confusion; the station shown as opening on 25 September 1882 at Tower Hill, for instance, was originally named Tower of London.

2 List of Underground Lines and Routes

	No of stations	Route miles
Metropolitan		
Aldgate-Amersham, branches to Chesham, Watford and Uxbridge	34	42
Hammersmith & City		
Hammersmith-Barking	28	16
District		
Upminster-Ealing Broadway, branches to Richmond, Wimbledon, Edgware Road and Kensington (Olympia)	60	40
Circle		
A combination of sections of the Hammersmith & City and District Lines, plus Aldgate and the Cromwell Road curve	27	13
East London		
Shoreditch-New Cross and New Cross Gate	8	5
Bakerloo		
Elephant & Castle-Harrow & Wealdstone	25	14
Central		
Ealing Broadway and West Ruislip-Epping, with a loop via Hainault	49	46
Jubilee		
Stanmore-Stratford, with a branch to Charing Cross (partly under construction)	27	24
Northern		
Morden-Edgware and High Barnet via Charing Cross or Bank, with a branch to Mill Hill East	49	36
Piccadilly		
Cockfosters-Heathrow terminal loop and branch to Uxbridge	51	45
Victoria		
Walthamstow-Brixton	16	14
Waterloo & City		
Waterloo and Bank	2	2
Docklands Light Railway		
Tower Gateway/Bank-Beckton and Stratford to Island Gardens	27	14

3 Royal Occasions

4 November 1890	Prince Edward (the future King Edward VII) visited Stockwell to open the City & South London Railway
27 June 1900	Prince Edward opened the Central London Railway, riding from Bank-Shepherd's Bush
26 February 1929	Prince Edward (the future King Edward VIII) visited Chiswick and Acton Works
14 February 1933	Prince Edward visited the Piccadilly Line eastern extension
15 May 1939 of	Princess Elizabeth and Princess Margaret rode from St James's Park-Tottenham Court Road and back as part of their education, accompanied by a lady-in-waiting and a governess
12 July 1968	Prince Philip and Prince Charles inspected tunnelling work under Vauxhall on the Brixton extension
7 March 1969	The Queen became the first reigning monarch to ride in the cab of a tube train, between Green Park and Oxford Circus, as she opened the Victoria Line
23 July 1971	Princess Alexandra opened the Brixton extension
16 December 1977	The Queen rode from Hatton Cross to Heathrow Central as she opened the airport extension
30 April 1979	Prince Charles opened the Jubilee Line, travelling from Charing Cross to Stanmore
28 March 1980	The Princess Royal opened the London Transport Museum at Covent Garden
1 April 1986	The Prince and Princess of Wales opened Heathrow Terminal 4
30 July 1987	The Queen opened the Docklands Light Railway, travelling from Island Gardens to Poplar, and thence to Tower Gateway

Left:
The Underground roundel as displayed at White City.
John Glover

Above:
The Underground roundel as displayed at Kennington.
John Glover

Above right:
The first all over advertising train was of Piccadilly Line 1973 stock. It was sponsored by United Airlines; the horizontal stripes are, alternately, dark blue and black. The train is seen here arriving at Acton Town from Heathrow on 19 June 1995, carrying invited guests on its first run
John Glover

Selected Further Reading

This brief guide can only skim the surface of the available literature, and those looking for a deeper understanding of various parts of the subject matter will have to explore further.

For a general overview of London itself, the series of books by Gavin Weightman and Steve Humphries *The Making of Modern London* (Sidgwick & Jackson, from 1983) is difficult to beat, while the standard work on London Transport is undoubtedly T. C. Barker and Michael Robbins' *A History of London Transport. Volume 1 The Nineteenth Century*, and *Volume 2 The Twentieth Century to 1970* were published by Allen & Unwin in 1963 and 1974 respectively, though both are long out of print. Mike Horne's current series of short histories of individual tube lines, published by Douglas Rose, is also excellent. Bringing in some recent history, though hardly in the same detail, is the present author's *London Transport Buses and Trains Since 1933* (Ian Allan, 1988). Those interested in the political machinations will find Paul E. Garbutt's *London Transport and the Politicians* (Ian Allan, 1985) of value. For a look at the wider railway scene, H. P. White's *Volume 3 Greater London* in the David & Charles series of *Regional Histories of the Railways of Great Britain* is an excellent historical account, while numerous HMSO publications, notably the *Central London Rail Study* (1989), give a glimpse into the future. *The Annual Report and Accounts of London Transport* are a mine of financial and statistical information; more recently from London Regional Transport they have been supplemented by the *Statement of Strategy* and the *Annual Business Plan.*

Dealing specifically with the Underground, the technical side of the rolling stock is dealt with in loving detail by J. Graeme Bruce in three complementary volumes: *Steam-Silver* (Capital Transport, 1983), *The London Underground Tube Stock* (Ian Allan, 1988), and *Workhorses of the London Underground* (Capital Transport, 1987). Fleet details and various statistics will be found in John Glover and Colin J. Marsden's *Motive Power Recognition: 4 London Transport Railways and PTE Systems,* (Ian Allan, 1985), but those interested in the number details of all the rolling stock will want to turn to Brian Hardy's *London Underground Rolling Stock,* (Capital Transport, 13th edition, 1993). Martin Smith's well illustrated *Steam on the Underground* (Ian Allan, 1994) provides extensive coverage on that topic.

Of the detailed company histories, few can compare with Alan A. Jackson's *London's Metropolitan Railway,* (David & Charles, 1986). From the same author, in conjunction with Desmond Croome, comes *Rails Through the Clay,* 2nd edition, 1994. A quite remarkable treatise on the stations, illustrated by many drawings, is Laurence Menear's *London's Underground Stations: A Social and Architectural Study,* (Midas Books, 1983).

Ken Garland's *Mr Beck's Underground Map* (Capital Transport, 1994) gives a detailed account of how the Journey Planner has developed, but as for establishing 'what opened when', Douglas Rose's splendidly detailed and privately published *The London Underground: A Diagrammatic History,* (6th edition, 1994) knows no equal. For detailed line by line drawings, the Quail Map Co's *Railway Track Diagrams 5: England South and London Underground* is most valuable.

'Official' publications presently in print are *London Underground Ltd: An Official Handbook* (1994) and the *Docklands Light Railway Official Handbook* (3rd edition, 1994). Both are published by Capital Transport.

Underground-related articles appear in *Modern Railways* and other magazines from time to time. Finally, *Underground News*, the monthly journal of the London Underground Railway Society, can be recommended as a record of current events.

INDEX